THE
BOYS
OF
'98

FORGE BOOKS BY DALE L. WALKER

Legends and Lies
The Boys of '98
Bear Flag Rising

THE
BOYS
OF
'98

THEODORE ROOSEVELT
AND THE ROUGH RIDERS

DALE L. WALKER

A Tom Doherty Associates Book
New York

THE BOYS OF '98:
THEODORE ROOSEVELT AND THE ROUGH RIDERS

Copyright © 1998 by Dale L. Walker

This book is printed on acid-free paper.

A Forge Book
Published by Tom Doherty Associates, LLC
175 Fifth Avenue
New York, NY 10010

Forge® is a registered trademark of Tom Doherty Associates, LLC.

Library of Congress Cataloging-in-Publication Data

Walker, Dale L.
    The boys of '98 : Theodore Roosevelt and the Rough Riders /
Dale L. Walker.
        p.   cm.
    "A Tom Doherty Associates book."
    ISBN 0-312-86479-5 (hc)
    ISBN 0-312-86847-2 (pbk)
    1. United States. Army. Volunteer Cavalry, 1st—History. 2. Spanish-
American War, 1898—Regimental histories. 3. Spanish-American
War, 1898—Campaigns—Cuba. 4. Roosevelt, Theodore, 1858–1919.
I. Title.
E725.45 1st.W35 1998
973.8'94—dc21   98-14626
                                                         CIP

Printed in the United States of America

0 9 8 7 6 5 4 3 2

TO THE LAST ROUGH RIDERS:

George P. Hamner (1873–1973)

Frank C. Brito (1877–1973)

Jesse D. Langdon (1881–1975)

What thoughts at heart have you and I
We cannot stop to tell.
But dead or living, drunk or dry,
Soldier, I wish you well.

A. E. Housman
A Shropshire Lad

CONTENTS

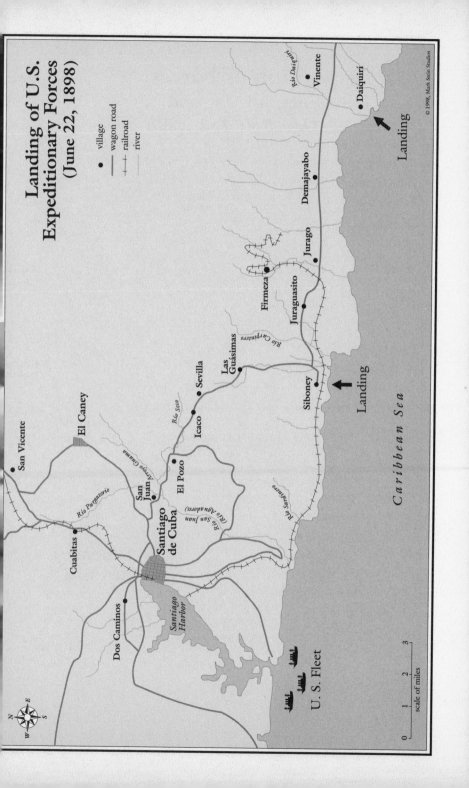

Landing of U.S. Expeditionary Forces
(June 22, 1898)

• village
+ + + railroad
wagon road
river

© 1998, Mark Stein Studios

Vinente

Río Daiquiri

Daiquiri

Landing

Demajayabo

Jurago

Firmeza

Juraguasito

Río Carpintero

Las Guásimas

Sevilla

Icaco

Río Seco

San Vicente

El Caney

Arroyo Guinia

Río Purgatorio

San Juan

El Pozo

Santiago de Cuba

Río San Juan (Río Aguadores)

Río Sardinero

Siboney

Landing

Cuabitas

Dos Caminos

Santiago Harbor

Caribbean Sea

U. S. Fleet

N
W · E
S

scale of miles
0   1   2   3

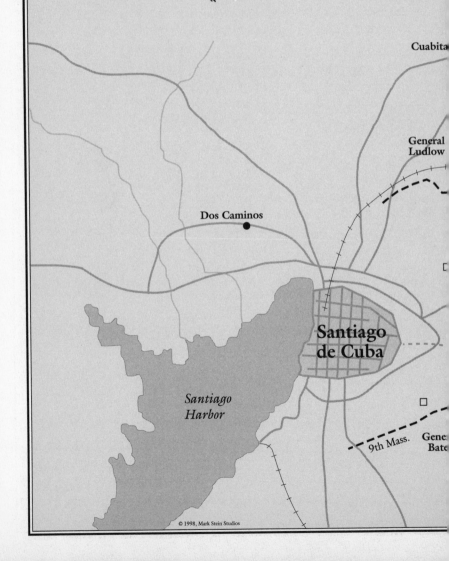

Disposition of Forces
at El Caney, July 1st, and
at San Juan, July 2nd, 1898

- – – American lines
- ● village
- —— wagon road
- ＋＋ railroad
- —— river
- – – – horse trail
- □ blockhouse
- 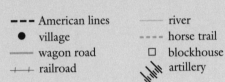 artillery

Cuabita

General
Ludlow

Dos Caminos
●

Santiago
de Cuba

*Santiago
Harbor*

9th Mass.

Gene
Bate

© 1998, Mark Stein Studios

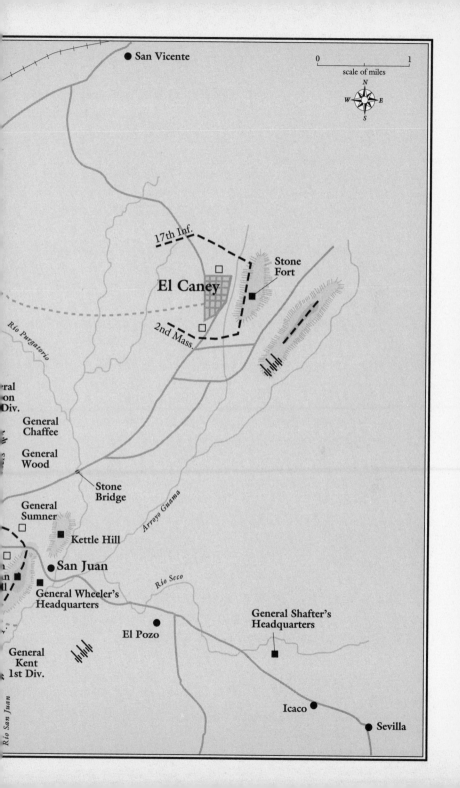

San Vicente

0   1
scale of miles

N
W   E
S

17th Inf.

Stone
Fort

El Caney

2nd Mass.

Río Purgatorio

eral
on
Div.

General
Chaffee

General
Wood

Stone
Bridge

General
Sumner

Arroyo Guama

Kettle Hill

San Juan

n

1

General Wheeler's
Headquarters

Río Seco

General Shafter's
Headquarters

El Pozo

General
Kent
1st Div.

Icaco

Río San Juan

Sevilla

INTRODUCTION

There is "Remember the *Maine*!" and *"Cuba Libre!"*

There is Commodore George Dewey's gentlemanly order to his flag captain at the opening of the Battle of Manila Bay, "You may fire when you are ready, Gridley."

There is "The Message to García."

There is the faint echo of that old minstrel song, "There'll Be a Hot Time in the Old Town Tonight," and the indelible image of Teddy Roosevelt waving his hat and yelling "Charge!" and leading his Rough Riders in a hell-for-leather footrace up San Juan Hill.

These are the traces—and they are fading—remaining in our collective memory of the 113-day Spanish-American War, the smallest and most popular of all our wars, begun and ended in the spring and summer of 1898.

It was a more important affair than the slogans and images signify and much more important than the exuberant characterization of it by John Hay, President McKinley's ambassador to the

Court of St. James, contained in a letter to Roosevelt after the guns were silent: "It has been a splendid little war, begun with the highest motives, carried on with magnificent intelligence and spirit, favored by that Fortune which loves the brave."

In fact, as all who fought in it learned, the war was anything but "splendid," the intelligence in which it was carried on considerably less than "magnificent." Even the motives were suspect.

Nor was the war "little." It is true that when the smoke cleared, only 369 American soldiers, ten sailors and six marines were counted dead in battle, scarcely more than fell with Custer in Montana in 1876; and even including the 2,000 others who died of wounds and disease, the casualties were those of but a few minutes on the Somme in 1916. A small sacrifice, some said, for such enormous gains. The war, after all, launched the U.S. on a colonial path and as a world power gained us the Philippines, Puerto Rico, Guam and Wake Island—and even created the martial milieu for annexing the Hawaiian Islands.

But for the common soldier, especially those of the volunteer regiments, the sacrifices were great, the gains unimportant. Charles Johnson Post, a New York *Journal* artist who served alongside the Rough Riders in Cuba with the Seventy-first New York Volunteers, wrote in his memoir, *The Little War of Private Post,* "for those who are in war and battle and on the fighting line, there is no triviality in shaking dice with death. It makes no difference whether a man gets his along with twenty thousand others, or falls on outpost duty all by himself. He is a hundred per cent casualty to himself."

Although it seemed a good idea, maybe even necessary, to devote considerable space to setting the scene for it, *The Boys of '98* is not a history of the Spanish-American War. The focus is the First U.S. Volunteer Cavalry Regiment—the Rough Riders—and the operations of the Fifth U.S. Army Corps in the Cuban campaign of June and July 1898. Thus, I have written as much here on Columbus's discovery of Cuba as on Commodore Dewey's naval victory at Manila Bay. Nor have I included more than a mention of the Puerto Rican "campaign"—a promenade compared to the rest of the war—or even of such actions in Cuba itself as the U.S. Marine Corps landing at Guantánamo, the naval engagements at Matanzas, Cienfuegos (a cable-cutting operation in which fifty-two Medals of Honor were awarded), and Santiago, or the lethal engagement at El Caney which served as the prelude to the attack on San Juan Hill.

My personal introduction to the Boys of '98 occurred in 1970, nearly three-quarters of a century after they fought their war in Cuba. In working on a book about one of the heroes of the regiment, I discovered there were three authentic Rough Riders still alive and in an amazing case of propinquity, found that one of them lived only forty miles upriver from my home in El Paso, Texas.

Five years before they laid Jesse James in his grave and fourteen months after the Little Big Horn battle, Frank C. Brito was born in the mining boomtown of Pinos Altos, in far western New Mexico Territory. He was the son of Santiago Brito, a Yaqui Indian prospector, and his Mexican wife Selma, and young Frank got his frontier education from *McGuffey's Eclectic Reader* and from work as a printer's devil on the Pinos Altos *Miner,* a weekly paper with a circulation of seventy-five hand-set copies.

We talked in silvery October sunlight in Las Cruces, New Mexico, in 1970, seated on weathered chairs on the edge of his porch while wind gusts whipped dust devils along the bald yard. Behind us, on the wall of his adobe house, a tin sign proclaimed this the "Home of Roosevelt's Rough Riders" and next to it, a *ristra*—a string of red chili peppers—was suspended from a roof beam together with an American flag with forty-five stars on a sun-bleached blue field.

Frank Brito was ninety-four when I spent that afternoon with him. He met me, reluctantly, at his home beside a rutted dirt byway called Tornillo Street, his son, Santiago, having made the arrangements. Santiago warned me, "He likes to be left alone so he might be a little impatient. Stand close to him and talk in his ear."

Mr. Brito, rooted like a cottonwood stump in his yard, stood by the gate, supported by two stout canes. His square Indian face was sun-baked and furrowed like old bark, his gray hair clipped short in military fashion. He was nearly blind from glaucoma but I felt his eyes boring into mine from beneath his green aviator sunglasses as his son introduced me.

We adjourned to his porch, and as he drew shapes in the dirt with his cane tip I asked questions in his ear and he answered without reflection, his impatience vanishing as good memories warmed him. He talked about Red Skelton and baseball games on television (his favorites until he couldn't see them anymore), of stray cats, Pat Garrett (who Mr. Brito, a former deputy sheriff of Dona Aña County, regarded as a friend), his own brittleness and fear of falling ("They don't make parts for this model anymore," he said), the many Britos who have served in America's wars, and the fiftieth anniversary reunion of the Rough Riders in Prescott, Arizona, when Boots Miller had too much to drink, broke into an Italian restaurant and smashed up all the crockery until he was hog-tied and thrown into the *calabozo* to sleep it off.

I came to ask about the Rough Riders and beat a circuitous path to the subject but he knew my mission and got to it in good time. He told me about being a $30-a-month cowboy on the Circle Bar spread "way out beyond" Silver City in April 1898, when he received a message from his father in Pinos Altos instructing him to come home at once.

"It took ten hours to get home on horseback," he said. "I got there near midnight and the house was all lit up. I was sure somebody had died. My dad came out and said he had news from Fort Bayard that we were going to war against Spain. He said there was a call for cowboy volunteers and he told my brother and me to ride to Silver City and sign up. In those days you didn't talk back to your father."

On May 6, he said, he and his brother Joe became privates in Troop H of the New Mexico Territorial contingent of the regiment the newspapers were already calling the "Rough Riders."

We talked about the Rough Riders the rest of the afternoon.

Toward the end of the day, Mr. Brito tapped his cane in the dirt and said, "The Colonel—we never called him 'Teddy'—had a nickname for everybody. He called me 'Monte,' short for Montezuma. I have nothing but good memories of him. One time, in Tampa, I think, a bunch of us had tossed a poncho on top of four bales of hay inside a big tent and, between unloading wagons, shot craps on it. The Colonel came by, peeked inside the tent flap and said, 'Be careful, boys, the adjutant is just around the corner.' He sure was, too, and we folded up our game just in the nick of time. The Colonel was a wonderful man."

He pointed to the tin "Home of the Rough Riders" sign. "There are just three of the boys left. George Hamner is in the VA hospital down in Florida and Jesse Langdon is up in New York. And here I am.

"I was born in 1877 and here it is 1970. I've seen a lot, been through a lot. But '98 . . . those were great times," he said as he walked me to the gate.

The Boys of '98 is the story of a regiment of Frank Britos, George Hamners and Jesse Langdons who heard the premonitory rattle of the sabre a century ago and formed up at the sound, as did their eastern seaboard comrades, creating as memorable an aggregation of volunteer fighting men as has been recorded in our history.

—Dale L. Walker
El Paso, Texas
April 10, 1997

PROLOGUE

"Ta-ra-ra-boom-der-ay: did you see my wife today?
No, I saw her yesterday: ta-ra-ra-boom-der-ay."

Rough Rider Frank Brito, when he was ninety-four, looked back to '98, when he was twenty-one, and pronounced it a "good time." All the nineties, he said, were "a good time."

To generations who were born too late to know them, they were "the Gay Nineties." Thomas Beer called the era "the Mauve Decade," to Mark Twain the years were part of "the Gilded Age," and Samuel Eliot Morison used the phrase "the Fecund Nineties."

It *was* a fertile time in America: We discovered dry cell batteries and the poems of Emily Dickinson, ate Leidercrantz cheese and Hershey's chocolate for the first time, saw the invention of basketball, carburetors and pneumatic tires, open-heart surgery, padded boxing gloves and the one-dollar Ingersoll pocket watch.

The years 1895–1898 alone gave us X rays, commercial electric power, discovery of the anopheles mosquito as the vector for malaria and of electrons in orbit around the nucleus of the atom.

In the nineties, gold was discovered along the Klondike River in the Yukon Territory of Canada.

William Jennings Bryan of Nebraska warned: "You shall not press down upon the brow of labor this crown of thorns, you shall not crucify mankind upon a cross of gold."

The New York Times introduced its motto, "All the News That's Fit to Print" and the *New York Sun* ran a column that began, "Yes, Virginia, there is a Santa Claus." Joseph Pulitzer of the *New York World* and the upstart William Randolph Hearst of the *New York Journal* jousted over the rights to a one-panel cartoon called "The Yellow Kid." This newsprint duel gave rise to a useful and enduring term to describe the outrageous newspaper coverage of the Cuban "problem" of 1895–1898—"yellow journalism."

People memorized San Francisco writer Gelett Burgess's verse, "I Never Saw a Purple Cow," read Stephen Crane's *The Red Badge of Courage,* Kipling's *The Light That Failed,* Arthur Conan Doyle's *The Adventures of Sherlock Holmes,* Anthony Hope's *The Prisoner of Zenda,* H. G. Wells's *The Time Machine* and *The Invisible Man,* Burt Standish's endless "Frank Merriwell" adventures, Mark Twain's *Pudd'nhead Wilson,* and the first issues of *Collier's Weekly* and *Field and Stream.* They listened to John Philip Sousa's marches, sang "The Band Played On" ("Casey Would Waltz with a Strawberry Blonde"), "Daisy Bell" ("A Bicycle Built for Two") and "There'll Be a Hot Time in the Old Town Tonight." They bought Cracker Jack and Tootsie Rolls, Lifebuoy soap and Campbell's condensed soup, Underwood typewriters, pocket Kodak cameras and all fifty-seven of Heinz's varieties.

Victorian mores were lessening. Men were growing fewer beards (and King Gillette was working on his disposable razor blade idea) and trying to emulate Charles Dana Gibson's *Life* magazine drawings of clean-shaven, clean-cut, all-American males whose up-tilted chins and flared nostrils seemed to signify they were detecting something in the air—success, perhaps, or the scent of someone beneath their station. Women were discarding their steel-reinforced corsets, puffed sleeves, bustles and multitudinous petticoats and undergarments. And both sexes were beginning to talk more freely about once-forbidden subjects just as painters, playwrights, writers and composers were becoming, in favorite words of the day, more "daring," even "risqué." Oscar Wilde's *The Picture of Dorian Gray* had a shockingly wide audience in America as well as England despite its critical condemnation as "decadent," "hedonistic" and "unmanly." Other artistic imports—Aubrey Beardsley's *art nouveau* drawings; paintings by Degas, Gauguin, Toulouse-Lautrec, Rousseau and Pissarro; Bram Stoker's *Dracula;* and Edmond Rostand's *Cyrano de Bergerac*—were much in demand. One tune, "Ta-ra-ra-boom-der-ay," from London's Gaiety Theatre, had verses so salacious they were believed known only by "depraved" men and "fallen" women, yet everybody sang them.

Naturally, not everything was lifesaving, timesaving, uplifting, educational, fun, naughty or delicious for the seventy-five million citizens of the United States in the nineties. There were plenty of bitter contrasts.

The hugest single vessel for these was the World's Columbian Exposition of 1893, which opened in Chicago along a stretch of beach edging Lake Michigan. Twenty-seven million people paid fifty cents to tour the 633-acre wonderland, thronging to ride the 265-foot-tall Ferris Wheel, to see a group of Dahomey natives alleged to be cannibals, to gaze up at an Egyptian obelisk and be taken along a specially constructed canal with genuine Venetian gondoliers poling the boat.

"Progress" was the theme of the Exposition, massively demonstrated by the mammoth engines and turbines of Machinery Hall, the Transportation Building and the Electricity Building.

But "Progress" must have seemed a paradoxical theme to many, even among those who could afford the price of admission. Here was a gaudy exposition opening during the most destructive economic depression in memory, a time when five hundred banks closed, millions were out of work and hungry, and Coxey's Army of unemployed began its march on Washington.

A roiling time of contrasts, the nineties. The western frontier had closed (officially in 1890, with the census that year) and wildernesses were becoming states of the Union. Indian conflicts were all but finished. Railroads now crisscrossed the continent. Industry was in revolution. Populists were demanding such radical things as the direct election of senators, public ownership of telephone and telegraph monopolies and a graduated income tax. There were strikes, work-stunted children, Jacob Riis's chilling exposés of poverty, vice, crime and disease in the slums, reported in the *New York Evening Sun* as "How the Other Half Lives," and, the Fifty-first Congress announced, for the first time, a billion-dollar federal budget.

This was the era of the Chinese Exclusion Act, Jim Crow laws, Eugene Debs's passionate socialistic oratory, the "Wobblies" of the Industrial Workers of the World . . . as well as of Sears Roebuck, General Electric, and "Stars and Stripes Forever."

Until middecade, the nineties stew of merriment and misery had a bittersweet domestic flavor. We were a self-satisfied, largely insular nation, rippling with muscle and edgy with pent-up power, but strangely inert, as if afflicted by a national torpor. Thirty years had passed since the tumult of the Civil War, time to ponder our place in the scheme of things, time to look outward to detect our Manifest Destiny, as we had in the great expansionist era of the 1840s.

In its April 1895, issue, a *Literary Digest* commentary on the renewed insurgency in Cuba, a mere ninety miles from the Florida Keys, bluntly asked a question about our strange malaise: "Are Americans Spoiling for War?"

Theodore Roosevelt, the president of the New York City Board of Police Commissioners, was even blunter about what was missing from the life and times of the United States when he wrote his friend, Massachusetts senator Henry Cabot Lodge, that year: "What this country needs is a war."

I

THE EVER-FAITHFUL ISLE

1

"It is the most beautiful land that ever eyes beheld."

He sailed south from Ragged Island in the Grand Bahama bank commanding three small caravels carrying ninety men and *marineros*—apprentice seamen—in the loftily named "La Armada de India." On October 27, 1492, the Genoese captain-general Cristoforo Colombo sighted the shimmering emerald hills off the bow of the *Santa María*. He signaled his ships to follow and his little fleet tentatively scouted the coast of the new land, finding many pristine, natural harbors, inlets and coves ringed by wide beaches of white sand backed by a loud wall of palms, flowers and foliage gorgeous beyond description.

On the 29th the *Santa María,* the *Niña* and *Pinta* found an anchorage at a place he called Puerto Gibara and the crew landed to fill water casks. Columbus and his men spent twelve days at Gibara before moving on to explore the coast to the east. He wrote exultantly of what he saw: "Everything is green as April in Andalusia. The singing of the birds is such that it seems as if one would never desire to depart. There are flocks of parrots that obscure the sun. There are trees of a thousand species, each having its particular fruit, and all of marvelous flavor."

But amidst this lush splendor, the captain-general had reason to be discouraged. He had fully expected to be greeted at some point along the coast by a fleet of junks carrying delegates from the Great Khan. The native Taino Indians called their big island "Colba," but Columbus was certain he had reached Mangi, the name Marco Polo gave to South China.

He was 13,000 miles from the fabled Indies.

As he sailed east toward the Windward Passage and Hispaniola, he watched from the stern of the *Santa María* as the land he had named Isla de Juana (after the Prince of Castile) disappeared in the mist. "It is the most beautiful land that ever eyes beheld," he wrote.

2

"Oh, the pity of it . . ."

The Spanish Empire in the New World broke up after 1808 but Cuba remained loyal to the Crown, survived many revolutions and came to be known as one (Puerto Rico the other) of "the Ever-faithful Isles" and "the Pearl of the Antilles." The resplendence of the island, its limitless resources, strategic location and great shipping port at Havana were for a century the subject of intermittant debate ninety miles north across the Florida Straits.

During the negotiations for what would become the Louisiana Purchase, Thomas Jefferson had advanced the idea that Spain might "with difficulty" relinquish Cuba. If attained by the United States, he suggested a column be erected on the southernmost edge of the island inscribed with the words "Ne Plus Ultra" to signify the utmost point of American expansion in the West Indies.

John Quincy Adams wrote of Cuba and Puerto Rico as "natural appendages of the North American continent."

In the mid-1840s, in the time of that fierce flexing of expansionist muscle which a New York editor called the nation's "manifest destiny," Americans were on the march to the Halls of Montezuma and the shores of Mexico's province of California. As if that were not enough, President James K. Polk, eyes darting around a map of the hemisphere, tendered an offer to Spain to buy Cuba for $100 million. The offer was declined, but Polk's successor, Franklin Pierce, renewed it in 1854, calling for a conference of ministers to be held in Ostend, Belgium, toward the view of "acquiring" Cuba. Pierce's successor, James Buchanan, was one of the signers of the Ostend Manifesto.

During the Polk administration, during the apex of the dizzying era of Manifest Destiny, New York City became the locus of the Cuban freedom movement in the United States. This was heralded by the arrival in the city, in the summer of 1848, of General Narcisco López, a once loyal officer of the army of Spain who became a passionate rebel after being sent to Cuba as a reward for a lifetime of service to the Crown. López could not have timed his advent more impeccably. He found Americans energized by the successes in the Mexican War and still hungry for conquest as he began recruiting followers and making his plans to invade the Pearl of the Antilles.

After a failed foray to the island with a small band of ne'er-do-well American followers in May 1850, López moved his operation to the south where his ideas of bringing Cuba into the Union as a slave state found more enthusiasm. In August 1851, after gathering a force of 300—many of them Americans—he sailed from New Orleans in the steamer *Pampero* to "liberate" the island. His second-in-command, W. S. Crittenden, was a twenty-eight-year-old West Point graduate and Mexican War veteran.

Spanish authorities learned their every move, dooming the mission before it began. López landed his men at Bahía Honda, west of Havana, and marched inland as Crittenden remained on the coast with a small force. The American and his fifty would-be insurgents, after fleeing in open boats, were captured at sea and following the failure of an appeal to the U.S. consul in Havana, all were executed by firing squad. López subsequently surrendered and was condemned to death by garrote in Havana. Forty-nine of his followers were shot and 106 chained and shipped to Spain and Africa for imprisonment. The others presumably escaped.

The failure of the expedition caused a riot in New Orleans and the sacking of the Spanish consulate.

In his message to Congress that year, President Millard Fillmore expressed great disapproval of the entire adventure, especially its aftermath. But, beginning in 1850, above the offices of the *New York Sun,* the Cuban flag, five bars and a single star, snapped in the wind, a signal that the issue of Cuba under the "Spanish yoke" would not be forgotten.

The Civil War diverted attention from governmental talk about buying or annexing the island but the insurgency there continued unabated, aided by numerous filibustering and gunrunning expeditions, many of them launched from New Orleans, Key West and eastern seaboard ports of the United States.

Cuban patriots proclaimed a revolution in October 1868, demanding freedom from Spanish rule and establishing a revolutionary "republic" in the hotbed eastern provinces of the island. It is estimated that two hundred thousand Spaniards and Cubans died in the Ten Years' War which followed the *grito* (cry) for independence, but the Spanish military held on to Havana and thus controlled most of the wealth of the island. Even so, the revolt was sustained by brilliant rebel leaders—Máximo Gómez, Calixto García, and Antonio Maceo among them—whose names would become even more familiar to Americans in the decades to come.

While the United States did not intervene in the Ten Years' War, one episode in it outraged the nation and solidified sympathy for the *insurrectos* and their cause.

The incident involved the *Virginius,* a sail-and-steam side-wheel vessel, and its captain, former Confederate officer Joseph Fry, a forty-seven-year-old native Floridian.

On October 31, 1878, Fry's *Virginius* steamed out of Port-au-Prince, Haiti, toward the Cuban coast carrying a damning cargo: five hundred Remington rifles and four hundred handguns, plus sabers, explosives and medical supplies, clearly intended for the revolutionary armies around Santiago, Manzanillo and Bayamo. Moreover, he had on board four insurgent officers and a hundred rebel soldiers.

In the Cayman Trench between Jamaica and the south Cuban coast, a Spanish gunboat spotted the *Virginius,* an American flag flapping from its topmast, and gave chase. Fry's crew, most of them Americans, tried to jettison the cargo but the ship was outrun, forced to surrender and follow the gunboat into Santiago Harbor.

Fry denied running guns, lamely claiming that he was heading for Costa Rica and that his capture in international waters was an unlawful act. The Spanish authorities were unmoved and on November 4, after a quick trial, the four rebel generals, one of them a Canadian, were shot, then beheaded, their heads placed on pikes for public display. Three days later, Fry and his men were tried and sentenced to death. He and fifty-two crewmen of the *Virginius* were executed by firing squad.

(Twenty years later an American army would fight a battle within walking distance of the place of execution.)

President Grant gave some thought to an "intervention" in Cuba over the *Virginius* imbroglio but settled for the strongly worded messages and veiled threats dispatched to Madrid by his secretary of state, Hamilton Fish.

There were no major battles in the Ten Years' War, only hit-and-run jungle skirmishes, cane-field burnings and similar guerrilla depredations. The war slogged on this way until 1878 when a treaty was signed in which Spain promised certain reforms. Slav-

ery was abolished on the island in 1886, but the other promises
were forgotten.

Veteran newspaperman Murat Halstead, once editor of the
Cincinnati Commercial Appeal, who had served as correspondent
in the American Civil War and the Franco-Prussian War, went to
Cuba in the mid-1890s and found Spanish rule of the island fatally
repressive. "Spain is stumbling down a dark and bloody road to
her doom," he wrote. "Persistent, long continued injustice, and
indifference or bitter hostility to all entreaties and demands for re-
dress, have caused the Cubans to become conspirators, revolu-
tionists, enemies and destroyers, all for self-government."

Halstead was saddened by what he witnessed in the
provinces—squalor, starvation, a grinding hopelessness—and observed, "It would have paid Spain well to have been occasionally
gracious, for the Cubans have suffered long every form of humil-
iation before they were incensed to fury, and goaded into a consummate purpose for redemption and vengeance."

Five hundred years of rule, Halstead said, had taught the rulers
nothing. "The Spaniard's fault is that he has not been able to escape from his own system. He is its slave as Cuba is its victim. Oh,
the pity of it, the disaster of it!"

Others saw the pity of it, too. By 1895, the "plight of Cuba"
had an international renown. It may have seemed to be an issue
exclusively American—American newspaper coverage of the island's revolutions gave that impression—but it was not.

3

"Here I might leave my bones . . ."

"What this country needs is a war," Theodore Roosevelt told
Senator Lodge in 1895 and another who felt that way about *his*
country was a young subaltern in the Fourth Hussars, a fashionable cavalry regiment of Her Majesty Queen Victoria's army.

He was a puny, freckled, delicate boy with wide-awake blue eyes, reddish hair and a matching ruddy complexion. He spoke with a faint lisp but animately and with a coiled-spring intensity. A descendent of the duke of Marlborough and the son of a peer of the realm, he affected some of the regimental airs of the day such as standing with his hands positioned on his hips under his gold-frogged uniform coat, elbows akimbo in a defiant posture, and he was known for asking too many questions of his superiors.

He had graduated from the Sandhurst Royal Military Training College and now, in November 1895, at age twenty, was suffering from his country's unusual peaceableness. There was no fighting to speak of anywhere, not even in the Sudan as yet, or the northwest frontier of India. He was restless, eager, had five months' winter leave on his hands and nothing to do.

"From early youth I had brooded about soldiers and war," he later wrote, "and often I had imagined in dreams and day-dreams the sensations attendant upon being for the first time under fire. It seemed to my youthful mind that it must be a thrilling and immense experience to hear the whistle of bullets all around and to play at hazard from moment to moment with death and wounds."

He searched the newspapers and consulted the maps. There had to be a war of some kind going on somewhere.

He found one, a tiny insurrection on the Caribbean island of Cuba, the ideal kind of thing in which a colonial soldier could experience his baptism of fire.

Rebel leaders with such names as José Martí, Máximo Gómez and Antonio Maceo were leading a revolt against Spanish rule; the commander of Spanish forces there, General Martínez de Campos, had occupied the principal towns and confined the guerrillas to the outlands and jungles far to the east of Havana.

That was enough to know for the present and the young officer wrote a letter to General de Campos, then requested permission from his superiors to spend his winter leave with the Spanish army in Cuba. The commander-in-chief of the British army, Lord

Wolseley, a veteran of wars from Burma to the Crimea, granted the request. He too, after all, had been an ambitious subaltern forty years ago.

The hussar next visited the London offices of the *Daily Graphic* and left with a commission to write reports, at five guineas each, on the rebel rising in Cuba. Then, on November 2, 1895, he sailed from Liverpool with a regimental friend and arrived in New York on the tenth. He put up in an apartment on Fifth Avenue in Manhattan, took in the sights, and after a few days boarded a train to Key West, Florida, where he embarked for Havana on the steamer *Olivette*.

"When first in the dim light of early morning I saw the shores of Cuba rise and define themselves from dark-blue horizons, I felt as if I had sailed with Captain Silver and first gazed on Treasure Island," he would later write. "Here was a place where real things were going on. Here was a scene of vital action. Here was a place where anything might happen. Here was a place where something would certainly happen. Here I might leave my bones."

On November 20, he stepped off the gangplank in the teeming Cuban capital and spent a day at the Gran Hotel Inglaterra before "setting out for the front," carrying copies of the letter he had written to General de Campos and his leave papers signed by Lord Wolseley.

The Spanish general met him at Santa Clara, 150 miles east of Havana, and sent him forty miles southeast to Sancti Spíritus, a town "beset by rebels" and decimated by yellow fever and smallpox. In the jungly village he met de Campos's officer-in-charge of the region, General Suárez Valdéz, who supplied the Englishman with horses and servants and invited him to accompany the Spanish troops in the field.

General Valdéz, with four battalions of infantry, two squadrons of cavalry and a mule-drawn gun battery, marched out of Sancti Spíritus in pursuit of a rebel band led by Antonio Maceo, a hand-

some, scholarly subordinate of Máximo Gómez, the iron-willed
Dominican professional soldier whose history of guerrilla fighting
dated back to the Ten Years' War of the 1870s.

On November 30, his twenty-first birthday, the hussar got his
fondest wish: He heard the pop of rifle fire and the buzz of bullets about his head when Maceo's rebel snipers opened fire as he
ate a skimpy breakfast with some Spanish officers. For four days
thereafter he followed Suárez Valdéz's force through the thick
jungle until, on December 3, at a machete-cleared place in the
thick brush called La Reforma, the general led an attack against
the Maceo rearguard, two thousand Spaniards killing thirty or
forty rebels and taking an insignificant hill.

In a bylined story from Havana that appeared in the *New York
World* on December 5, the Englishman wrote of the skirmish at
La Reforma and how the rebels turned and fled when the
Spaniards were within shooting distance. In subsequent articles in
the *Daily Graphic* after he returned to England in January 1896,
he sympathized with the oppressed Cubans and pontificated on
the corruption among Spanish administrators of the island. He
said the revolt was justifiable.

For his services with the Spanish army at the "battle" of La Reforma, Second Lieutenant Winston Spencer Churchill of the
Fourth "Queen's Own" Hussars received a medal, the Cruz Roja,
for gallantry.

II

SPOILING FOR WAR

1

1895: "Peanuts"

Eighteen Ninety-five, which Lieutenant Churchill's little adventure with the rebels closed out, began with news of renewed insurrection in Cuba. In February, *El Porvenir (The Future),* the New York newspaper devoted to the rebel cause, excitedly announced in the spring of the year that the provinces of Matanzas, on the north coast east of Havana, and Santiago de Cuba, on the southeastern coast, were under martial law. Insurgents had landed on the coast and the *grito* of freedom was again being heard across the island from Punta Maisí to Cabo Corrientes.

The resonance of the *grito* may have been exaggerated but the shrillness of the Cuban junta in New York was not. This revolutionary society, using its lawyer's shabby, cigar-perfumed office at 88 Broadway, was one of thirty stretching from Key West to New York, from Chicago to San Francisco. The New York club had as its main business sending agents across the country to make speeches and collect money for the great *causa de Cuba Libre.* Another important junta function was to disseminate concocted

snippets of "news" about atrocities committed against the innocent citizens of the island by their brutal Spanish overlords, and
about the countless "victories" against the Spanish soldiery by
rebel "armies." These snippets were called "peanuts" by New
York newspapermen and the junta office became known as "the
Peanut Club."

In February and through the spring of 1895, the juntas
worked around the clock producing "peanuts."

The great dailies in New York were also busy, the *Times, Tribune, Sun, Herald* and *World* among them. That February, the papers began carrying long dispatches, many of suspicious origin,
from Madrid and Cuba about Spain's rushing reinforcements to
the island. By March 13, after a month of relatively dull news, a
real "outrage" occurred worthy of banner headlines. On that day,
the American steamer *Alliança* arrived in New York with the story
that it had been chased and fired upon in the Windward Passage
by a Spanish gunboat. Spanish authorities said that only blanks
had been used and the purpose, entirely legal, was to warn the
steamer to heave to for inspection for contraband. These expla-
nations fell on deaf ears. The *New York Sun,* edited by the combative Charles A. Dana, long a proponent of Cuban independence, urged action, writing, "The next Spanish gunboat that
molests an American vessel ought to be pursued and blown out of
the water."

Even President Grover Cleveland, determined that there
would be no war over Cuba in his administration, was angered by
the *Alliança* incident and notified Madrid by diplomatic cable
that such interference with American vessels would not be tolerated.

While the tocsin of Cuban liberty sounded on February 24, the
first real act of insurgency involved the landing in April in the
eastern Oriente Province of three immortals of the revolution,
José Julián Martí, Máximo Gómez and Antonio Maceo.

Martí, forty-two years old in 1895, was an accomplished poet and a revolutionary from his teenage years when he spent time in a Spanish prison as a subversive. Educated at the universities of Madrid and Salamanca, he lived in exile in Mexico, Central and South America, served as a diplomat and newspaper correspondent (for Dana's *Sun*, among other papers) and by 1891 had become the acknowledged leader of the Partido Revolucionario Cubano (Cuban Revolutionary Party) whose two thousand or so members were scattered in the various juntas, most of them in the United States.

Martí's compatriots were two tested veterans of the Ten Years' War, the Dominican Máximo Gómez, seventy-two, living in Santo Domingo in 1895, and the "Bronze Titan," Antonio Maceo, forty-seven, a brilliant mulatto *insurrecto* leader in exile in Costa Rica with his band of Cuban nationalists.

Martí, Gómez, and their small force of rebel soldiers landed near Santiago de Cuba on April 11 and were joined near Guantánamo a few days later by Maceo and his troops. The combined army of several hundred men marched west toward Manzanillo on the Gulf of Guacanayabo to merge with a third group of local guerrillas.

On May 20, at a place called Dos Ríos, the insurgents encountered Spanish troops and in the skirmish that followed, Martí was killed.

With the death of the poet and spiritual chief of the revolution, Máximo Gómez, as *generalísimo* of the rebel army, changed tactics. He introduced a slash-and-burn guerrilla warfare aimed at the chief source of the island's wealth, the sugar industry (in which Americans had a fifty-million-dollar investment), and his scorched-earth policy of torching cane fields, dynamiting railroad lines and capturing arms and supplies had an almost instantaneous success.

Spain's counterstrategy, put into effect by its great hero of the Ten Years' War, General Arsenio Martínez de Campos, was to contain the *insurrectos* in the far eastern Oriente Province by building forts and blockhouses along a *trocha* (defensive line) and reinforcing the number of Spanish troops in the area.

By the end of 1895, Gómez's general commanding the army in eastern Cuba, the battle-scarred Calixto García, continued to test Spanish patience.

Another who arrived on the scene late in the year was a big, shambling, sad-eyed newspaperman out of San Francisco named William Randolph Hearst, the new owner of the *New York Morning Journal*. The son of a California mining magnate, he had been expelled from Harvard after sending each of his instructors a chamber pot with the professor's name inscribed on the bottom, had worked briefly for Joseph Pulitzer's *New York World,* and in 1880, searching for a career, was handed a newspaper— building, presses, and staff—as a gift from his father. The paper was the *San Francisco Examiner,* an anemic sheet used by the elder Hearst to further his political career. Within a few years, "Willie" turned it into a raucous, sensation-mongering success. Now, with an inheritance of $7.5 million from his father's estate and paying a meager $180,000 for another decrepit paper, the *Morning Journal,* he turned his considerable talents and bottomless bank account to girding up for battle in the New York newspaper wars. In this, he developed two early passions that were to have a curious future connection. He opposed Police Commissioner Theodore Roosevelt's enforcement of laws on closing saloons on Sundays (he wrote of the commissioner in his paper as "King Roosevelt I, ruler of New York and Patron Saint of dry Sundays") and in San Francisco he had become a Free-Cuba boomer and was now determined to out-Cuba his former employer, Joseph Pulitzer, on that and every other circulation-gaining issue.

Hearst came to town in September and the same month, in Washington, arrived a man whose name would appear often in his paper—and all the others—two-and-a-half years hence. This was Captain Leonard Wood, a thirty-five-year-old New Hampshire-man and Harvard medical graduate. He had served as army contract surgeon during the Geronimo campaigns in the Southwest and had earned a Medal of Honor for valorous services in the Indian wars. Now he had been assigned as physician to President Cleveland.

Lithe and fit, Wood loved to walk for exercise and in this pasttime would soon meet a man who could keep up with him walking, easily outpace him talking, the former Dry Sunday New York police commissioner Theodore Roosevelt.

Toward the end of 1895, the U.S. Naval War College came up with a strategic paper enumerating plans on the navy's role in the event of a war with Spain. Among the options outlined: an attack on Spain itself, an attack on Spanish possessions in the Pacific, an attack on Cuba and Puerto Rico. The latter option included suggestions that American forces be landed on the northern coast of Cuba to seize Havana, leaving the eastern provinces of the island to the insurgents, whose efforts, it was said, would need to be supported by U.S. financing. Key West, Florida, the paper stated, would be the navy's advance base for Cuban operations, Tampa the army's. Navy strategists suggested that 30,000 regulars and 250,000 volunteers would be needed to capture Havana.

2
1896: "Infamies of bloody debauchery"

A year into the new revolution in Cuba, Hearst, Pulitzer, Dana of the *Sun,* James Gordon Bennett of the *New York Herald,* their like-minded Park Row brethren, and the Peanut Club on Broadway, received an unexpected blessing. It came in the form of a man who would come to represent, among American newspapermen at least, the apogee of Spanish repression, a man who would drive politicians to furious rhetoric and goad the *Cubanos,* as the island-watcher Murat Halstead observed, "into a consummate purpose for redemption and vengeance."

In Madrid, the ministry recalled General Martínez de Campos, a worthy old warrior but one apparently not decisive enough for the new conservative government, and, on February 10, 1896, the new governor-general in Cuba took over. General Valeriano Weyler y Nicolau was a handsome, fifty-eight-year-old Majorcan of German-Spanish ancestry, a grimly deliberate professional with a fine set of mutton-chop whiskers and eyes that those who saw him at close range said were as black and unemotional as a shark's. He had served as military attaché in Washington during the Civil War and knew things about the United States, its people and government, most of which he did not like.

An American news service reporter in Cuba named Rapplyea had an early audience with the governor-general in Havana and described Weyler as "lean, diminutive, shriveled, ambitious for immortality irrespective of its odor, a master of diplomacy, the slave of Spain."

In the eastern jungles of the island, Máximo Gómez welcomed his new foe. The shrewd old revolutionary knew Spain had made a great mistake, perhaps a fatal one, in assigning this cold, fierce-visaged militarist to "pacify" Cuba.

Within a week of his taking office, Weyler earned the enmity of the American press by imposing a strict censorship on news reports leaving the island. More importantly, he issued a *bando* (decree) putting into motion a radical program which ordered all Cubans in villages known to be rebel strongholds, from Sancti Spíritus to Santiago, to be "reconcentrated" in fortified towns, their cattle to be confiscated, their homes razed. By this harsh measure Weyler planned to put scorched earth between the rebels and their source of food, supplies and recruits, while he massed his forces along the *trochas,* the fortified roads cutting the island north to south, designed to deprive the insurgents free movement westward.

The effect of Weyler's decree was to convert the eastern end of the island into a vast concentration camp with all the attendant horrors of such confinement. (Before the *reconcentrado* effort ended in 1898, an estimated one hundred thousand Cubans died of starvation and disease in the fortified camps.)

Reconcentrado—the word alone quickly sufficed to describe the policy—galvanized American opinion against Weyler and the government he represented. Americans, reading of the inhumanity of the system in their daily newspapers—the stories grotesquely and unnecessarily amplified by the creative fictions of the "Peanut Club" and by its dupe, the yellow press—responded with money, relief efforts and pressure on the Cleveland, and subsequently, the McKinley, administrations to intervene, by diplomatic means or armed force, in the "matter of Cuba."

Hearst's *Journal* led the anti-Weyler reportage, printing voluminous dispatches denouncing the governor as "the most cruel and bloodthirsty general in the world" and creating the nickname "Butcher" for him. A typical *Journal* story was that of February 23, 1896, less than two weeks after Weyler's advent on the island: "Weyler, the brute, the devastator of haciendas, and the outrager of women . . . is pitiless, cold, an exterminator of men. . . . There is nothing to prevent his carnal, animal brain from running riot with itself in inventing tortures and infamies of bloody debauchery."

Not long after this story ran, Hearst stepped up his personal war to free Cuba by dispatching two of his best correspondents to the island. They were not to be thwarted by Weyler's gag order; they were to use whatever devices necessary to get news to the *Journal*.

At the Democratic Party Convention that summer the "Boy Orator of the Platte," William Jennings Bryan of Nebraska, stilled the Chicago Coliseum throng into an almost palpable silence, then to an ecstasy that rocked the building, with his evangelical "Cross of Gold" oration, and was nominated as the party's standard-bearer for the November presidential elections. In June, William McKinley of Ohio, an expert on the protective tariff and a man suspected of being a "tool of the trusts," won the Republican Party nomination.

In St. Louis on a steamy July 22, one thousand four hundred delegates to the People's Party Convention decided to "fuse" with the Democrats and support Bryan's nomination.

Among the Populist delegates at the city's cavernous auditorium was the former sheriff of Yavapai County, Arizona Territory, William Owen O'Neill, entering his second race for a seat in Congress.

He had come out to Arizona in 1879 from Washington where his father, a distinguished soldier in Meagher's Irish Brigade in the Civil War, served as provost marshal for the District of Columbia. Young O'Neill had read newspaper reports about opportunities in the territories and in the past seventeen years had made the most of them. He became a newspaperman in Phoenix, Tombstone (and was there during the O.K. Corral gunfight in 1881) and Prescott; a deputy marshal, court reporter, sheriff, Grand Canyon explorer and guide, civic leader, politician and local legend in the gambling hells of Prescott's "Whiskey Row." His propensity for "bucking the tiger"—going for broke—at the faro tables earned him the nickname "Buckey" (which he used and spelled with the "e").

Tall and darkly handsome at age thirty-six, with deep brown hair and eyes, a silky black mustache and a perpetual roll-your-own cigarette dangling from his lips, he was "dashing" to his wife Pauline and to other female admirers, who were legion in his town of Prescott, where he owned and edited the stockman's newspaper *Hoof and Horn*. Gregarious, ambitious and a combative politician, O'Neill, among his many offices, served as captain of the Prescott Grays, a splendidly uniformed and epauletted local militia group. He had a thirst for military glory.

Newspaperman James McClintock, who had come to Arizona from Sacramento the same year as O'Neill, shared Buckey's enthusiasms. The two met often to discuss politics, the military life, and local scuttlebutt. O'Neill, boots up on the desk in his *Hoof and Horn* office, would roll a butt from his Bull Durham bag and would forever open the conversation by saying, "Jim, gimme a match."

He returned to Prescott from the St. Louis convention and waged an exhausting campaign for the delegate's seat in Congress. McClintock said his friend traveled "by long passes across deserts, malpais, mesas, and unbroken forests, secluded hamlets where the spellbinder was a stranger, a new 'critter' and met upward of ninety percent of the voters in Arizona Territory."

But he lost the election—coming in, following the typical Populist trend of 1896, third in a field of three.

Undaunted, he returned to Prescott and the next year ran for mayor and won in a walk.

McClintock, a frequent visitor to Mayor O'Neill's office, later remembered their talks and how both had attended an appearance in Prescott of a group of Cuban junta leaders who came to tell about the plight of the island, the atrocities resulting from General Weyler's pitiless starvation camp program, and to collect money for their cause. The newspapers were by now full of Cuba and there was a deepening sense, even in the remoteness of Arizona Territory, that the United States, with *"Cuba Libre!"* ringing in its collective ears, would go to war.

3

1897: "There is no war."

On the sunny afternoon of New Years' Day 1897, in Jacksonville, Florida, the notorious epicenter of gunrunning to Cuba, a thin, chain-smoking man in a wrinkled linen suit climbed aboard the sea-going tug *Commodore,* tied up at wharfside on the St. Johns River. Stevedores had finished loading the boat with a ten-thousand-dollar cargo of four hundred rifles, two hundred thousand cartridges, one thousand cannon shells, one thousand pounds of dynamite and three hundred machetes—"loaded up as placidly as if she were going to carry oranges to New York, instead of Remingtons to Cuba," the man, who was traveling under the name "Samuel Carlton," would later write.

He was officially listed on the *Commodore* papers as an "able seaman," one of twenty-nine crew members, but "Samuel Carlton" was in fact the celebrated author Stephen Crane. He had seven hundred dollars in gold in his possession and the mission of getting to Cuba to write about the insurrection there for the Bacheller Syndicate, which had serialized his masterpiece novel, *The Red Badge of Courage,* in newspapers.

Crane, the preacher's son from Newark, led an urgent life, levering into his days an astonishing amount of work, study and travel with the perfervid passion of one who suspects his time is limited. He had attended a seminary, a military school and Syracuse University, without staying long at any of them. He began writing newspaper sketches for the *New York Tribune* in 1891, lived in the New York slums and wrote his first novel, a dark and daring story of a prostitute's life titled *Maggie of the Streets,* in 1892. *Red Badge* appeared two years later together with a stunning book of doleful blank verse, *The Black Riders and Other Lines.* Along the way he had gained the admiration of such literary men as William Dean Howells and Hamlin Garland, and the interest of such men of station as Theodore Roosevelt, the New York City police commissioner, whom Crane met at the Lantern Club in Manhattan in 1894. Crane had since published other novels, stories and newspaper work, and by the time he threw his valise aboard the *Commodore* at the Jacksonville dock, was an established, if slightly shabby and impecunious, man of action and of letters.

The tug slipped its moorings that New Years' afternoon and butted its way down the St. Johns channel to the Atlantic where it was to make its way south, its destination Key West, thence into the Yucatan Channel, and on to Cienfuegos, on the southern mid-coast of Cuba.

On January 2 the *Commodore* sprung a leak in a sudden squall twelve miles off Daytona and, with its pumps failing, foundered. Many of the crew jumped overboard to attempt to swim to shore while others managed to lower lifeboats. Crane, together with the boat's captain, cook and oiler, comandeered a ten-foot dinghy and rowed away from the sinking tug. Crane saw seven men die in the water, including one man who was shoved away from an overcrowded boat.

The dinghy, battered by high winds and rollers for over a day, finally overturned in the slashing surf off Mosquito Inlet Light. The oiler drowned but Crane and the others made it to shore.

Back in Jacksonville on January 6, Crane turned the incident into a first-person essay for his syndicate and subsequently mined the experience for one of his finest short stories, "The Open Boat," published in *Scribner's Magazine* later that year.

Eighteen months would pass before he would make his way to Cuba, this time without incident and not as a would-be filibuster. This time he shipped out in comfort, as a bona fide correspondent covering a war, and in particular the work of a peculiar regiment put together by Theodore Roosevelt, his Lantern Club acquaintance and fan.

At about the time Crane arrived in Jacksonville to board the *Commodore,* William Randolph Hearst, who had a flair for finding the best writers and artists for difficult assignments, and who had the money to buy their services, assigned two of his choicest acquisitions to the Cuba story. They were to make their way to the rebel army of Máximo Gómez in Santa Clara province, five hundred miles east of Havana.

This formidable team consisted of the artist-writer Frederick Sackrider Remington and the veteran newspaperman and book author Richard Harding Davis. They were busy men with sought-after talents but by December 1896, Hearst had them kicking their heels in Key West, the town Crane's biographer Thomas Beer described as a "mangy little city filled with journalists, harlots and mosquitos."

Remington, thirty-six, a burly, affable former Yale football star from Canton, New York, had quit school in 1880 and with money inherited from his father's estate had gone out to Montana Territory to sketch and write and see the Old West, its "wild riders and vacant land," which he knew would soon vanish forever. He failed at ranching in Kansas but wandered through the West and Southwest, sketching cowboys, Indians, cattle herds, river crossings, frontier posts, towns and settlements. When he returned to New York in 1885 with three dollars in his pocket and a fat portfolio of drawings under his arm, he found work instantly as a magazine illustrator. His work appeared in *Harper's Weekly, Outing* (its editor, Poultney Bigelow, son of a former ambassador to France), *Century, St. Nicholas,* and other of the best periodicals of the day, all hungry for images of the still-exotic western frontier. By 1896, Remington's earnings were rising as illustrator and fine artist; he had married, published his first book and produced his first sculptures. He was a companionable man, well recognized in New York clubs as a lover of good food, cigars and scotch.

Remington could write, but Hearst hired him to make sketches and depended upon Richard Harding Davis for the words to go with them.

Davis was a born celebrity and enjoyed the status all his life. A talented and likeable thirty-four-year-old Philadelphian, his father was a newspaper editor and his mother, Rebecca Harding, a popular novelist. He attended Swarthmore and Lehigh and Johns Hopkins, played football, and in 1886 began working for the *Record,* then the *Press,* in his home city. He moved to New York

in 1889 for a stint on Dana's *Evening Sun* and there created a series of enormously popular stories about a suave and chivalrous
man-about-town and society Robin Hood named Cortland Van
Bibber. Square-jawed, handsome and elegantly dressed, "Richard
the Lion Harding" became a sort of living incarnation of Van
Bibber, so much so that Charles Dana Gibson used him to per-
sonify the male counterpart to the "Gibson Girl," the all-
American woman of the age.

Davis had served for a time as managing editor of *Harper's
Weekly* and was author of such books as *Gallegher and Other Stories,* about an enterprising office boy, *Van Bibber and Others,* and
the novel *Soldiers of Fortune,* which he had written in Santiago de
Cuba during one of his several visits to the island.

While Stephen Crane was working on his *Commodore* narra-
tion in Jacksonville, Davis and Remington finally found passage
south out of Key West on the Plant Company steamer *Olivette,* the
same ship which had carried Lieutenant Winston Churchill to the
island two years before, and on January 9, 1897, landed in Havana. They checked into the Hotel Inglaterra on the ocean-front
promenade called the Prado and paid a call on the U.S. consul in
the capital, Fitzhugh Lee, the corpulent sixty-two-year-old
nephew of Robert E. Lee, and himself a Civil War brigadier general and senior cavalry commander of the Army of northern Virginia.

Before moving east on their assignment, Davis managed to
win a rare interview with Governor-general Weyler and Remington made a sketch of the man Davis described as "a black appari-
tion—black eyes, black hair, black beard—dark, exceedingly dark
complexion; a plain black attire, black shoes, black tie, and soiled
collar and not a relief from the aspect of darkness anywhere on his
person."

With Weyler's sanction, Davis and Remington left Havana to
travel the countryside and on January 19 their train reached Santa
Clara. Although they were now in a war zone, neither had had a

Churchillian experience under fire—that would come later. Davis did, however, witness the pre-dawn execution of a rebel soldier by Spanish musketry. The condemned man, Adolfo Rodríguez, the twenty-year-old son of a cane farmer, had been found guilty of treason against the government. He stood stoically before the firing squad in the classic stance, smoking a cigarette, Davis wrote, "with the nonchalance of a man who meets his punishment fearlessly, and who will let his enemies see they can kill but cannot frighten him."

Davis traveled about the island by rail as far east as Morón, taking notes and writing pieces for Hearst on Gómez's sugarcane field burnings and on Weyler's starvation camps.

Remington was disgusted by all he saw and was anxious to get home to his clubbish world of scotch, cigars and boon companions. According to *New York World* correspondent and veteran Cuba hand James Creelman, Remington cabled Hearst in New York, "Everything is quiet. There is no trouble here. There is no war. I wish to return."

To this, the *Journal* proprietor politely replied, "You furnish the pictures and I'll furnish the war."

III

THE INFERNAL MACHINE

1

"Two dollars"

On the evening of March 4, 1897, after the inauguration of William McKinley as the twenty-fifth president of the United States, he and his predecessor, Grover Cleveland, had dinner together at the White House. The festering issue of Cuban independence had a high place on their agenda.

Cleveland had pursued a "non-interference" policy, opposing the rising congressional belligerence toward Spain and overt support of the *insurrectos*. He had demanded strict enforcement of laws against filibustering expeditions involving American citizens, matériel and debarkatation points and urged that this policy continue. Every effort, he said, no matter how odious to the press or public opinion, should be exerted to prevent a war over the island.

McKinley, whose mind dwelled on domestic issues, seemed sympathetic to Cleveland's views on Cuba and reportedly said, "Mr. President, if I can go out of office at the end of my term with the knowledge that I have done what lay in my power to avert this terrible calamity, with the success that has crowned your patience and persistence, I shall be the happiest man in the world."

McKinley knew about war. He had enlisted at age seventeen as a private in the Twenty-third Ohio Volunteers, serving under another Ohio-born future president, Rutherford B. Hayes, and saw action on the bloody ground of Antietam.

A lawyer, former U.S. congressman and governor of Ohio, he had won the Republican Party nomination for president at the St. Louis convention in 1896 and handily defeated his Democratic opponent, William Jennings Bryan. McKinley was a homebody and felt entirely comfortable conducting his campaign from the front porch of his house in Canton.

Age fifty-four when he took office, he was a short, stout, well-tailored man addicted to cigars (but never photographed with one) and to such eye-glazing political esoterica as tariff reform, international bimetallic agreements and the gold standard. He exuded a palpable charm, had a presidential bearing and a natural dignity, but to all but his closest Ohio cronies, he seemed reserved if not cold. Those who knew his history spoke of his stoicism. He had endured the tragedy of his two daughters dying in infancy and doted on his beloved wife Ida, afflicted with terrible migraines and epilepsy, refusing to permit these illnesses to exclude her from White House dinners and banquets. (When Ida McKinley suffered a petit mal seizure at one of these dinners, the president placed a napkin over her contorting face until the seizure subsided, doing this, to the astonishment of his guests, without breaking stride in the table talk.)

He felt destined for greatness but in his ambition seemed to many to be too malleable and without firm convictions, determined to please everybody and earn no enemies. Joseph G. "Uncle Joe" Cannon, the autocratic speaker of the House of Representatives in McKinley's time, said the president had his ear so close to the ground it was full of grasshoppers.

The president did not grant interviews and was never to be quoted directly although he was accessible to reporters and had a deftness in handling them. They knew he favored annexation of the Hawaiian Islands and was pushing hard for this measure during his first term in office; knew, as the months of 1897 passed that he had made unsuccessful overtures to Spain about purchasing Cuba as a means to end the strife there.

McKinley and the antiwar faction of Congress saw a chance for peace after the assassination in Madrid, in August 1897, of Spain's conservative prime minister, and the rise of a liberal ministry. Although announcing that it would not countenance "foreign interference in our domestic affairs or with our colonies," Spain began showing signs of appeasing the United States by reaching some kind of accord with Cuba's revolutionaries.

By the end of the year, McKinley felt progress had been made on his chief foreign policy problem. "War should never be entered upon until every agency of peace has failed," he said, and with "Butcher" Weyler recalled to Spain, and a modified form of autonomy being granted to the island by its mother country, he entertained hope that intervention might be unnecessary.

The previous April, the president had resolved a minor problem, the selection of someone to serve as assistant to Navy Secretary John D. Long. McKinley had been courted on this minor appointment by no less an eminence in Congress than Senator Henry Cabot Lodge of Massachusetts. "Cabot," as his wide circle of friends and admirers called him, was the eminent former editor of the *North American Review,* author of biographies of Washington, Daniel Webster and Alexander Hamilton, a Harvard professor, and a stellar figure in Republican politics. Lodge suggested that his good friend, the capable and energetic New York police commissioner Theodore Roosevelt, would be a good choice as assistant secretary of the navy. Among other qualifica-

tions Lodge mentioned, Roosevelt had served several years with
the New York National Guard and was author of a fine book on
the navy's role in the War of 1812.

The combative commissioner had been suggested to him by
others as well and McKinley, who had some reservations, agreed
on the appointment.

"Absolutely the only thing I can hear averse," Lodge wrote
Roosevelt, "is the fear that you will want to fight somebody at
once."

By the end of the year, from his office in the Navy Department on
Sixteenth Street, Roosevelt was excitedly reading the official cables
and dispatches ordering the North Atlantic Squadron to winter
maneuvers off Key West. The squadron had been preceded there
by the heavily gunned battleship *Maine,* which had weighed anchor at Hampton Roads, Virginia, on December 11.

The U.S. consul in Havana, Fitzhugh Lee, a Cleveland administration holdover who McKinley felt was too vociferously
pro-rebel, had littered desks at the State Department and White
House for over two months with cables about riots in the capital
and warnings that the city was seething with unrest. Lee felt that
the *Maine* might need to be sent down for a "friendly visit" to
give assurance to the Americans on the island that their government was concerned for their safety. In mid-December, the
Maine's skipper, Captain Charles D. Sigsbee, had made arrangements with Lee, with the blessing of the squadron's commanding
officer, on a signal which would indicate the battleship needed to
proceed to Havana. If Sigsbee received the message "Two dollars"
from Lee, the *Maine* would steam south.

All hands were on deck, yawning and stuffing shirttails into
trousers, on the early morning of January 25, 1898, as Captain
Sigsbee and his officers stood on the *Maine* quarterdeck watching
the gray-green hills of Cuba rising out of the mist. At nine-thirty,

with the crew manning their duty stations, the big white-hulled ship slid past Morro Castle, the fort built in 1597 atop a rocky pinnacle on the portside of the channel entrance. The captain ordered two salutes be fired and after these were answered by the Spanish flagship *Alfonso XII,* a pilot boat guided the *Maine* to Buoy 4, four hundred yards off Machina Wharf in Havana Harbor. There, a chain was rove through the buoy and by ten, the first U.S. Navy warship seen in Havana in three years swung at its anchorage.

The "friendly visit" of the *Maine,* arranged by Consul Lee after sending the "two dollar" message to Sigsbee at Key West on January 12, did come, as the consul had said, in a time of worrisome unrest in the island capital. There had been a riot in Havana a few weeks before in which old-islanders, anti–U.S. factions, the military and other partisans of Spanish rule reacted to the news of autonomy and the recall of Governor-general Weyler—the hardwon concessions the McKinley administration had prised from the new ministry in Madrid. Newspaper offices had been vandalized, shops closed, and mobs had roamed the streets chanting "Long live Weyler! Down with autonomy!"—1898 versions of "Yanqui go home!"

Sigsbee was acutely aware of the tremulous climate of the capital and the necessity as a gunboat diplomat of maintaining the strictest decorum during the *Maine*'s stay in the capital. He dressed in his best uniform and carried his cocked hat under his arm as he greeted the bowing and saluting Spanish naval dignitaries coming aboard his ship, and accepted their welcoming gift of a case of Jerez sherry.

The captain's gig took him ashore later in the day where he made official calls, met with Consul Lee, and accompanied Spanish officials to a bullfight (which Sigsbee called "a savage spectacle" in a letter he wrote to his wife) held in his honor. As the party departed the *Plaza de Toros,* somebody pressed a broadside into his hand which he had translated. It read,

Spaniards! The moment of action has arrived. Do not go to
sleep. Let us teach these vile traitors that we have not yet
lost our pride, and that we know how to protest with the
energy befitting a nation worthy and strong, as our Spain is,
and always will be! Death to the Americans! Death to
autonomy! Long live Spain! Long live Weyler!

Sigsbee returned to the *Maine* disturbed by the message but
in a few days he and his officers and sailors settled down to a
routine anchorage. "The atmosphere was heavy; the easterly
trade wind has fallen flat. Occasionally I heard the sound of a
ferry boat. Otherwise the harbor was very quiet," he wrote in his
daily journal.

The *Maine* was only nominally a "battleship." It had been built
in the Brooklyn Navy Yard at a cost of $2.5 million and its
keel laid in 1888, but seven years passed before its official com-
missioning, in September 1895, as a "U.S. Steel Armored
Cruiser."

The ship was twin-masted and twin-stacked, 324 feet long and
57 at the beam, displacing 6,650 tons. Its coal-fed boilers pres-
sured its engines above nine thousand horsepower and gave the
ship a top speed of eighteen knots. Its main guns were the four
ten-inch monsters in rotating steel turrets fore and aft, the turrets
extending several feet over the sides of the ship so that each had
a 180-degree firing range. Its other armament were six six-inch
breech-loading "rifles," seven six-pounder rapid-firing guns, eight
one-pounders, four Gatling machine guns and tubes for four torpedoes.

If not a battleship, a ship certainly built for battle, the *Maine*
had a crew of 31 officers and 346 sailors. (Age sixteen was the
legal age for enlistment, fourteen for apprentice seamen; average
pay for enlisted men: nine dollars a month.)

When commissioned, the *Maine*'s first skipper, Captain A. S. Crowninshield, read his orders aloud to the gathered ship's company and ended the ceremony with the revered proclamation of Horatio Nelson, "I expect every man to do his duty."

As a ship of the North Atlantic Squadron, the *Maine*'s common sea-lane ran from Tomkinsville, New York, to Key West and the Dry Tortugas and around the Florida Straits to New Orleans. Frequent days for coaling, refittings and refurbishings took place in New York Harbor, Hampton Roads and Norfolk Navy Yard, Virginia; Charleston and Port Royal, South Carolina; and other eastern seaboard ports.

Captain Charles Dwight Sigsbee took command of the ship in April 1897, at Hampton Roads. He had compiled a distinguished career in the navy—Annapolis '63, veteran of the Mobile Bay and Fort Fisher ironclad engagements of the Civil War. He was a hydrographic specialist and discoverer of the Sigsbee Deep, the deepest spot in the Gulf of Mexico; a veteran of six pre-*Maine* seagoing commands, a favorite of the Navy Department, an intelligent, iron-willed and cool officer in trying times.

Just before he received his orders to steam from the squadron's anchorage in the Dry Tortugas on the ninety-mile straight-south passage to Havana, Captain French E. Chadwick, commander of the flagship *New York*, came aboard the *Maine* for a visit. Chadwick, who knew of the impending orders to Cuba, said, "Look out, Sigsbee, that those fellows over there don't blow you up."

2

"The worst insult . . ."

The friendly visit, a bore for everyone after two weeks in harbor, at least gave Captain Sigsbee and his officers ample time for

visits ashore and for receiving visitors on board the ship. Among these, on February 9, arriving in Havana on the cruiser *Montgomery,* was the indefatigable Clara Barton, founder of the American Red Cross.

"Miss Barton," as everybody called her, impressed everyone who met her. She had been everywhere, seen everything: nurse in the Civil War and Franco-Prussian War, the yellow fever epidemic in Florida in 1887, the Johnstown Flood of 1889, the Russian famine in 1891. A tall, frail, seventy-six-year-old packet of energy, she had come to Cuba with the blessings of both the Spanish ministry and President McKinley to determine what the Red Cross could do to assist the sick, homeless and helpless refugees now swarming into Havana and other populated areas. She likened the plight of the starving Cubanos to what she had witnessed in Armenia after the Turkish massacres in 1892.

She came out to the *Maine* in the captain's gig to have dinner with Sigsbee and during the meal spoke of the irony of being served at a polished table with fine china and cut glass while the victims of the revolution were starving and dying in squalor just a short distance across the harbor.

Miss Barton's arrival was duly noted by the newspapermen lounging at the outdoor cafe of the Hotel Inglaterra and strolling about Havana's Prado and Parque Central. Among them were Sylvester Scovel of the *New York World,* a seasoned Cuba watcher and atrocity specialist who had been in and out of the island since 1895 when he found Máximo Gómez's rebel force at about the same time Lieutenant Winston Churchill found them; and George Bronson Rea of the *New York Herald,* author of a new book, *Facts and Fakes about Cuba,* in which he denounced "news" reports manufactured by the war-mongering New York junta and its lapdog, the sensationalistic American press.

No longer banned from the capital or censored, as during the Weyler regime, the correspondents had to dig for news, wait for it, or resort to the yellow journalist's special skill, inventing it.

Except for the refugee problem and the unrest over the autonomy issue, the island seemed unnaturally calm. There had been but one break in the tedium in recent weeks, this the publication in the *New York Journal* on February 9 of something called "the de Lôme letter."

The previous December, the Spanish minister to Washington, Enrique Dupuy de Lôme, wrote to a friend, José Canalejas, editor of the Madrid newspaper *Heraldo*. In the letter, written on official Washington legation letterhead, Dupuy de Lôme shared with his friend observations on U.S.–Spanish relations and specifically the state of affairs in Cuba. He stated that he opposed negotiating with the rebels or the "autonomists" or bowing in any way to the American "newspaper rabble" and its strident militarism. He also characterized President McKinley as "weak" and "a bidder for the admiration of the crowd, besides being a would-be politician who tries to leave a door open behind him while keeping on good terms with the jingoes of his party."

Canalejas carried the letter with him during a visit to the United States and Cuba. In Havana the letter disappeared, then surfaced in the possession of the chief of the New York junta. This man, instantly recognizing its explosive propaganda value, promptly delivered it to both the *World* and *Journal*.

On February 8, upon learning that his damning letter had fallen into the hands of the New York press, Dupuy de Lôme resigned. The next day the full text of the letter appeared in facsimile in Hearst's *Journal* under the headline

WORST INSULT TO THE UNITED STATES IN ITS HISTORY

and with a rousing ladder of subheadings, the last of which said "Send De Lôme Home at Once in Disgrace," accompanied by a doggeral verse containing such lines as:

Just pack your few possessions and take a boat for home
I would not like my boot to use but—oh—get out, de Lôme.

McKinley brushed the matter aside and six days after the big story was published, something much bigger and more "insulting" had moved it off page one.

Dupuy de Lôme had taken a suite in a New York hotel to await arrival of the liner which would return him to Spain when he was awakened by reporters and told about the terrible news from Havana.

After three weeks in harbor, the heaviest scuttlebutt on the *Maine* had nothing to do with Cuban problems; it concerned the happy prospect that the ship would be weighing anchor soon and heading for New Orleans, where shore liberties would be granted during Mardi Gras.

February 15 began with the routine sailor's work of scraping paint, busting rust, polishing brass, airing bedding and hammocks, scrubbing decks, standing watches and answering the musters for inspection, meals and the day's orders. There was a fine easterly breeze that day, the sky overcast, the air sultry. The ship bobbed at ebb tide in thirty-six feet of water, drawing twenty-two, swinging at its buoy with the bow facing the city. Faint music came from the Ward Line steamer *City of Washington,* a hundred yards distant. Taps sounded at 2110 hours.

In his cabin, Captain Sigsbee had finished a report to Assistant Navy Secretary Roosevelt on the "advisability of continuing to place torpedo tubes on cruisers and battleships" and was writing a letter to his wife when taps sounded. "I laid down my pen to listen to the notes of the bugle, which were singularly beautiful in the oppressive stillness of the night," he later wrote.

At three bells—nine-thirty P.M.—most of the crew were in their bunks and hammocks, some asleep, some chattering about New Orleans and Mardi Gras and shore leave and getting home.

In his cabin, the *Maine*'s chaplain, John P. Chidwick, had settled down for a quiet reading of Rea's *Facts and Fakes* book before a hot night of fitful sleep.

At nine-forty, Sigsbee had just folded the letter when he felt the ship shudder. A rumbling sound followed, lasting a fraction of a second, then a "bursting, rending, crashing roar"—no direct lightning strike could have been more ear-shattering or frightening. The *Maine* seemed to list instantly to port and when Sigsbee ran topside he saw flames and black smoke billowing from the bow and saw the main deck awash. He grabbed the rail and pulled his way forward on the starboard.

On the *City of Washington*, the noise brought crewmen and passengers to the deck. Some were already there and had witnessed the explosion that lifted the *Maine*'s bow out of the water for a second, followed by a bright spout of fire and smoke and a hot rain of metal pieces spanging against the hull of the steamer. Within minutes the harbor was littered with burning debris from the battleship, together with human bodies and parts of bodies.

Sigsbee, on the rising starboard side of the stricken ship, could see little—there was a wall of black smoke shrouding the bow and superstructure. He made his way aft, joined by other officers whose quarters were located there, saw the flames and billowing smoke amidships and shouted orders for the flooding of the forward ammunition magazine. He was told the magazine was safe—already under water—and that the after ammunition lockers were flooding as well. From his vantage point on the starboard rail, the captain could see dim shapes of twisted metal—stairways, hatches, bulkhead and deck plating in a jagged chaos—and one of the ship's great funnels lying in the water below him. He could hear the thrashing and screams of the men in the water, the high-pitched whine and hiss of air being pushed from once watertight compartments now rent by the explosion.

The *Maine*'s wounds were mortal and the ship's port list was

so severe there was danger of her heeling over entirely. Sigsbee
gave the order to abandon ship and the three boats which had survived the explosion were lowered. Meantime, the *City of Washington* and the *Alfonso XII* also had boats in the water to pick up
survivors and Chaplain Chidwick was picking his way along the
deck giving comfort and prayers to dying men. A seaman named
Holzer who served as his altar boy found Chidwick on the deck
and said, "Look at me, Father, I'm all burned." The chaplain ordered the boy into one of the boats. (Seaman Holzer died of his
burns ten days later.)

The captain's launch was brought alongside and several officers boarded it, Sigsbee last, reluctant to leave. The gig and the
other boats headed for the *City of Washington* as the *Maine* continued to wallow and settle in the harbor mud, the crack and pop
of small explosions still echoing across the water as the crawling
fires found ammunition bays still above water.

Ashore, the explosion caused the ground to shudder and win-
dows to shatter along the waterfront and deep into the city. The
newspapermen, Scovel and Rea, found the Havana chief of police
and convinced him to take them along in a harbor boat to the
stricken ship, then on to the *City of Washington*.

On the steamer, Sigsbee's executive officer, Lieutenant Commander Richard Wainwright, ordered a muster and found that
252 of the *Maine*'s crew were dead or missing. (Eight others died
in Havana hospitals in the days to come. Clara Barton and her volunteers worked feverishly at one of them, the San Ambrosio Hospital, nursing the burned and maimed casualties.)

3

"There is no other big news."

On the *City of Washington*, Sigsbee borrowed a cabin to write
a cable to navy secretary John D. Long:

Maine blown up in Havana harbor at nine forty to-night
and destroyed. Many wounded and doubtless more killed or
drowned. Wounded and others aboard Spanish man-of-war
or Ward line steamer. Send Light House Tenders from Key
West for crew and few pieces of equipment above water. No
one has clothing other than that upon him. Public opinion
should be suspended until further report.

The captain must have known the last sentence was little more
than a forlorn hope as he handed the pencil-scribbled message to
Herald correspondent George Bronson Rea, whom he knew and
trusted, and asked Rea to see that it was transmitted.

Reports of the *Maine* disaster reached Washington, via Key
West, at one A.M. on February 16. Secretary Long and his wife had
attended a ball the night before and were asleep in their rooms in
the Portland Hotel when awakened by a Navy Department
courier with the news. By three, Long, his assistant secretary Roosevelt, and Navy Department aides arrived at the White House
and met with the president, Secretary of War Russell Alger, and
other cabinet and congressional officers.

An hour earlier an Associated Press bulletin from Havana
reached New York and within an hour Pulitzer's *World* had an edition on the street with a four-column heading,

U.S.S. MAINE BLOWN UP IN HAVANA HARBOR

and in the next edition a few hours later appeared Sylvester
Scovel's dispatch and Sigsbee's cable to SecNav.

William Randolph Hearst, the story goes, had been out on the
town the night of February 15 and after returning to his apartment in Manhattan's Worth House was informed by his valet that
the *Journal* office needed him to call on an urgent matter.

Hearst talked with the night editor and learned of the *Maine*
catastrophe.

"What have you done with the story," Hearst asked.

"We have put it on the first page, of course."

"Have you put anything else on the front page?"

"Only the other big news."

"There is no other big news," the proprietor said. "This means war."

The first headlines in the *Journal* were matter-of-fact but in two days began to reflect a strident insistence that something nefarious lay behind the explosion. The February 17 issue of the *Journal*, which had a circulation of over a million copies, carried an above-the-nameplate announcement,

$50,000 REWARD—WHO DESTROYED
THE MAINE?—$50,000 REWARD

and the headline below it read,

DESTRUCTION OF THE WAR SHIP MAINE
WAS THE WORK OF AN ENEMY

accompanied by a fanciful six-column-wide line drawing of a submarine mine resembling a steel oil drum tethered to the harbor floor under the *Maine*. The caption read, NAVAL OFFICERS THINK THE MAINE WAS DESTROYED BY A SPANISH MINE, and above the drawing was a teasing heading,

ASSISTANT SECRETARY ROOSEVELT
CONVINCED THE EXPLOSION OF
THE WAR SHIP WAS NOT
AN ACCIDENT.

The Journal Offers $50,000 Reward for the Conviction of the Criminals Who Sent 258 American Sailors to Their

Death. Naval Officers Unanimous That
the Ship Was Destroyed on Purpose.

The *Journal*'s headline writers worked zealously in the days to come to maintain the level of stridency:

THE WARSHIP MAINE WAS SPLIT IN TWO BY
AN ENEMY'S SECRET INFERNAL MACHINE

and,

THE WHOLE COUNTRY THRILLS WITH THE WAR FEVER,
YET THE PRESIDENT SAYS "IT WAS AN ACCIDENT."

Pulitzer's *World* ran an enormous page one drawing of the *Maine* blowing to smithereens, bodies and debris flung in the air, but tempered its banner heading:

MAINE EXPLOSION CAUSED BY BOMB OR TORPEDO?

By midmorning on the day after the event, *Maine* news was appearing in extras and special editions of newspapers across the country and abroad. "The world's press went mad with all the brilliance of its eternal parochialism," Thomas Beer wrote, and as the days passed, the handling of the story in the *World* and *Journal* provoked a deadly comment from one of New York's smaller-circulating papers. Edwin Godkin of the *New York Post* wrote, "Nothing is so disgraceful as the behavior of these two newspapers this past week has ever been known in the history of journalism. . . . No one—absolutely no one—supposes a yellow journal cares five cents about the Cubans, the *Maine* victims, or any one else. A yellow journal is probably the nearest approach to hell existing in any Christian state."

* * *

Six days after the smoke cleared everywhere but in the yellow journals, a U.S. court of inquiry convened in Havana to determine the cause of the explosion. Eighteen days were occupied in hearing the testimony from officers, crew members, eyewitnesses, experts on ship construction and divers who had inspected the underwater wreckage.

Among the journalists swarming at the scene, the least popular, if most rational, theory was that the explosion might have been the result of spontaneous combustion in the ship's ill-ventilated bituminous coal bunkers. These storage bins were located near the forward ammunition magazines and such fires were not unique on naval ships of the era.

But even Captain Sigsbee was dubious of any such notion and, privately at least, placed the responsibility on unnamed "outside" forces. Buoy 4, the ship's anchorage, he said, might have been "mined" in advance of the *Maine*'s arrival in the harbor.

The inquiry board's report to President McKinley, completed on March 21, supported Sigsbee's idea, concluding that the *Maine* had been destroyed by "the explosion of a submarine mine which caused the partial explosion of two or more of her forward magazines." The weighty report, filled with arcane statistics and data, did not speculate on who might be responsible for placing the infernal device on or near the ship.

But the press and a large segment of governmental and popular opinion had already named the culprit and composed the battle cry. Poet Richard Hovey employed the slogan, soon ubiquitous on recruiting posters, homemade signs and newspaper headlines, when he wrote:

> *Ye who made war that your ships*
> *Should lay to at the beck of no nation,*
> *Make war now on murder, that slips*
> *The leash of her hounds of damnation!*

Ye who remembered the Alamo,
Remember the Maine!

In England, Lieutenant Winston Churchill, now packing his kit to debark to Egypt to join Lord Kitchener's "reconquest" of the Sudan, told a reporter, "America can give the Cubans peace, and perhaps prosperity will then return. American annexation is what we all must urge, but possibly we shall not have to urge long."

And in Waco, Texas, after the *Maine* blew up, William Cowper Brann, editor of a venomous little journal called *The Iconoclast*, wrote: "We must either close our ears to Cuba's cry for assistance or we must go to her side with the naked sword. There are but two ways to deal with the Spanish Don: One is to ignore his barbarities, and the other is to break him in twain and feed the better half to the buzzards."

In the Navy Department, ten days after the *Maine* settled to the bottom of Havana Harbor, Theodore Roosevelt, acting in the absence of Secretary Long, sent a cable that demonstrated his, and the nation's, attitude on what the tragedy meant in the high scheme of things. The cable was dispatched to Commodore George Dewey, commanding the Pacific Squadron from his flagship *Olympia* near Hong Kong. "Keep full of coal," Roosevelt directed. "In event of declaration of war with Spain, your duty will be to see that the Spanish Squadron does not leave the Asiatic coast, and then offensive operations in Philippine Islands. . . ."

IV

JINGO

1

"The light went from my life forever."

The *Maine* calamity placed the nation on its first surge toward war since the Union divided in 1861 and on its first foreign war footing since the invasion of Mexico fifty years before. President McKinley, awaiting the findings of the *Maine* inquiry board working in Havana, in March 1898, told his physician Leonard Wood, "I pray God that we may be able to keep peace. I shall never get into a war until I am sure God and man approve. I have been through one war; I have seen the dead piled up; and I do not want to see another."

Others close to the president held out hope that war might be averted. The inquiry board's conclusion that the *Maine* sank from an external explosion, probably caused by a submarine mine, was equivocal. It did not pin blame or even speculate on possible motives for what it had identified as an act of sabotage. Navy Secretary John D. Long's diary notation, "I am satisfied that the Spanish government is not responsible for the disaster," echoed the attitude of many unmoved by press and pubic hysteria, including Pope Leo XIII, who was said to be ready to serve as mediator between the contending nations.

Just a few steps down the hall from Secretary Long's office and a few blocks from the White House worked a man who shared neither of his employers' beliefs or aspirations. But there was no irony in it. The president and the secretary knew where Theodore Roosevelt stood in the matters of Spain, Cuba, the *Maine* and war. It would have been difficult not to know.

On March 26, one week after the *Maine* report was delivered to the president, a Gridiron dinner was held in the capital and among the speakers were Senator Mark Hanna, the Ohio industrialist who was McKinley's closest advisor and friend, and Assistant Navy Secretary Roosevelt. Hanna told the invitees at the private dinner of his opposition to a war and spoke of the cost of such a war, in human lives and treasury funds, and that the best course, as in all undertakings, was to proceed with negotiations with Spain and to exercise patience and caution.

When Hanna finished, the president of the club introduced his next guest, saying, "At least we have one man connected with this administration who is not afraid to fight—Theodore Roosevelt," and when TR gripped the podium in his customary style and leaned toward the audience, his head outthrust like a bulldog's, he wasted no time stating his position: "We will have this war for the freedom of Cuba, Senator Hanna, in spite of the timidity of commercial interests."

There has been a suggestion in studies of Roosevelt's life that his passion for military glory derived from his wish to erase a blot on his family escutcheon: His beloved father, a glass importer and philanthropist, had not served in the Civil War. He had hired another to take his place.

It is significant that Roosevelt, when he wrote his *Autobiog-*

raphy in 1913, made no mention of his father's Civil War years and may have regarded Theodore Senior's nonparticipation as "unmanly" (a favorite Rooseveltian word of disapproval). If so, it was the single instance in which he found a flaw in "the best man I ever knew."

At the time he made his Gridiron dinner speech, Roosevelt was already the best-known national specimen of the "strenuous life" he advocated. At age thirty-nine he exemplified strength in thought as well as deed, but few people then knew that he had risen to his philosophy out of personal experience and against the odds.

Born into a prosperous family of Dutch lineage in New York City on October 27, 1858, he was called "Teedie" as a child and he had to fight to live. He was weak and sickly, homebound and lonely, a chronic asthmatic struggling for breath. Told by his father, who spent countless nights ministering to the pale, frail, wheezing boy, that he would have to overcome his weakness by main strength, of will and body, Teedie began daily workouts in the "gymnasium" his father set up for him—body and wind-building apparatus on the back porch of the family home. The elder Roosevelt died in 1878, living to see Teedie outgrow his nickname and his infirmities: Theodore Junior had emerged as a vigorous young man, deep-chested, bull-necked and muscular, a skilled boxer, hiker, swimmer, horseman, hunter and self-taught outdoorsman and naturalist.

He graduated from Harvard in 1880, made a Grand Tour of Europe, kissed the pope's ring, visited Egypt and the Holy Land and married a beautiful young woman, nineteen-year-old Alice Hathaway Lee of Massachusetts. In 1882 he was elected to the New York Assembly as an Independent Republican and published his first book, *The Naval War of 1812, or, The History of the United States Navy During the Last War with Great Britain*.

In his midtwenties he had found supreme happiness: a wife he adored, a baby daughter born on February 12, 1884, and a life's pursuit—politics—with a limitless vista for a young man of character, energy, intelligence and wit.

But his world fell to pieces two days after the birth of little Alice when he received a telegram in Albany instructing him to come home at once. He reached his mother's house on West Fifty-seventh Street in Manhattan just before midnight on February 14 and found his wife barely conscious, stricken by the kidney failure called Bright's disease, while in another room, his mother fought valiantly against typhoid fever. At three A.M. on the 15th, Martha Bulloch Roosevelt, called "Mittie" in the family, died. Theodore spent the next eleven hours holding his wife in his arms. Alice Hathaway Lee Roosevelt died at two P.M.

He never spoke of her again, not even to their daughter as she grew up. Roosevelt biographer Carlton Putnam suggests this silence "seems pathologically rigorous," a "discipline approaching cruelty."

But perhaps he could not bear the memory her name evoked. Perhaps he meant what he said when he wrote of her that last time, in a private memorial, "And when my heart's dearest died, the light went from my life forever."

2

"Hasten forward quickly there!"

He found solace in the West, still a great blank land in the 1880s where anyone who could abide its rigors could lose himself in its lonely grandeur.

Roosevelt, a dedicated hunter from his youth, had first gone out to Dakota Territory to kill buffalo in September 1883, stepping off the train at the Little Missouri station (called "Little Misery" by the scattering of residents there) in his derby hat and Brooks Brothers suit, and wearing his thick pince-nez eyeglasses. If the tailoring did not mark him as a greenhorn, the glasses did.

Before long the cowboys, ranchmen and others among the horny-handed denizens of the Badlands were calling him "Four-Eyes" and "that dude Rosenfelder," and were amused no end by his Harvardish language, his spurning of tobacco in any form, and hard liquor, and his idea of swearing—an occasional "Damn!" more often a "By Godfrey!" uttered in a tinny-tenor voice.

Although he occasionally employed a mild form of it, he hated profanity and there are stories, some resembling dime novel tales, in Roosevelt's *Autobiography* attesting to this. Once a drunk accosted him in a Dakota hotel and in a stream of vile language and with six-guns drawn, announced that "Four-Eyes is going to treat!" Roosevelt, by now accustomed to the "Four-Eyes" name, listened to the man for a moment, got up from his chair and punched the drunk with a short combination, right and left hands working like pistons. The man slid to the floor and the story of the incident spread almost as quickly. It did that dude Rosenfelder's reputation no harm.

"Hell-Roaring" Bill Jones, sheriff of Billings County, was another who felt the tenderfoot's wrath on the matter of the mouth. Roosevelt admired Jones, saying he was "a thorough frontiersman, excellent in all kinds of emergencies, and a very game man," and "a thoroughly good citizen when sober." But in the offices of the *Bad Lands Cowboy,* the newspaper in the Dakota town of Medora, Jones was regaling Roosevelt and a group of cowpunchers with some stories which Roosevelt regarded as filthy. He listened awhile then interrupted the sheriff, saying, "I can't tell you why in the world I like you, for you're the nastiest-talking man I ever heard." Sheriff Jones, who had shot men for lesser insults, was so taken aback at this gritty statement that he ended up allowing, meekly, "I don't mind saying that mebbe I've been a little too free with my mouth."

Roosevelt's own choice of language was long remembered. During his first roundup, some cowboys heard him shout, "Hasten forward quickly there!" and the phrase entered the Badlands lexicon with countless barflys thereafter bellowing to saloon keepers to "hasten forward quickly there" with their shot of whiskey or schooner of beer.

The dude simply wore them down. He learned to rope, bulldog and brand steers, stay aboard a bucking horse and breathe trail dust through a bandana. He learned to ride long distances—a hundred miles in a day—and while he never sat a horse with the lazy and confident ease of a cowpuncher, he won a grudging admiration. One waddy who saw him in the saddle recalled that "He was not a *purty* rider, but a helluva *good* rider." They saw he had the strength—muscular shoulders and arms, a big chest and bull neck—and the will and self-confidence to take his place among them.

After a time, cowmen along the Little Missouri got used to his raspy voice, his habit of telling a story as if on the stump exhorting for votes, pounding his fist into his hand, his big grin full of blunt white teeth and blue-gray eyes behind the pince-nez flashing. So eager was he to learn and become one of them, the Bad Landers even managed to put up with the outlandish costume he occasionally affected: a fringed and beaded buckskin shirt and matching trousers, broad-brimmed sombrero, horsehide chaps, boots with silver spurs and a pearl-handled revolver in a tooled holster.

Between duties in Albany, Roosevelt returned often to Dakota Territory and after his three terms as New York assemblyman ended in 1884, he spent most of the next two years working on his own Elkhorn Ranch cattle enterprise on the Little Missouri in which he invested over fifty thousand dollars.

In this period, while working furiously to make his ranch profitable, he found time to serve a stint as deputy sheriff of Billings County under foul-mouthed "Hell-Roaring" Bill Jones and made a respectable record as a lawman. One of his most talked-about exploits occurred after thieves stole a thirty-dollar boat from his

Elkhorn spread. Roosevelt, who carried a copy of *Anna Karenina* and a collection of Matthew Arnold's works in his saddlebags, riding with a posse, trailed the thieves for several days, captured the three men and delivered them to the sheriff's office in the town of Dickinson.

His western experiences were etched deeply on him. Although he sold his ranching interests and property in 1897 (at a loss of about twenty thousand dollars, which he never regretted), he returned on hunting trips to the Badlands many times in the years to come. The land and its people never failed to invigorate him. "For healthy exercise," he told a reporter, "I would strongly recommend some of our gilded youth to go West and try a course of riding bucking ponies and assisting at the branding of a lot of Texas steers."

He returned east early in 1886, "as brown and tough as a hickory nut," to campaign as Republican candidate for mayor of New York City and to resume his book-writing and his courtship of Edith Carow, a long-time friend whom he had admired from afar in his Harvard days. They were married in London that December.

During one summer on his ranch in 1886 he became preoccupied with the possibility of "trouble with Mexico" and in his correspondence wrote of his dream of raising a cavalry regiment, or at least a troop, from among the "harum-scarum rough riders of the West," to go to war, if necessary. These rough riders, he said, would be "as utterly reckless a set of desperadoes as ever sat in the saddle." Later he said this idea originated with his friend, Baron Hermann Speck von Sternberg, who came out to the Little Missouri on a hunting expedition. Von Sternberg, a professional soldier who had served at age seventeen as a hussar in the Franco-Prussian War, became German ambassador in Washington and a frequent guest at Roosevelt's Oyster Bay home where they matched skills at the firing range and talked politics. "It was he,"

Roosevelt said in his *Autobiography*, "who first talked over with me the raising of a regiment of horse riflemen from among the ranchmen and cowboys of the Plains."

3

"Every true patriot . . ."

Roosevelt lost his bid for the mayoralty of New York in 1886 but felt no ignominy in finishing last in a three-candidate race. There had been a time, after he left the legislature in Albany, when he would write his friend Henry Cabot Lodge, "My chance of doing anything in the future worth doing seems to grow continually smaller," but in fact no man of his time had a surer sense of his destiny to accomplish great things. As to the defeat in New York City, he knew all about such matters as overcoming adversity, rising when knocked down, regarding defeat as but a small impediment en route to victory.

What he knew nothing about was biding time. He was ever the impatient man, governed by nervous energy, and for a time he channeled it into his writing—"extremely irksome work," he called it—and his family and their new home, the twenty-three-room Sagamore Hill, on Oyster Bay, Long Island.

In the Dakotas, between hunts, roundups and brandings, ranch and law work, he managed to keep up a prolific correspondence with friends back east. He completed a biography, *Thomas Hart Benton*, on the Missouri senator and expansionist in whom Roosevelt found a philosophical blood brother, and wrote such other books as *Hunting Trips of a Ranchman* (published in 1885) and *Ranch Life and the Hunting Trail* (1886).

In New York he produced *Essays in Practical Politics*, which dealt with state political reform in New York, and in 1888, *Gouverneur Morris*, a biography of the influential politician and diplomat of Revolutionary era New York. He also began work on what would become a four-volume work, *The Winning of the West,* the first two volumes of which appeared in 1889.

In these latter books Roosevelt's lifelong romantic notions of western frontiersmen poured forth in frothy descriptive passages: Daniel Boone was a "tall, spare, sinewy man with eyes like an eagle's and muscles that never tired," and of John Logan, the great Cayuga Iroquois chief, Roosevelt saw a man of "straight-forward honesty," a "skilled marksman" with a "splendid appearance . . . straight as a spear-shaft" and a "countenance brave and manly."

In the fall of 1888 he borrowed time from his writing, hunting trips, and family matters to campaign for the election of Benjamin Harrison of Indiana, the Republican candidate nominated to oppose the incumbent president, Grover Cleveland. Roosevelt worked strenuously in the Midwest for Harrison and although the candidate lost the popular vote, he won the election and took office in January 1889.

Cabot Lodge almost immediately went to work to find a place in the new administration for his friend Theodore and spoke to Harrison's new secretary of state, James G. Blaine, on Roosevelt's behalf. The outcome of this collaring, and those by other of Roosevelt's friends in Congress, was the post of civil service commissioner, which, despite its meager $3,500 annual salary, Roosevelt accepted, taking office in May.

His two-fisted approach to the then-obscure office, his battles against what he called "the spoils-mongers"—these including Harrison's own postmaster general—drew newspaper attention and the president's dismay. Harrison later reflected on his turbulent appointee, saying that the only trouble he ever had in managing Roosevelt was that "he wanted to end all the evil in the world between sunrise and sunset."

The commissioner rented a house on Connecticut Avenue and during his six years in the office invited there new and old friends and a circle of wealthy political and literary luminaries. These included the poet-diplomat John Hay, who had served as Lincoln's private secretary and biographer; Judge William Howard Taft of Ohio; British diplomat Cecil Spring-Rice (who had served as his best man in his London marriage to Edith Carow); Harvard historian Henry Adams; Senator William E. Chandler of New Hampshire; *New York Sun* editor Charles A. Dana, and his star feature writer, Richard Harding Davis; and Roosevelt's closest friend, correspondent and inspiration, Henry Cabot Lodge, junior senator from Massachusetts.

In his always-voluminous reading, during this first Washington period no book more captivated him than *The Influence of Sea Power upon History* by Alfred Thayer Mahan of the U.S. Navy. In the book, published in 1890, Captain Mahan proposed that a nation's growth and prosperity depended upon its navy, that America needed a great fleet to take command of the seas, needed a canal across the isthmus of Central America, and needed colonial expansion as a natural and necessary step in national growth and power, to open foreign markets to trade and provide coaling stations for the new American navy.

Roosevelt, mesmerized by Mahan's theories and in thorough agreement with them, began a correspondence with the author and subsequently established a personal friendship with the "New Navy" intellectual. The disciple was honored to learn that Mahan was an enthusiastic admirer of Roosevelt's *The Naval War of 1812*.

Their friendship and mutual admiration was the product of their bellicose nationalism and patriotism. They were brother jingos, in the purest sense of that felicitous word coined in a London music hall ditty composed during the Crimean War:

> *We don't want to fight yet by Jingo!*
> *if we do*
> *We've got the ships, we've got the men,*
> *and got the money, too!*

Roosevelt remained civil service commissioner even after Grover Cleveland returned to office, but he resigned in the spring of 1895 to become commissioner of New York City's four-man Police Board. His two-year tenure at police headquarters on Mulberry Street could best be described as "pugnacious." He took his work seriously—too seriously, some thought—fighting police corruption and lazy cops by tramping New York's streets into the wee hours and appearing suddenly in saloons and tenements, questioning everybody in sight. In these forays he was often accompanied by his friend Jacob Riis, the *Evening Sun* reporter and author of such exposés of the city's slums as *How the Other Half Lives* and *Children of the Poor,* or that splendid muckraker-in-the-making, Lincoln Steffens of the *Evening Post.*

Commissioner Roosevelt's one-man campaign to enforce such laws as that requiring the city's saloons to close on Sundays was opposed by the city's German community, by Tammany Hall and Republican machine politicians, and by such influential newspapers as Whitlaw Reid's *Tribune* and Joseph Pulitzer's *World.* Among his admirers were such reporters as Richard Harding Davis of the *Herald* and Edward Marshall of the *Journal,* whose boss, William Randolph Hearst, was noisily opposed to the commissioner's work and had dubbed Roosevelt the "Patron Saint of dry Sundays."

Another occasional newspaper writer Roosevelt met in this period was Stephen Crane, whose shocking novel, *Maggie of the Streets,* Crane had self-published in 1893 and whose Civil War masterwork, *The Red Badge of Courage,* had just appeared in book form. Roosevelt met the skinny, ardent twenty-four-year-old author at the Lantern Club in Manhattan, a supper club frequented by Park Row newspapermen, and expressed admiration for Crane's work. He was especially impressed with *Red Badge,* and a short story with a western setting Crane had sent Roosevelt for a critique. Unfortunately, while the war of Crane's *Red Badge* joined them temporarily, the real war in Cuba would divide them permanently.

While battling corruption in New York, Roosevelt's attention never strayed far from national and international matters and he missed no occasion to voice his opinions in his voluminous correspondence or in the press. In world affairs he was as belligerent a nationalist as any man of his time, his eye forever cocked toward America's real or perceived enemies. He was nervous over the "Yellow Peril," "alive to the danger of Japan" and the growing Japanese population in the Hawaiian Islands; saw "big problems" in the West Indies; was alarmed at potential dangers to the United States fomented by Spain, Germany and France; and in 1886, when newspapers were carrying stories of U.S.–Mexican problems, he wrote about organizing a cowboy cavalry from his ranch in the Dakotas and heading for the Rio Grande.

Nor did the British escape his ire during the "Venezuelan Boundary Crisis." This episode had begun in 1886 when England declared that some 23,000 square miles of border territory belonged to its colony of British Guiana and not to Venezuela, which claimed the mineral-rich lands. A U.S. offer to arbitrate the matter was rebuffed and after nine years of dispute, the issue flared anew in 1895 when President Cleveland's secretary of state notified the British prime minister that the United States would resist "any sequestration of Venezuelan soil by Great Britain."

New York Police Commissioner Roosevelt, seemingly an odd spokesman for the Monroe Doctrine, was quoted in newspapers praising the Cleveland administration, the Senate and House, for their "spirit of broadminded patriotism" in opposing the British incursion into South America. As to conjectures that English warships might attack American coastal cities and "hold them at ransom," he said this speculation "is too foolish to me for serious consideration" but gave such preposterous rumors credibility nonetheless. "American cities may possibly be bombarded, but no ransom will be paid for them," he said. "It is infinitely better to see the cities laid level than to see a dollar paid to any foreign foe to buy their safety."

In such an event, Roosevelt suggested a startling scenario: "We might suffer a check or two at first, in time, [but in] a very short time, Canada would surely be conquered, and, once wrested from England, it would never be restored."

"Every true patriot," he said later when Cuba had replaced Venezuela as the issue of the moment, "every man of statesman-like habit, should look forward to the day when not a single European power will hold a foot of American soil."

He wearied of the trivial municipal politics that hampered his work as police commissioner and welcomed the opportunity for service on a larger, national, scale. In the summer of 1895 he campaigned for the election of William McKinley against the oro-tund Orator of the Platte, William Jennings Bryan. He called the Chicago "Cross of Gold" convention which nominated Bryan "a witch's sabbath," and hurled himself into the effort to defeat the Nebraska Democrat, whose candidacy, he believed, posed the greatest threat to the nation since the Civil War.

After McKinley's sweeping victory, and with the assistance of Cabot Lodge and other influential friends, Roosevelt returned to Washington.

The timing of his taking office as Navy Secretary John D. Long's assistant in April 1897, was fatefully perfect for him. He had risen in politics during an era of a renewed national sense of Manifest Destiny and was a recognized spokeman for expansion-ism, a disciple of Mahan's theories on the preeminence of naval power, author of numerous books celebrating Americanism, pa-triotism, national destiny, the "brave and manly" virtues of the American character. (In 1897, upon publication of his book *American Ideals,* Speaker of the U.S. House of Representatives

Thomas B. "Czar" Reed told him, "If there is one thing more than another for which I admire you, Theodore, it is your original discovery of the Ten Commandments.")

To some, Roosevelt's public pugnacity—as civil service and police commissioner, as oft-heard voice in the Venezuelan and Cuban affairs—was scary. Toward the end of 1897, after less than eight months in the Navy Department, the *Boston Globe* observed that while he was an "entertaining performer" and "a man to watch," "it would never do . . . to permit such a man to get into the Presidency. He would produce national insomnia."

4

"A man of imdomitable pluck"

Just over a month after his inauguration, on April 6, 1897, McKinley sent Roosevelt's name to the Senate and the confirmation vote quickly followed. The *Washington Post* predicted that the new assistant secretary would bring with him to Washington the "machinery of disturbance and upheaval" which, the newspaper said, was as much a part of him as "the very air he breathes." Despite this anxious beginning, the editorial ended in praise: "He is inspired by a passionate hatred of meanness, humbug, and cowardice. He is a fighter, a man of indomitable pluck and energy, a potent and forceful factor. . . . A field of immeasurable usefulness awaits him—will he find it?"

He found it, often to the discomfort of his kindly, indolent boss, John D. Long, who, as the months passed, became alternately amused and exasperated—but never really angry—at the trying "ardor" of his whirling dervish of an assistant.

Roosevelt produced a blizzard of paperwork in his thirteen months in the Navy Department. He wrote letters and suggestions to department personnel, memos, pronouncements and suggestions to Long, speeches, minutes, and a staggering personal correspondence. His subjects ranged from Mahan-inspired pleas for increased appropriations for the navy and ideas on a canal across the Isthmus of Panama, to ship construction matters, assignment of torpedo-boat commanders and, above all, the navy's role in a war with Spain and how, in the event of such a war, the Pacific Fleet could occupy Cuba while a "Flying Squadron" could be sent to menace Spain itself.

"His typewriters had no rest," Long wrote in his journal, adding that Theodore, "like most of us, lacks the rare knack of brevity."

For his part, Roosevelt had great affection for Long, writing of him as "a perfect dear" even after being called on the carpet by the secretary for some public pronouncement Long considered intemperate. Roosevelt said these "wiggings" were only as severe as Long's "invariable courtesy and kindness would permit." Certainly they did nothing to dampen his ardor for preparing for the war he felt was inevitable even before the *Maine* blew to pieces in Havana Harbor.

There could be no mistaking that his references were Spain and Cuba when he spoke to officers of the Naval War College a few months after he took office. In this perfect forum, he leaned over the podium and with teeth and pince-nez flashing preached to a choir of like-minded militarists. He said that "cowardice in a race, like in an individual, is the unpardonable sin," that "a willful failure to prepare for danger may in its effects be as bad as cowardice," and that "the timid man who cannot fight and the selfish, shortsighted or foolish man who will not take the steps that will enable him to fight, stand on almost the same plane." He ended his address in the trademarked Rooseveltian crescendo, smacking his fist in his palm and declaring that "no national life is worth having if the nation is not willing, when the need shall arise, to stake everything on the supreme arbitrament of war, and to pour out its blood, its treasure, its tears like water rather than to submit to the loss of honor and renown."

Such speeches, containing such bellicosities as "the diplomat is the servant, not the master, of the soldier," not only made Long uncomfortable but their reverberations reached the White House where the president and his advisors were distracted from Roosevelt's hortatory by the search for diplomatic means to prevent a war with Spain. Owen Wister, a close friend from Harvard days, said Roosevelt became "an uneasy thorn in the side of the Administration," and the Harvard philosopher Henry James would later say of his former student that in his public war making, Theodore was "still mentally in the *Sturm und Drang* period of early adolescence."

Two months after taking office in the Navy Department, Roosevelt met a man to whom he would soon become bonded in a lifetime friendship, beginning with the shared addiction to hiking and football, later as comrade-in-arms. This new companion and confidante was the president's physician, Captain Leonard Wood, and the two met at a dinner party and were inseparable thereafter. In a letter to Cabot Lodge, Roosevelt wrote, "You will be pleased to hear that I have developed at Washington a playmate who fairly walked me off my legs; a Massachusetts man moreover, an army surgeon named Wood."

In fact, Wood was a New Hampshire man who had graduated from the Harvard Medical School in 1884 and shortly after joined the Army Medical Corps. He was assigned as assistant post surgeon at Fort Huachuca, Arizona Territory, in 1886, toward the end of the Geronimo campaigns, and received a company command in an infantry regiment actively engaged in chasing Apaches in northern Sonora, Mexico. Wood distinguished himself by carrying dispatches through Apache country, on one occasion making a ride of seventy miles and walking another thirty to deliver important intelligence reports to his commanders. He earned a Medal of Honor for his exploits (awarded in April 1898) and the admiration of such important officers as Henry W. Lawton and

Nelson A. Miles, who became his champions at critical points later in his career.

Wood was a handsome, stoutly built, broad-chested man, eager for tasks and responsibility, intensely ambitious and given to cultivating influential friends. In Washington, he demonstrated little interest in national affairs but was a dedicated expansionist, seeing in a conflict with Spain an avenue for personal advancement.

In Roosevelt, Wood discovered a soul mate who shared his hunger for military glory, and the two, during their long walks around the capital and lunches at the Metropolitan Club, talked tirelessly about Cuba. Each confided in the other their plans in the event of war: Wood intended to ask for an assignment as a line officer, transferring to a volunteer regiment if necessary, as a step toward a regular army billet; Roosevelt had already notified Secretary Long and President McKinley that when war came, he planned to seek a volunteer officer's commission. He had, in fact, been in contact with an old family friend, Colonel Francis Vinton Greene of the Seventy-first New York Regiment, offering his services "in some capacity" in the event of war with Spain. He had proposed that Greene raise a volunteer regiment and serve as its colonel and consider selecting Roosevelt as lieutenant colonel. "I know that under a man like yourself I could do first-class work," he wrote.

Roosevelt and Wood's close friendship and like-mindedness did not escape the attention of the president and during the war hysteria after the sinking of the *Maine,* McKinley asked his physician, "Have you and Theodore declared war yet?" Wood, who for all his military starchiness had a muted sense of humor, did not mind the joke. "No, Mr. President," he answered, "but we think *you* should."

Another military man who came into Roosevelt's circle of friends in Washington and who shared his and Wood's expansionist views, was sixty-year-old Commodore George Dewey, president of the navy's Board of Inspection and Survey. White-haired with a bushy white walrus mustache, Dewey, a Vermonter, had by the time of his Washington assignment in 1895 a respectable and unblemished, if not particularly distinguished, thirty-five-year navy career. He had served under David Farragut in the Gulf of Mexico and on the steam frigate *Colorado* during the attack on Fort Fisher in the Civil War; had a good record with the European Squadron on the sloop-of-war *Kearsarge;* five years at the Naval Academy at Annapolis; a Gulf of California surveying expedition; a stint as lighthouse inspector. He was a robust, physically fit specimen of a sailor thinking of retirement when he met Roosevelt at the Metropolitan Club in 1897.

The two became fast friends, meeting periodically at the club and on horseback-riding excursions in Washington parks and paths. Dewey struck Roosevelt as a heroic figure with an unrealized potential for greatness. He saw in him the perfect officer to command the Asiatic Squadron when the war with Spain came, the one who would pounce on the Philippines "like a wolfhound from a leash." As second-in-command in the Navy Department, Roosevelt seized the opportunity to make his voice heard on the matter of the Asiatic Squadron command and wrote letters and called upon influential lawmakers, lobbying for Dewey's appointment. Then, after the powerful Vermont senator Redfield Proctor, a man Roosevelt described as "very ardent for the war," talked with McKinley, Dewey received the assignment and on New Year's Day 1898, reported aboard his flagship *Olympia*, at anchor in the harbor at Nagasaki, Japan.

Six weeks later the commodore received a cable announcing the *Maine* disaster and ten days after that, on February 25, received another message, this one from "acting secretary of the navy" Theodore Roosevelt, ordering him to Hong Kong: "In the event of declaration of war, Spain, your duty will be to see that the Spanish Squadron does not leave the Asiatic Coast and then offensive operations in the Philippine Islands."

Secretary Long, out of the capital when his assistant took this bold initiative, learned of it upon his return and gave Roosevelt a gentlemanly "wigging." Afterward, the secretary wrote in his journal that Theodore had "gone at things like a bull in a china closet."

But Long did not rescind the order.

The wiggee wrote to Cabot Lodge, "I have continually meddled with what was not my business, because I was willing to jeopardize my position in a way that a naval officer could not."

Roosevelt had no patience with the *Maine* inquiry board and its work in Havana to determine the cause of the explosion on February 15. He had even urged Long to advise the president against such an investigation, making no secret of his conviction that the ship "was sunk by an act of dirty treachery on the part of the Spaniards." In a private letter that sounded precisely like the work of a yellow journal editor, he said, "the blood of the Cubans, the blood of women and children who have perished by the hundreds of thousands in hideous misery, lies at our door; and the blood of the murdered men of the *Maine* calls not for indemnity but for the full measure of atonement which can only come by driving the Spaniard from the New World."

V

THE CLANK OF THE SABER

1
"The supreme triumph of war"

John D. Long thought it patently ridiculous that his ob-
streperous protégé, a rising star in Washington politics, would
abandon an important government post, one that would be intimately involved in the event of a war with Spain, to march off to
soldier. "His heart is right and he means well," the secretary wrote
in his journal, "but it is one of those cases of aberration-desertion-
vainglory, of which he is utterly unaware." Cabot Lodge also
urged Roosevelt not to resign and to think of the potential injury
to his political career, and even McKinley twice asked him to re-
consider his decision. But Roosevelt had long been angling for
"active service" when war came. As early as 1895, while still police commissioner, he had written to New York Governor Levi P.
Morton asking for a captaincy of volunteers in the event of a war
with Spain over Cuba. He was in touch with his friend Colonel
Francis V. Greene of the Seventy-first New York Regiment, hoping for an appointment "in some capacity," and lately had been

nagging War Secretary Russell A. Alger and army general-in-chief Nelson A. Miles for a commission of some kind. Ironically, for such a student of naval history he gave no serious consideration of a naval commission. "I shall be useless on a ship," he said.

While John D. Long loyally followed the administration's tread-softly line toward Spain, and while the president sought a diplomatic solution to the Cuban problem, Roosevelt seemed to spend all his waking hours writing and speaking and devising plans for war. His operations plan for the navy, based on the one prepared by the Naval War College in 1895, typified a miscellany of plans which he shared with Long and Lodge: blockade Cuban ports, send four cruisers to the coast of Spain, send the Asiatic Squadron to capture Manila.

Roosevelt considered McKinley's post-*Maine* willingness to continue negotiations with Spain "mollycoddling" and "shillyshallying" and he said, privately, of course, that the president "has no more backbone than a chocolate éclair." In mid-April, a few days before Congress issued its war resolution, he crowded the pages in his personal diary with observations on McKinley's "painfully trying for peace," the president's "weakness and vacillation," the army's "awful" condition and the War Department's "utter confusion." Secretary Alger, he wrote, "has no force whatever, & no knowledge of his department. But he wishes for war, at least." General Miles he dismissed as "merely a brave peacock," and he scorned Alger and Miles's claim that they could "put 100,000 men in Tampa in 24 hours!"

He had exhibited no such vacillation or "weakness," had advocated intervention in Cuba in plain language and remained deaf to any other argument, using words like "cowardice" and "timidity" to characterize the words and actions of those who differed with him, while accusing Spain of "dirty treachery," no matter the outcome of the *Maine* inquiry.

He made speeches to naval cadets about preparing for war, warning them that the nation's honor was at stake and exhorting them that "no triumph of peace is quite so great as the supreme triumph of war."

For years he had lost no opportunity to take a podium to extoll America's manifest destiny to expand its borders and seize its rightful place in the world scheme.

He sent Dewey to Japan to prepare to pounce on the Philippines.

He wanted war and wanted to fight in it.

"There was always a clank of the saber in his discourse," H. L. Mencken wrote of the Theodore Roosevelt of 1898.

The president's best diplomatic efforts failed in the end—"not in the conduct of his diplomacy," McKinley biographer Margaret Leech wrote, "but in restraining the belligerence of Congress and the American people"—and on April 11, after much agonizing, he sent a high-minded if somewhat murky message to Congress asking sanction "to authorize and empower the President to take measures to secure a full and final termination of hostilities between the government of Spain and the people of Cuba." The presidential paper asked the lawmakers to "secure in the island the establishment of a stable government" employing "the military and naval forces of the United States as may be necessary." Eight days later, Congress issued a declaration "for the independence of the Cuban people," demanding that Spain "withdraw its land and naval forces," and authorizing the president "to carry these resolutions into effect."

McKinley signed the document on April 20 and the ultimatum was handed to the Spanish minister and cabled to Madrid that day. The demands were peremptorily rejected by Spanish Premier Práxedes Sagasta and his government, and, since it regarded the ultimatum as a declaration of war, Spain ended diplomatic ties to the United States.

On April 22, with the war now official, the *New York Evening Journal* declared "NOW TO AVENGE THE MAINE!" and

Queen Victoria jotted in her diary her opinion of the opening of hostilities: "It is monstrous of America." Within days a naval blockade of the principal ports of Cuba went into effect, the president called on the War Department to publish a call-to-arms for 125,000 volunteers, and a congressional War Revenue Act authorized a two-hundred-million-dollar appropriation for the war effort and expansion of the regular army to 61,000 men.

"Seldom can history have recorded a plainer case of military aggression," Walter Millis, a historian of the war, wrote in 1931, "yet seldom has a war been started in so profound a conviction of its righteousness."

In fact, the nation was unprepared to wage war. In April 1898, the regular army consisted of a meager force of 28,000 men, most of them spread thinly around western frontier forts. There were few units of regimental size and only the dwindling number of Civil War veterans still on active service remembered a unit as large as a brigade. Militia and National Guard companies, about forty of them, each under the control of the governors of their states, numbered under one hundred thousand infantrymen with obsolete equipment and little training. The War Department, its once-aggressive ideas dulled after the Civil War and as the Indian campaigns ended, had no discernible mobilization plan and little knowledge of the Spanish forces in Cuba (believed to number about eighty thousand regulars), or their deployment on the island. The number, location and dependability of the insurgents, who would presumably assist an American invasion force, were unknown, as were details on the topography and the terrain of the island and the overland approaches to its main population centers. Even accurate maps of Cuba were nonexistent. Moreover, with the island a prime objective, no American army had managed a major amphibious operation on a foreign shore since the landings at Vera Cruz in the Mexican War fifty years past.

While these matters preoccupied the War Department and

army strategists, they were of little interest to the press. Between concocting new Armaggedon-sized daily headlines, newspaper editors everywhere were concentrating merrily on various preposterous ideas to assist the War Department to fight the Spaniards. Among the proposals given serious credence, in the press and nowhere else, was that of the celebrated frontiersman and Wild West showman William F. "Buffalo Bill" Cody, who announced in the *New York World* that he was prepared to raise a force of thirty thousand veteran scouts and Indian fighters, equip this awesome army with horses and guns, and lead them into battle. He estimated that the Spaniards would flee Cuba in sixty days. Hearst's *Journal* suggested that prizefighters James J. Corbett and Bob Fitzsimmons, baseball star Cap Anson and other such professional heroes could command a regiment of athletes for the war ("Think of a regiment composed of magnificent men of this ilk!"). Elsewhere, Frank James, brother of the late Jesse, offered to organize a company of cowboys to fight the Spaniards, and another story announced that six hundred Sioux Indians were prepared to go on the warpath and collect Spanish scalps.

But while these journalistic volunteers got newspaper space, the matter of actual volunteers had the serious attention of the War Department. The initial call for 125,000 men was raised to 267,000 and authorization was given for National Guard organizations to serve as volunteer units at the discretion of governors. In addition, after lobbying and appeals from Judge Jay L. Torrey of Wyoming and Melvin "Milt" Grigsby, adjutant general of South Dakota, the original Volunteer Bill was amended. The revised document empowered the president "to authorize the Secretary of War to organize companies, troops, battalions, or regiments, possessing special qualifications" from among the western territories. After the bill's passage, Secretary Alger specified that three cavalry regiments be formed "exclusively of frontiersmen possessing special qualifications as horsemen and marksmen." The First U.S. Volunteer Cavalry Regiment was to be raised in the

four territories—Arizona, New Mexico, Oklahoma and Indian
Territory. The other two, designated the Second and Third, were
to be formed in Wyoming under Judge Torrey, a colorful rancher
and legislator, and Colonel Milt Grigsby, the Civil War veteran of
South Dakota.

(Ironically, neither of the two men most responsible for pro-
moting the idea of cowboy volunteers got their regiments into the
fighting. Torrey's "Rocky Mountain Riders" and "Grigsby's Cowboys" spent the war at Camp Thomas, Georgia, and Chickamauga
Park, Tennessee, drilling and hoping for mobilization.)

Roosevelt's public pronouncements on quitting his post to
seek active campaign service, his dogged pestering of the War Department for a commission, and his reputation as a man who knew
the West from first-hand experience, paid dividends within days of
the Volunteer Bill. Alger, quickly swamped with requests from
would-be warriors for assignments in the army, called Roosevelt to
his office and offered him a colonelcy and command of the First
Volunteer Cavalry Regiment. There is no record of the precise
conversation between the two men—each wary of the other—but
what happened astonished Alger: Roosevelt expressed gratitude at
the offer, was greatly honored, etc., etc., but said he must decline
the offer to command the regiment. He said he had compelling
duties in the Navy Department to finish before resigning and that
he had no experience in the intricacies of organizing a regiment—
although he felt he could learn these quickly. Before the secretary
could recover from his shock at this example of utterly uncharac-
teristic modesty from the younger man, Roosevelt said he had a
perfect counterproposal: that their mutual friend, Captain
Leonard Wood, a man with battle experience on the western frontier, be given the regiment and that he, Roosevelt, would be honored to serve as Wood's second-in-command.

Wood was Alger's family physician as well as McKinley's and
the secretary knew Wood's military history. He also knew that
such an appointment would have the full support of Nelson Miles,

commanding general of the army, under whom Wood had served in the Apache campaigns.

Roosevelt's proposal made sense and Alger approved it.

On April 25, John D. Long wrote in his journal:

> My Assistant Secretary, Roosevelt, has determined upon re-signing, in order to go into the army and take part in the war. He has been of great use: a man of unbounded energy and force, and thoroughly honest, which is the main thing. He has lost his head to this unutterable folly of deserting the post where he is of most service and running off to ride a horse and, probably, brush mosquitoes from his neck in the Florida sands. . . . He thinks he is following his highest ideal, whereas, in fact, without exception, every one of his friends advises him, he is acting like a fool. And, yet, how absurd all this will sound if, by some turn of fortune, he should ac-complish some great thing and strike a very high mark.

And at their home at 1810 N Street, opposite the British Embassy, Edith Kermit Carow Roosevelt, in fragile health after the birth of their fifth child, valiantly supported her husband's decision to go to war. She could scarcely do otherwise.

Many years later, Roosevelt confessed to a friend, "I know now that I would have turned from my wife's deathbed to have answered the call." The war, he said, was "my chance to cut my little notch on the stick that stands as a measuring-rod in every family."

2

"Death or a star!"

Two days after the war declaration and call for volunteers, Secretary Alger sent a telegram to Myron T. McCord, governor of Arizona Territory: "The President directs that Captain Leonard

Wood of the United States Army be authorized to raise a regiment
of cowboys as mounted riflemen, and to be its Colonel, and has
named Hon. Theodore Roosevelt as Lieutenant Colonel. All
other officers will come from the vicinity where the troops are
raised. What can you do for them? Answer immediately."

The governor must have read this message smiling, perhaps
seeing in it the hand of his friend and former legislative colleague,
William McKinley. McCord, a Pennsylvanian by birth, a banker
and lumberman in Wisconsin, had been elected to the House of
Representatives in 1888 and formed a close friendship with the
Ohio congressman McKinley. After failing in his bid for reelection,
McCord moved to Phoenix where he purchased an interest in the
Phoenix Gazette and kept active in Republican politics, champi-
oning McKinley's bid for the presidency and working for his nom-
ination at the St. Louis convention in 1896. A year later,
McKinley, now president, reached out to his friend and supporter
and appointed McCord to the Arizona governorship.

A week after the *Maine* news reached the territory, McCord
began bombarding the president and the War Department with
ideas on raising an entire regiment of Arizona volunteers and asking official permission to do so. In these efforts, he was in league
with other prominent Arizonans, one of whom had recently
caused McCord considerable grief and embarrassment. This was
the former sheriff of Yavapai County, newspaper editor, Populist
candidate for Congress, terror of faro tables, and current mayor of
the former territorial capital of Prescott, William O. "Buckey"
O'Neill.

In that forested high country town, seat of the vast Yavapai
County, a hundred miles northwest of Phoenix, Mayor O'Neill,
after the *Maine* news, had practically suspended municipal business to lay plans for organizing a volunteer unit for the war every
soul in in the territory knew was inevitable. O'Neill's military aspirations had never been realized although he had served as captain of the Prescott Grays, the local militia group, and as adjutant

general of Arizona, a mostly ceremonial appointment. He was
now thirty-eight years old and had missed the Apache campaigns
in the south of the territory, missed chasing Geronimo, had been
refused permission to organize volunteer troops to serve in the
Sioux wars. He was the son of a hero of the Irish Brigade at Fred-
ericksburg, a student of war—England's Gordon of Khartoum
was one of his heroes—and one who dreamed of military glory.
No man in Arizona was more attentive when Cuban junta agents
came through Prescott to plead the cause of *Cuba Libre;* no man
was more moved by the news of the *Maine.* At a gathering at the
Yavapai County Courthouse that February, of the *Maine* he said
he was "ready and willing to shed his heart's last drop" for his flag
and country, and those who knew him knew it was not empty
rhetoric.

Governor McCord appreciated Mayor O'Neill's fervor but
nursed a strong distaste for the popular Populist of Prescott.
O'Neill had earned the governor's enmity in the fall of 1897 when
he launched a bitter attack on McCord's plan to build an irriga-
tion canal near Yuma using convict labor from the Territorial
Prison. Buckey was not alone in suspecting the governor of ben-
efitting personally from the project, but had infuriated the governor by publishing, in the classic traditions of freewheeling,
libelous, frontier journalism, a venomous "open letter" in which
he accused McCord of being a possible "fugitive timber thief"
and "rogue."

Fortunately, when it came to McCord's dream of organizing
an Arizona volunteer regiment, he could avoid dealing directly
with his Prescott nemesis. O'Neill had among his cronies a man
McCord trusted, a former professional soldier, now a prominent
territorial mining engineer, Alexander Oswald Brodie.

More than McCord, O'Neill or the Phoenix newspaperman
James McClintock—all prominent figures in the genesis of the
Arizona contingent of volunteers that became the heart of the
regiment soon to be called the "Rough Riders"—the forty-nine-

year-old Brodie was the key to its organization. He was a New York and 1870 West Point graduate who had served at Fort Apache with the First Cavalry and compiled a distinguished record in the 1872–1873 campaign against the Apaches in the Tonto Basin of Arizona, and in pursuing the Nez Percé in Idaho in 1877. After his wife's death, Brodie resigned from the army and for a time ranched in Kansas. In 1883 he returned to Arizona with the Sixth Cavalry and served again in the border Apache campaigns. Then, after leaving the army in 1884, he became a colonel in the Arizona National Guard.

From the beginning, this tall, dour, sun-baked professional was the uncontested choice to organize the Arizona volunteers for the war with Spain and to be its regimental colonel.

Brodie needed no prodding. On March 3, six weeks before the call for volunteers, he had written to both Governor McCord and President McKinley offering his services "in the event of war" and requesting permission to raise a regiment of Arizonans. On April 2, McCord asked McKinley to appoint Brodie as a colonel of volunteers and to sanction organization of the Arizona contingent. "No better material can be found anywhere in the world, than among the cowboys of Arizona," he wrote, and thereafter sent a barrage of letters and telegrams to Washington, listing reasons why his frontiersmen were ideal volunteer troopers: expert horsemen and marksmen who would require little training; self-reliant men accustomed to outdoor camp life; many of them veterans of the Indian wars; many who could speak Spanish; all Southwesterners accustomed to the sun and tropical weather conditions.

Brodie, working with his friends O'Neill and McClintock, planned a full regiment of cavalry—over a thousand men total in three squadrons of four troops each, each troop of eighty-five men led by a captain and two lieutenants—and began taking enlistment pledges while waiting for war to be declared.

But the Volunteer Bill of April 22 proved to be a great disappointment. There would be no full regiment from Arizona; in fact, as plans for the three volunteer cavalry units evolved, Leonard Wood's First U.S. Volunteer Cavalry was initially designated to have 780 men, only 170 of them to be enlisted in Arizona, an equal number from Indian Territory, 340 from New Mexico Territory, and 80 from Oklahoma Territory. Even when the total was eventually raised to 1,000 men and Arizona's share 200 of that number, only a fifth of McCord's and Brodie's dream was to be realized. Secretary Alger did notify the governor that he could name the officer to command the Arizona contingent, but the rank could be only that of major.

McCord immediately selected Brodie to the command and Brodie in turn named O'Neill and McClintock as troop captains.

In the days that followed instructions from Leonard Wood, now a colonel of volunteers and preparing to leave for San Antonio, Texas, the designated training area for his regiment, the troop commanders began screening recruits. McClintock did his work in Phoenix while O'Neill set up his desk in the Aitken and Robinson Cigar Store in downtown Prescott. Potential enlistees had to be expert horsemen and marksmen, between eighteen and forty-five years of age, and physically fit. They came from all corners of the territory, traveling to the rendezvous point of Prescott by horseback and train. Those selected to be among the elite two hundred were quickly marched off to Whipple Barracks, the old fort three miles northeast of the town which had once served as headquarters of the army's Department of Arizona, there to await their swearing-in.

In Phoenix on April 27, Governor McCord awarded O'Neill and McClintock their captain's bars and joined them and Major Brodie at a banquet held that evening. There, the territorial adjutant general raised his glass and said, "Now we drink the soldier's toast—death or a star!" At this, Buckey O'Neill rose to his feet and said, alluding to the dream of Arizona statehood, "Who would not gamble for a new star!"

At Whipple Barracks two days later, O'Neill took his oath, becoming volunteer number one, the first man to volunteer for service in the war against Spain.

On the 30th, the entire Arizona contingent was sworn in and on May 4 marched out of Whipple, lining up four abreast in the town square, standing in a semblance of military order, a rough-looking crowd of men in cowboy mufti—baggy pants, galluses, blanket rolls, wrinkled shirts, sweat-stained hats and trail-scuffed boots, carrying their sparse belongings in cardboard suitcases and canvas bags. Each wore a hatband proclaiming "1st U.S. Volunteer Cavalry—Arizona Column," otherwise they might have been mistaken for a group of cowpunchers heading out on a trail drive.

While the recruits stood as much at attention as could be expected, Governor McCord was introduced and held up a large homespun flag, the work of the Women's Relief Corps of Phoenix. The banner "shall be carried into the battlefields of Cuba or elsewhere," he said, adding that he had promised the ladies who made it that "it would be found like the plume of Henry of Navarre waving in the front of the battle."

Next, a feisty young mountain lion named Florence was led to the grandstand and presented to the Arizonans by Robert Brow, a Prescott "Whiskey Row" saloonkeeper well-known to the recruits. After a few more ceremonial words, the volunteers tramped to the train station where the cars were decorated with bunting and "Remember the Maine!" slogans and stocked with food and a large supply of corncob pipes. Just after seven that evening, the train chuffed out of the station heading east while the town band played "The Girl I Left Behind Me" and other martial airs.

Four days after the Arizonans departed Prescott for San Antonio, New Mexico Territory's four troops of volunteers for Wood's regiment left Santa Fe by special train headed in a somewhat roundabout way, via Colorado, Kansas and Indian Territory, for the Texas training ground.

The call for volunteers by New Mexico Governor Miguel Otero had produced, as in Arizona, Indian and Oklahoma Territories, a flood of eager recruits. Among the officers who came forward to lead the New Mexicans were two of the territory's most lustrous figures. Maximiliano Luna was among the earliest of New Mexicans to be commissioned. A thirty-seven-year-old sheriff of Valencia County, he was a descendent of conquistadors and the son of a congressman. ("The Captain's people had been on the banks of the Rio Grande before my forefathers came to the mouth of the Hudson or Wood's landed at Plymouth," Theodore Roosevelt said of him.) George Curry, another man of substance and renown, also came forward to serve. A Louisianan by birth, he had a spectacular career as a post trader, sheep rancher, territorial senator, one-time sheriff of Lincoln County and a fringe figure in the Lincoln County War who counted among his friends Billy the Kid, Pat Garrett, Governor Lew Wallace and cattle baron John Chisum.

Other volunteer officers in the New Mexico contingent included Thomas P. Ledwidge, an Illinois carpenter who had a unique distinction: he had fought in Cuba as a soldier of fortune, serving with Máximo Gómez and other *insurrecto* immortals; William Henry Harrison Llewellyn of Las Cruces, a Wisconsin-born wanderer who came to New Mexico and made a career as lawman, agent to the Mescalero and Jicarilla Apaches, rancher and a lawyer; Henry B. Hersey, a Vermonter, lately adjutant general of New Mexico Territory; and Thomas Littlepage Ballard, Roswell rancher and deputy U.S. Marshal.

The 340 men of the New Mexico Squadron were mustered into service on May 6–7 and left Santa Fe on the eighth.

One of the raw troopers who boarded the train headed for San Antonio that day was twenty-one-year-old Frank C. Brito of Pinos

Altos, a mining camp in the southwest corner of New Mexico Territory. He had been cowboying in the Silver City area when his father got a message to him, calling him home and instructing him and his brother Joe to enlist in the New Mexico volunteers which the newspapers said was being organized to fight the Spaniards. Frank and Joe Brito were assigned to Captain George Curry's Troop H.

Another of the New Mexico volunteers, a long way from home, was George Hamner, a native of Faber's Mill, near Charlottesville, Virginia. The youngest of ten children, he was a well-traveled twenty-four-year-old telegrapher, a trade he learned from a retired railroader back home. He worked for Western Union and the company had sent him to such exotic places as Kenova, West Virginia; Minneapolis and Duluth, Minnesota; and Wagon Mound, New Mexico. His most memorable assignment had been his telegraphic reportage of all twenty-one rounds of the John L. Sullivan–James J. Corbett heavyweight championship prizefight in New Orleans on September 7, 1892. Hamner was working in Wagon Mound when he got the news of the squadron the territory was organizing for the war against Spain. He quit his job, made his way the hundred or so miles southwest to Santa Fe and on May 6 signed up. He was assigned to Troop F.

In Oklahoma Territory, volunteers were mustered in by Lieutenant Allyn K. Capron of the Seventh U.S. Cavalry, son of a serving artillery officer. He represented the fifth generation of Caprons to serve as professional soldiers, his forebears having fought in the Revolutionary War, the War of 1812, the Mexican War and Civil War. Lieutenant Capron, soon to be captain and adjutant of the First U.S. Volunteer Cavalry, was a native of Brooklyn, twenty-six years old, married, and an eight-year veteran of the regular army.

That April and May, wrote Kansan William Allen White, editor of the *Emporia Gazette*, "everywhere in this good and fair

land, flags were flying. Trains carrying soldiers were hurrying—
and little children on fences greeted the soldiers with flapping
scarves and handkerchiefs and flags . . . the fluttering of flags
drowns the voice of the tears that may be in the air."

3

"Let the young men go to war . . ."

At nine A.M. on April 25, 1898, Commodore George Dewey,
standing on the bridge of his flagship *Olympia* in a fresh, white
uniform, binoculars fixed to his eyes, led the U.S. Asiatic
Squadron from its anchorage in Hong Kong to Mirs Bay to take
on ammunition, then into the open sea for the five-day voyage
south to the Philippines. As of three days ago there was a war to
be fought and the navy had the welcomed duty to perform the
first large-scale hostile act of it, an attack on the Spanish Fleet in
Manila Bay. This plan had been an open secret since January
when, after Dewey took command of the squadron in Nagasaki,
Japan, the Spanish military attaché in Washington notified his
government that if war was declared, the Americans would make
their first strike at Manila.

It seemed clear from the beginning that the war would be
fought on two fronts, with the navy in the vanguard on the Pacific
side and taking a significant role in the Caribbean as well. There,
Admiral William T. Sampson's Atlantic Squadron had been dispatched to blockade Havana, Matanzas, and other of Cuba's main
ports. The army's role did not seem so well-defined to the
newspaper-reading public, but Cuba clearly seemed to be the primary objective of land forces, with troops to be landed on the island, perhaps to capture Havana or the Oriente Province capital
of Santiago. Whatever the objective, it would have to be done
with dispatch since, if the Cuba experts who were massively
quoted in the press were correct, the island's summer rainy season

and its deadly fevers and disease could decimate an army unaccustomed to the tropics.

Among the newspaper correspondents who knew about such
things was Richard Harding Davis, whose familiarity with the island dated to 1886 when he wrote a novel while vacationing in
Santiago. Now, just four days after the war was declared, he had
a press billet on Admiral Sampson's flagship *New York*, in blockade duty off Havana, and was writing his mother that while he
hadn't submitted anything on the war as yet, he was getting ten
cents a word from *Scribner's Magazine* and four hundred dollars
a week plus expenses from the *New York Herald*. "I expect to get
rich on this campaign," he said. "I am going to travel en suite with
an assistant and the best and gentlest ponies; a courier and a servant, a tent and a secretary and a typewriter. . . ."

Stephen Crane, representing the *New York World*, also had a
press space on the *New York* and had become reacquainted with
Davis, whom he had met in Greece during the Greco-Turkish
War the year before. Crane was not being paid as well as Davis, did
not expect to travel so sumptuously, nor to get rich from the war,
but he did share his colleague's boredom in the wait for the Spanish response to the American blockade.

The nation and its armed forces may not have been prepared for
war, but the War Department had not been idle and in April, after
the official declaration of hostilities, it moved with unaccustomed
alacrity. On the fifteenth, twenty-two regular army infantry regiments were ordered to New Orleans, Tampa and Mobile, and six
cavalry regiments and most of the army's artillery units were
massed at Chickamauga Park, Tennessee. Moreover, on the 26th,
the regular army complement was increased to nearly 65,000,
more than doubling its strength.

Among the War Department's most important early decisions
was the appointment of sixty-three-year-old Major General

William Rufus Shafter to organize and command the Cuban invasion force. This officer had the endorsement of General Nelson A. Miles; of Henry C. Corbin, adjutant general of the army; and of War Secretary Alger, all of whom felt this veteran of Union Army and Indian War battles to be a dependable, level-headed and, importantly, nonpolitical, officer. He could, it was argued, handle the exigencies of working with the navy for a quick amphibious landing on the Cuban mainland and lead an assault on whatever objective was assigned to him. He had led assaults before, after all, although admittedly only against such foes as Confederates, Comanches and Apaches.

In his favor, Shafter had as remarkable a record of army service as any active officer available for command. A native of Kalamazoo, Michigan, he was commissioned in 1861, at age sixteen, as a first lieutenant in the Seventh Michigan Infantry. At Fair Oaks, Virginia, in May 1862, he led an open-field charge against the Confederates, concealed his wounds for three days to continue the fight and in 1895 received the Medal of Honor for the exploit. He ended the war a brevet brigadier general and in 1866, as a regular army lieutenant colonel, took command of the all-Negro Twenty-fourth Infantry on the Texas frontier. He led the Twenty-fourth in scouting expeditions across the Staked Plain of Texas to the Pecos River in New Mexico—earning the nickname "Pecos Bill"—fought Comanches and Lipan Apaches, and, serving under General Nelson Miles, helped restore peace at Pine Ridge, South Dakota, in the winter of 1890–1891 following the Wounded Knee battle.

An army colleague called Shafter an "energetic and thorough officer," said his manner was "vigorous, nervous, abrupt," his language "inelegant," and his appearance "not distingué, being short and corpulent." This euphemistic description was later to be more freely translated, especially by the newspaper correspondents who ran afoul of him: Shafter was fat, coarse, abrasive, boozy, and a sulpherous swearer who "hated slackers" and who had twice pushed his troops so unmercifully he was brought before court-martial proceedings.

At the time of his appointment by Secretary Alger, Shafter weighed over three hundred pounds—was in the words of commissary officer John F. Weston, "beastly obese"—and suffered from gout and varicose veins. He came up from New Orleans to Washington on April 27 to visit President McKinley, then departed for Tampa, Florida, the jumping-off place for the Cuban invasion. He made his headquarters in the Tampa Bay Hotel, there to organize and provision his command, the Fifth Army Corps, one of eight such corps created by the War Department to wage the war with Spain and one of only two which would leave the United States.*

The day before he met with Shafter, the president invited to the White House another distinguished soldier, one who could have fit snugly in one leg of Shafter's massive khaki trousers.

Congressman Joseph "Fighting Joe" Wheeler of Alabama had graduated near the bottom of his West Point Class of '59. He received his poorest grades in cavalry tactics, yet had risen to a major generalcy in the Confederate Army at the age of twenty-six, serving as chief of cavalry in the Army of Tennessee and a man who Robert E. Lee considered one of the two best cavalry leaders in the war (the other being J. E. B. Stuart). Now a wealthy planter, influential Democratic politician and one of the foremost *Cuba Libre* jingos in the capital, Wheeler wanted a role in the war. He had been among the first to offer his services to McKinley, writing the president, "In case of trouble with Spain, remember that my tender of services is on file in the War Department."

When called to visit the president on April 26, Wheeler was sixty-one, a white-bearded, frail-looking elf five-foot-five inches

---

*The Eighth Corps saw active service in the Philippines.

tall and weighing 120 pounds, but still exuding the pacing, clenched-fisted energy known to his colleagues in Congress and on the House Ways and Means Committee, which Wheeler chaired.

He was described as "game and fearless" and McKinley offered him the command of the cavalry in Shafter's Fifth Corps for those reasons and one other: the president said, "There must be a high officer from the south. There must be a symbol that the old days are gone. You are needed."

In his memoir on the Cuban campaign, Charles Johnson Post told the story that Wheeler's family gently tried to persuade him to stay home. "Father, you surely had fighting enough to do from 'sixty-one to 'sixty-five," one daughter said to him. "Let the young men go to war this time."

"Daughter," the peppery "Fighting Joe" said, "if a fish had been out of water for thirty-three years, and suddenly came in sight of a great pond, he'd wiggle a little, at any rate."

He accepted the major generalcy and cavalry command and although he didn't tell the president, he had no intention of being a mere symbol of the Confederate south. They called him "Fighting Joe" and he aimed to get in the fight.

In his headquarters in Tampa, the army's assembly point for the Cuban campaign, Shafter's Fifth Corps began taking shape. It consisted of three divisions, each with three brigades, each brigade with three regiments. The two infantry divisions were to be commanded by Brigadier Generals J. Ford Kent and Henry W. Lawton, who had campaigned with Shafter in the Southwest Indian wars. The cavalry division would fall under the command of Joe Wheeler and an independent brigade would be led by Brigadier General John C. Bates.

In all, there were to be seventeen thousand officers and men distributed among eighteen regular army and two volunteer infantry regiments, ten regular and two volunteer cavalry regiments, a battalion of engineers, a Signal Corps detachment, an observation balloon detail and four light artillery batteries equipped with eight field mortars, four siege guns, four seven-inch howitzers, four Gatling guns, a pneumatic dynamite gun and a Hotchkiss revolving cannon.

And all this had to be massed and moved quickly to the Cuban beaches where the enemy, in unknown numbers and with unknown resolution to defend their island, lay waiting.

VI

HEROES AND STALWARTS

1

"I have the Navy in good shape."

The announcement that Leonard Wood would lead the First U.S. Volunteer Cavalry Regiment, with Theodore Roosevelt as his second-in-command, was made on April 25, 1898, and the news produced in a few weeks twenty-seven sacks of mail—applications from potential recruits. Most of the letters were addressed to Roosevelt. "He, Secretary Alger, the President, and Congress might imagine Wood to be the true commander of the regiment, but the American public was not fooled," Roosevelt biographer Edmund Morris said, and the *New York Press* summed up the situation memorably: "Colonel Wood is lost sight of entirely in the effulgence of Teethadore."

Indeed, newspaper coverage of the announcement paid only lip service to Wood and his distinguished record in the Southwestern Indian campaigns. During the time when troops were being formed in the territories of the West and weeks before the volunteers were organized in San Antonio, the ever-inventive press devoted countless column inches to suggesting alliterative labels

for the regiment, virtually all of them spun off Roosevelt's nickname (which he disliked): "Teddy's Terrors," "Teddy's Terriers,"
"Teddy's Riotous Rounders," "Teddy's Cowboy Contingent,"
"Teddy's Texas Tarantulas" and "Teddy's Gilded Gang," the latter apparently a reference to the number of wealthy New England
sportsmen and Harvard friends who announced their intention of
joining the regiment. "Wood's Wild Westerners" cropped up in
one newspaper but didn't catch on.

On April 21, the Tucson *Arizona Star* inadvertently landed on
the magic name, quoting Governor Myron McCord's reference to
"Colonel Brodie's regiment of Rough Riders." This perfect word-
pairing, used by Roosevelt himself—"harum-scarum rough riders
of the West"—in his correspondence from the Black Hills in
1886, perhaps derived from the garish posters advertising the
"Congress of Rough Riders" in Buffalo Bill Cody's Wild West
Show. In any event, "Rough Riders" and more often "Roosevelt's
Rough Riders," was the name that stuck. (Spanish newspapers, in
an unaccidental translation, later called them "rough rioters.")

Roosevelt had some momentary concern about the name-
coining, although not, it appears, over the use of his name over
Wood's: "The objection to that term," he told newspapermen in
Washington before he left the capital, "is that people who read it
may get the impression that the regiment is to be a hippodrome
affair. . . . The regiment may be one of rough riders, but they will
be as orderly, obedient, and generally well-disciplined as any equal
number of men in any branch of the service."

Wood, by nature a private man with a professional soldier's pri-
oritized mind, didn't seem bothered by being slightly out-of-focus
in the press coverage. In early May he left Washington to travel to
Texas to prepare for receiving and training his regiment. He was
content to leave his lieutenant colonel in the capital to handle
such matters as ordering khaki uniforms and prying from the War
Department a shipment of the new Krag-Jörgenson carbines and
the smokeless powder cartridges to go with them.

* * *

In fact, before his official resignation date of May 6, Roosevelt had more important duties to perform than scrounging uniforms and rifles.

"I have the Navy in good shape," he wrote in his journal in those frantic early days of the war, and despite its characteristic immodesty, there was truth in the statement. He knew the whereabouts of the navy's fleet of ninety ships, out of which forty-two were in commission and serviceable. He was involved in the navy's purchase or leasing of ninety-seven merchant vessels to be refitted and refashioned to serve as transports, colliers and auxiliary cruisers. He studied the manpower tables—the 13,500 sailors and 1,000 line officers forming the pool to fight the two-ocean war.

The immediate need in the Atlantic was the blockade of Cuba and Secretary Long assigned that duty to William T. Sampson, now commanding the North Atlantic Squadron with the rank of rear admiral. From his flagship cruiser *New York*, Sampson and his squadron ranged the island's northern coast from Bahía Honda to Cárdenas, with Havana in between, and to Cienfuegos on the southern midcoast, returning to Key West when necessary to re-coal.

The first hostile act of the war occurred on April 22 when the U.S. cruiser *Nashville,* steaming southeast of Key West bound for Havana, spotted a cargo ship flying Spanish colors. The cruiser bore down on it and after an authorizing signal flag from the *New York,* fired a blank shot across the Spaniard's bow. A live shell followed and the enemy ship, the *Buena Ventura,* bound for Rotterdam with a lumber and cattle cargo, hove to and was captured. Interned in Key West, the value of ship and cargo was estimated at five hundred thousand dollars.

The blockade duty was uneventful with the exception of an incident on April 27 when the *New York* and two other of Sampson's ships lobbed some shells at a Spanish battery at Matanzas,

fifty miles east of Havana. The bombardment gave two correspondents on the *New York,* Richard Harding Davis of the *Herald* and Stephen Crane of the *World,* something to write about.
Crane likened the blockade to "a huge game, with wide and lonely
stretches of ocean as the board, and with great steel ships as counters."

On the 29th, the counters who would do battle with Sampson
on the board of the ocean departed the Cape Verde Islands
headed for Puerto Rico. This was the Spanish Squadron of four armored but undergunned cruisers and three torpedo boat destroyers commanded by Admiral Pascual Cervera y Topete, a
distinguished old-navy officer who steamed toward the inevitable
battle with the Americans utterly pessimistic about its outcome.
When ordered from the Cape Verdes to the Caribbean, Cervera
cabled his superiors in the Ministry of Marine, "I shall do all I can
to hasten our departure, disclaiming all responsibility for the consequences."

"Keep full of coal," Roosevelt had written to Dewey ten days after
the *Maine* explosion. "In event of declaration of war with Spain,
your duty will be to see that the Spanish squadron does not leave
the Asiatic coast, and then offensive operations in Philippine Islands. . ."

John D. Long supplemented the order on April 24, cabling
the Pacific Squadron commander, "War has commenced between
the United States and Spain. Proceed at once to the Philippine Islands. Begin operations at once, particularly against the Spanish
fleet. You must capture vessels or destroy. Use utmost endeavors."

On his flagship *Olympia,* the commodore led his nine-ship
squadron out of Hong Kong on the 26th to Mirs Bay, thirty miles
distant, to take on ammunition and for a day's target practice before proceeding south on the six-hundred-mile voyage to Luzon.
At daybreak on April 30, Dewey spied the mountains of the largest
island in the Philippine Archipelago and the entrance to Manila

Bay where the fleet of Spanish Admiral Patricio Montojo lay at anchor. The commodore, pleased at the timing of his arrival, turned to the captain of the *Olympia,* Charles Gridley, and said, "Now we have them."

The next morning, May 1, the Asiatic Squadron steamed past the Corregidor forts defending the bay and at 5:40 A.M., with Dewey's words, "You may fire when you are ready, Gridley," the *Olympia* and the eight other American warships opened fire on the Spanish ships and shore defenses.

Two hours later the battle was over, the guns silent, a pall of oily smoke rising above the bay. The Spanish defenders had lost seven ships and 381 lives; Dewey's squadron had suffered fifteen hits from Spanish fire but suffered only eight casualties.

"Mr. Dooley," the Irish bartender in the celebrated column by Chicago newspaperman Finley Peter Dunne, might wonder what the Philippines were—"islands or canned goods?"—and even President McKinley may have had to consult a globe to find them, but soon everybody knew about Manila Bay as the news of the first great victory of the war, and its first great hero, made its way home.

May Day 1898 produced another hero, too. His accomplishments paled in contrast with Dewey's mighty victory, but his exploit, on the island to be invaded by American troops in six weeks' time, illustrated the lack of preparedness for war that Roosevelt and his jingo brethren had harped on for years.

Two weeks before the war declaration, Andrew Sumner Rowan of the War Department's fledgling Military Information Bureau was sent on a secret, and potentially dangerous, mission to Cuba. His assignment was to determine what assistance an American expeditionary force might expect from the *insurrectos* on the island. The one man who could answer this question was Calixto García y Iñiguez, the old revolutionary whose stronghold near Bayamo, northwest of Santiago, lay in an remote jungle camp far from all ordinary means of communication. Rowan had to find

García, deliver the War Department communication, and return with the answer.

He was an odd choice for the job. An 1881 West Point graduate, Rowan had spent seventeen uneventful years in the army and had risen only to the rank of lieutenant. His single qualification for the critical mission lay in his co-authorship of a little book, *The Island of Cuba,* published in 1896 at the height of the *Cuba Libre* hysteria. Rowan had never been to Cuba but the book was well researched and came to the attention of the head of the Military Information Bureau, who recommended the author to Secretary Alger.

Rowan left Washington on April 8 and took a British steamer to Jamaica where he awaited orders. On the 20th he boarded a small fishing boat to carry him the one hundred miles across the Cayman Trench to the Cuban coast through waters patrolled by Spanish launches armed with pivot guns. On the 24th he landed at Turquino, west of Santiago, and with a party of rebel guides began a six-day trek through the mangrove swamps to Bayamo. He reached García's camp on May 1 and later, in his laconic account of the mission, recalled his momentous meeting with the great revolutionary: "At the door of the headquarters I was met by General Calixto García. I gave him my papers, made a short statement of my business, and was given a glass of rum and invited to breakfast. . . . Then, we went to work, and by nightfall the return dispatches were ready."

Rowan pushed on north, reaching the seaport of Manatí where he was escorted in an open boat to Andros Island in the Bahamas, thence via a commercial schooner to Key West, where he arrived on May 13. Two days later, five weeks after he had departed the city, he limped into the War Department offices, handed over the García dispatches and made his report to Secretary Alger. President McKinley personally congratulated the lieutenant, saying, "You have done a brave deed," and subsequently,

General Nelson Miles wrote to Alger that "in my judgement Lieutenant Rowan performed an act of heroism and cool daring that has rarely been excelled in the annals of warfare."

Except for such encomia and some glowing accounts of his exploit in the press, Rowan's mission might have vanished quickly from a public consciousness already grown accustomed to newspaper war heroes. But the story did not die, thanks to an irrepressible optimist and supersalesman who published a "Periodical of Protest" called *The Philistine* from his farm in update New York.

Elbert Hubbard was a forty-two-year-old Illinois-born eccentric who latched on to the Rowan exploit while searching for filler material for his magazine. He had read Rowan's artless memoir of the mission in *McClure's* and *Leslie's Weekly* and in an hour of inspiration Hubbard composed a one-thousand-five-hundred-word editorial that he said "leaped hot from my heart" about a man who got an order to deliver a message to García and who delivered it without even asking, "Where is he at?"

With its leitmotif of being "loyal to a trust, to act promptly, concentrate their energies, do the thing" unquestioningly—in brief, a sermon on blind obedience to orders—"A Message to García" sold two million copies in pamphlet form within a few months of its publication and a hundred million by the time of Hubbard's death on the *Lusitania* in May 1915.

2

"The Fifth Avenue Boys"

Roosevelt was anxious to join Wood in San Antonio and spent his last days in Washington attending to the "Eastern volunteers" who were crowding his Navy Department office, writing letters and maneuvering requisitions through the Ordnance and

Quartermaster bureaucracies of the War Department. He was particularly determined that the Rough Riders would have the best
weapons available.

At the fifteen sites named as assembly points for the Fifth Army
Corps—Chickamauga Park and Tampa chief among them—infantry volunteers, national guardsmen and some regular army
troops were armed with the Model 1873 Springfield rifle, a
.45–70-caliber single-shot breechloader using cartridges as big as
a man's finger, each packed with seventy grains of old-fashioned
black powder. Charles Johnson Post, the *New York Journal* illustrator and private in the Seventy-first New York Regiment, gave a
good account of the old weapon. He said, "You jammed a cartridge in, snapped the butt of the Springfield hard against your
shoulder—for the recoil was like a hurled brick—and pulled the
trigger." With each discharge, Post said, "there burst forth a cloud
of white smoke somewhat the size of a cow." Firing the Springfield, he concluded, "could, properly directed, knock down two
men, the one it hit and the one who fired it."

The weapon Roosevelt determined to have assigned to his and
Wood's volunteers, and the one the army had adopted for its regulars, was the .30–40-caliber, five-shot Krag-Jörgensen, patterned
after the military rifle of Denmark. The Krag used smokeless ammunition and was less traumatic to fire, but while it had been in
use since 1894, only fifteen thousand of them had been issued by
1898.*

Roosevelt, meantime, armed and outfitted himself. A friend
had given him a revolver salvaged from the *Maine;* he purchased
a dozen pair of steel-rimmed pince-nez eyeglasses and gave his
haberdasher-of-choice, Brooks Brothers, an order for leggings
and "a blue cravenette regular Lieutenant-Colonel's uniform

*The rifle was used in the Philippine Insurrection of 1899–1902 against the
Moros and other tribes opposed to American intervention and inspired a ditty
containing the lines, "Underneath the starry flag, civilize him with a Krag."

without yellow on the collar"; he bought a floppy-brimmed campaign hat from a Manhattan hatter and had several pairs of his pince-nez sewn inside it. He also took out a life insurance policy with Edith as the beneficiary.

Knickerbocker and Somerset Club cronies, Harvard classmates ("a swarm of applications from it that I could not take one in ten," Roosevelt said), wealthy athletes and playboys, hunting partners, political and social friends, drifted in and out of his Navy Department office. These "clean-cut," "gallant," "fine boys" were each looking to join Roosevelt as gentlemen rankers in the forthcoming adventure and some, he said, were "men who belonged neither to club nor to college, but in whose veins the blood stirred with the same impulse which once sent the Vikings over sea."

Among these stalwarts, known to their western counterparts as the "Fifth Avenue Boys," were men from well-known, monied families:

Roosevelt's Harvard friend Woodbury Kane was a thirty-eight-year-old New York City bachelor, a cousin of John Jacob Astor, a polo player and horseman who chased foxes in both New England and England and raced yachts against the prince of Wales.

William Tiffany of Manhattan was a nephew of the eminent banker, art connoisseur and sportsman, August Belmont, and grand-nephew of Commodore Oliver Hazard ("We have met the enemy and they are ours") Perry. He had a cattle-ranching business out west and shared with Roosevelt a love of the rough country of the western territories. He and Kane used their own money to buy a pair of Colt "rapid-firers," a sort of machine gun newly developed by Samuel Colt.

James Robert "Rob" Church was a physician and the son of the U.S. Senate's librarian. He had been a noted Princeton halfback, was a skilled horseman and had served as an army contract surgeon at Fort Myer, Virginia. He came to Roosevelt to serve as surgeon for the Rough Riders.

Craig Wadsworth of Genesco, New York, age thirty-five, was

another wealthy bachelor, a horseman and "successful cotillion leader."

Others Roosevelt signed up included Townsend Burden, a college footballer, the son of a Troy, New York, iron-steel magnate; Hamilton Fish, Jr., the ex-captain of the Columbia University racing crew and grandson of Grant's secretary of state; Reginald Ronalds, who played varsity football at Yale, listed his address as the Knickerbocker Club, New York, and was the son of tobacco tycoon Pierre Lorillard Ronalds; and Dudley Dean, who Roosevelt said was "perhaps the best quarterback who ever played on a Harvard Eleven."

Guy Murchie of Maine, a Harvard coach and old friend of Roosevelt's brought together such volunteers as Charles and Henry Bull, brother Harvard crewmen; David M. Goodrich, heir to the rubber fortune and another Harvard crewman; and Stanley Hollister, the half-miler. Other athletes who came directly to Roosevelt to enlist were Horace Devereaux of Princeton football, golfers Sumner K. Gerard and Kenneth Robinson, and tennis champions Bob Wrenn and Bill Larned.

Roosevelt was particularly pleased that the Harvard, Yale and Princeton men did not ask for commissions. "With hardly an exception," he wrote, "they entered upon their duties as troopers in the spirit which they held to the end, merely endeavoring to show that no work could be too hard, too disagreeable, or too dangerous, for them to perform, and neither asking nor receiving any reward in the way of promotion or consideration."

Among those "who belonged to neither club nor to college" were a number of New York policemen who knew Roosevelt from his commissioner days, and a few ordinary citizens who traveled long distances to Washington to see the man whose name was by now synonymous with the Rough Riders. Among these was a big, sunbaked seventeen-year-old out of Fargo, Dakota Territory, named Jesse D. Langdon. He caught up with Roosevelt on the stairs of the Navy Department, introduced himself, said he had hobo'd his way east to join the Rough Riders. Langdon reminded Roosevelt that they had "met" once before, more than ten years ago in Medora, when the senior Langdon, a veterinarian, came out to Roosevelt's ranch to inspect some cattle suspected of having Texas fever.

He remembered and sent Langdon upstairs to put his name on the roll and get a chit for boarding the Baltimore & Ohio cars on May 7 that would take the eastern enlistees to San Antonio.

Roosevelt wrote of the Fifth Avenue Boys, "They went down to San Antonio, where our regiment was to gather and where Wood preceded me, while I spent a week in Washington hurrying up the different bureaus. . . ."

He was anxious to go to war, especially after Dewey's sudden, smashing victory in the Philippines. He worried that it might be over before he could get into it.

VII

SAN ANTONIO

1

"There'll Be a Hot Time . . ."

The War Department thoughtfully gave the name "Camp
Wood" to the training area in San Antonio set aside for the First
U.S. Volunteer Cavalry Regiment. But for those unfamiliar with
the name of the titular commander of the regiment, at the railroad
station a hand-painted sign proclaiming "This Way to Camp of
Roosevelt's Rough Riders" pointed the direction to the site.

Camp Wood lay on a flat, grassy, six hundred-acre tract of state
fairgrounds land called Riverside Park, three miles south of the city
on the banks of the San Antonio River. Near the center of the
park, made picturesque by patches of cottonwood, sycamore,
hackberry, pecan and live oak trees, stood the cavernous, two-
story Exposition Hall, command tents around it, the area skirted
by a high board fence. The building had a mess hall, bunk-and-
belongings areas for the arriving volunteer officers, floor space
for the bedrolls of the enlisted men.

A few mile distant lay Fort Sam Houston, on Government

Hill, a leading cavalry training post which would assist Colonel Wood in acquiring horses for his regiment. Also, the Alamo was located only a few miles north of Camp Wood and local newspapers never tired of reminding readers that "Remember the Alamo!" and "Remember the Maine!" had a historical relationship.

Leonard Wood arrived at Camp Wood on May 5, followed by most of the animals and matériel, the enormous cargo of a cavalry regiment going to war. On the sixth he supervised the unloading of a pack train of 189 mules which arrived from St. Louis on the International and Great Northern under the care of the regiment's chief packer, Mickey O'Hara, an old friend of Wood's from Apache campaigns in the Southwest.

The Arizona volunteers, the first to rendezvous in San Antonio, came into camp at dawn on Saturday, May 7, riding out from the train station to Riverside Park in Edison Car Company streetcars draped with banners proclaiming them, in a rare bow to the colonel, "Wood's Woolies." The Oklahoma contingent arrived later in the day, the eighty-three troopers led by Captain Robert D. Huston, a Guthrie lawyer. On Monday, a number of eastern volunteers stepped off the train in the wilting San Antonio sun. Some of these "dudes" were nattily attired in expensive suits and straw boaters, and carried fine leather valises, portmanteaux and hat boxes. Unlike the territorials, who sought out the camp mess hall, many of the easterners dined at the Menger Hotel, a favorite gathering place for officers from Fort Sam, before taking the trolley out to Riverside Park.

The San Antonio *Express* later wrote exaggeratedly of the eastern "swells": "Ninety percent of them carry a large wad in their side pockets with which to play a little game of draw and large bank accounts behind them. Some of them have their 'men' with them to care for their uniforms and top boots at a salary of $60 a month, also to cook at $100 a month."

Actually, there were few body servants (Roosevelt brought one) and personal cooks in evidence at Camp Wood—a good thing given the number of cowboys there whose thirty-dollar-a-month cow camp salaries were now reduced to the thirteen-dollar monthly pay of a volunteer cavalry trooper.

The 340 New Mexicans arrived on May 10, the four troops commanded by Major Henry B. Hersey, who had resigned as territorial adjutant general to volunteer. In Dodge City, Kansas, en route to San Antonio, his troopers were joined by a formidable gentleman named Benjamin Franklin Daniels. He was a gotch-eared (the ear was "bitten off" was all he would say of it) former marshal of Dodge, "a very large, hawk-eyed man," Roosevelt called him, who had survived as lawman in the toughest town in the West and who now was determined, despite recurring problems with a hernia, to get to San Antonio to enlist in the Rough Riders.

On the 14th, the arms, uniforms and saddlery shipment came in: cotton underwear and socks, heavy blue flannel shirts, thick, baggy, khaki trousers, jackets of a ducklike material, cartridge belts, gray campaign hats, canvas leggings, high-topped brogans, ponchos, blankets, tin canteens, mess pans and cups, and dog tents consisting of two shelter halves that snapped together, forming, with a tent pole, a canvas tent for two men, four foot high by six-and-a-half long. A couple of forks of straw covered by a blanket made a mattress home for bugs and lice.

Horse accoutrements were also issued: McClellan saddles (unpopular among cowboys accustomed to the large, comfortable stock saddles), saddlebags, rifle boots, grooming kits, bridles, stirrups, surcingles, picket pins, latigo cinch straps, halter shanks, horse blankets and nose bags.

A signal event at Camp Wood was the arrival and issuing of the Krag-Jörgensen carbines and the first firing practices with the .30–40-caliber bolt-action weapon. Cavalry-style .45-caliber pistols and machetes were also issued. Some of the Westerners brought along personal weapons—Winchesters and Colt side arms—and were permitted to use them.

The 170 Indian Territory troopers were the stragglers, arriving in town on the 17th under the command of Captain Allyn Capron. This blond-haired, blue-eyed boxer, horseman and athlete, was to Theodore Roosevelt, the very "archetype of the fighting man" and his Indian Territorials were some of the scruffiest and fiercest-looking of all the volunteers. The officers at Camp Wood were dazzled by the polished young officer's ability to lead such a rough band. "He had under him two companies . . . and he soon impressed himself upon the wild spirit of his followers," Roosevelt said. "He got them ahead in discipline faster than any troop in the regiment. . . . [he] required instant obedience, and tolerated not the slightest evasion of duty, but his mastery of the art was so thorough and his performance of his own duty so rigid that he won not merely the admiration, but that soldierly affection so readily given by the man in the ranks of the superior who cares for his men and leads them fearlessly in battle."

When he wrote his book on the regiment, Roosevelt named Capron "the best soldier in the regiment."

Wood's arrangements with the Fort Sam Houston cavalry experts produced two hundred head of feisty horses—the number later to swell to a voracious hay-fueled machine of over one thousand head—purchased from local ranchers and driven in a herd to Riverside Park. The animals were a minimum of four years old, averaging fifteen-and-a-half hands high and weighing 1,100–1,250 pounds—"good-sized cow ponies," Captain George Curry of Tularosa, New Mexico, called them. Curry's second lieutenant, Charles L. Ballard, "known as an expert judge of horses," was assigned as receiving agent for the herd. He was a Roswell rancher and city marshal, a former U.S. deputy marshal and sheriff of Lincoln County, celebrated in New Mexico for his involvement in bringing to bay the notorious Black Jack Gang of stage, train and bank robbers who ranged through Oklahoma, New Mexico and Arizona in the mid-'90s.

Most of the horses purchased for the troopers were acceptable, although some were barely broken and tended to buck off anybody boarding what one Rough Rider called their "hurricane decks." The horses, which were assigned to enlistees (officers had to provide their own) soon came under inspection by a veteran cavalryman, William W. Greenwood, first sergeant of Buckey O'Neill's troop of Arizonans. The forty-four-year-old Greenwood, called "Grandma" by his troopers, had been a sergeant in the First Cavalry, serving in the Apache campaigns with Alex Brodie, and was one of seven regular army sergeants who would help Wood and Roosevelt get the regiment in a semblance of fighting trim. Greenwood knew horses and after giving the Fort Sam remuda his gimlet-eyed treatment, pronounced a number of them "totally unfit for service."

With the massing of the horse herd and nearly a thousand men to ride them, on May 11, while still awaiting the arrival in camp of his second-in-command and of the balance of his volunteers, Colonel Wood was able to announce the preliminary makeup of his regiment. There would be three squadrons of four troops each, the first two squadrons made up of men already in training, the third consisting of the volunteers coming from Indian Territory, leftovers from oversized troops and the "Fifth Avenue Boys" from the East. Major Alexander Brodie of Arizona was named to command the First Squadron; Major Henry Hersey of Santa Fe would lead the Second, and Major George M. Dunn, a Denver native, a "master of hounds" from Chevy Chase, Maryland, and a close Roosevelt friend, the Third.

The twelve troops, each with sixty-five men at the beginning, were given letter designations. The Arizonans had Troops A, B and C; New Mexico Troops E, F, G and H. Troop D was made up of volunteers from Oklahoma, ten states and Washington, D.C.; Troop I had the overflow of New Mexicans and volunteers from twenty-three states; Troop K was made up mostly of the "Fifth Avenue Boys"—also called by the crusty Westerners the "lah-de-dah boys," "dudes" and "society swells"; and Troops L and M were composed largely of the Indian Territorials.

At 5:30 on the eve of Roosevelt's long-awaited arrival at Camp Wood, San Antonio mayor Callaghan, his city councilmen and a dozen townspeople arrived at Riverside Park on a special streetcar. With them came the city's immensely popular German bandmaster, "Professor" Carl Beck, and his brass-and-drum musicians. The delegation marched directly to Wood's command tent and while the politicians and civic leaders exchanged greetings and welcomes with the colonel and his officers, the splendidly uniformed Professor Beck led his band in playing stirringly loud renditions of "Manhattan Beach," "Yankee Doodle" and "The Star-Spangled Banner."

The Rough Riders loved Beck and practically adopted him. Captain Jim McClintock of the Arizona volunteers said of the tireless bandmaster, "His greatest joy was to come to the camp at the fairgrounds, take station before the colonel's tent, and noisily execute some stirring warlike composition just about the time the Colonel and his officers were in serious consultation."

One of the professor's favorites, the minstrel show tune, "There'll Be a Hot Time in the Old Town Tonight," played boisterously and frequently, became the unofficial anthem of the Rough Riders, its chorus known to every trooper:

> *When you hear dem-a bells go ding, ling, ling,*
> *All join 'round and sweetly you must sing,*

And when the verse am through, in the chorus all join in,
There'll be a hot time in the old town tonight.

2

"These men are wild."

Roosevelt arrived in San Antonio at 7:30 on Sunday morn-ing, May 15, hopping off the Southern Pacific coach resplendent in grin and uniform, his khaki trousers stuffed into spit-polished cordovan boots, the stiff collar of his epauletted, fawn-colored, khaki jacket bearing the initials "U.S.V." beside embroidered crossed sabers surmounted by the number 1, the brim of his shapeless campaign hat rakishly pinned up on the side with a huge crossed-sabers badge. He pumped the hands of Colonel Wood and his officer retinue, and doffed his hat to the newspapermen and city dignitaries who greeted him, and to the ubiquitous Professor Beck and his clamorous bandsmen who were already wilting in the steamy railroad station and the rising heat of the day.

After a brisk walk to the Menger Hotel and breakfast with Wood and other regimental officers, Roosevelt, accompanied by his black servant Marshall, an old veteran of the Ninth Cavalry, was taken by buckboard to Riverside Park. There, after a round of introductions, he was given a tour of the camp. A throng of peo-ple—several thousand according to newspaper reports—their buggies, wagons and horses tethered all around the spacious fair-grounds, had gathered to catch some random rays from "Teddy's" effulgence.

To some, including some of the Rough Riders who saw him for the first time that day, he turned out to be somewhat of a dis-appointment, a far different figure than the sword-wielding Mars of Washington depicted in newspaper drawings and cartoons. He was squat and bandy-legged, had a round, neckless head, a clench-jawed smile full of blocky white teeth and funny little eyeglasses pinched to his nose, the black ribbon attached to them disappearing somewhere inside his tunic. And when he opened his mouth to speak, which was often, his brushy blond mustaches twitched and the words came out in Harvard-heavy, high-pitched tenor tones, queerly raucous, like his laugh, a single explosive syllable—"Hah!"

For all that, his reputation had preceded him. The Westerners had heard tales of his exploits as a rancher and sometime lawman in the Dakotas, and he exuded such enthusiasm and energy, seemed so genuinely friendly and approachable—everyone, Rough Rider and well-wisher, warmed to him in an instant.

On that first day in camp, Roosevelt's message to the regiment drew a roaring cheer: "The eyes of the entire civilized world are upon you and I want your watchword to be 'Remember the *Maine!*' "

By the time of Roosevelt's advent in Camp Wood, nearly a thousand men had reported for duty. A muster was made on May 17 and the paperwork showed the regiment consisted of men from forty-two states, four territories and several foreign countries. Their professions and skills ranged from cowboy to lawyer, stonemason to stockbroker. There were former lawmen (and a few former outlaws), yachtsmen, physicians, politicians, barkeeps, butchers, bakers, barbers, soldiers-of-fortune and civilians-of-misfortune, men with prominent professions and addresses in New York, Boston and Philadelphia, mixed with men with no fixed address or employment record. There were a number of Indians on the muster roll, a scattering of former Texas Rangers, some veterans of the Riel rebellion in Canada, some men who had served with the British army in South Africa, at least one Australian with service in the New South Wales Mounted Rifles, and a couple of professional foreign war soldiers, one of whom served as the regimental trumpeter. This was Emilio Cassi, age twenty-seven, born in Monte Carlo, Monaco, a musician and one-time bandmaster who enlisted in Jerome, Arizona. He had served in the Italian army and in a French regiment of Chasseurs d'Afrique in Algeria, Egypt and China.

Chris Madsen of El Reno, Oklahoma Territory, had a history even more far-flung than Cassi's. Born in Copenhagen in 1851, Madsen had fought as a foot soldier in the Danish-Prussian and Franco-Prussian wars, with the French Foreign Legion in Algeria, and with the Fifth U.S. Cavalry. While with the Fifth he served with scout William Frederick "Buffalo Bill" Cody and helped bury the troopers of Custer's Seventh Cavalry slain in the Little Big Horn battle. In 1891 he became a deputy U.S. marshal out of El Reno and, with legendary lawmen Bill Tilghman and Heck Thomas, became one of the "Three Guardsmen" of Oklahoma history. He was named quartermaster sergeant of the Rough Riders.

Roosevelt was never happier than during those hand-shaking, speech-making first days of camaraderie at Camp Wood. He never seemed to sleep, spent every hour talking, questioning and listening. He could never learn enough, whether catching up on the histories of old friends, such as Fred Herrig of Kalispel, Montana, his guide and hunting companion in the Badlands, or learning about new ones. He grilled the senior regimental officers—Majors Alexander Brodie of Arizona, Henry Hersey of new Mexico, George Dunn of Colorado, and that "perfect game-cock," Micah Jenkins of South Carolina—all of whom left lasting impressions on him. He was greatly impressed by such other officers as Captain Buckey O'Neill, mayor of Prescott, Arizona ("a wild, reckless fellow, soft-spoken, and of dauntless courage and boundless ambition"); the tall, yellow-haired beau ideal soldier, Captain Allyn Capron of Brooklyn, now commanding L Troop of the Indian Territory volunteers; Captains Luna, Llewellen, Ballard and Curry of the New Mexicans; Reverend Henry A. Brown of Prescott, an Oberlin College man who came to San Antonio to serve as the Rough Riders' regimental chap-

THE BOYS OF '98

121

lain; and Dr. James Robert Church, former Princeton footballer, former contract surgeon at Fort Myer, Virginia, now surgeon to the First U.S. Volunteer Cavalry Regiment. "Rob" Church and "Buckey" O'Neill soon became fast friends. Roosevelt was impressed by O'Neill's "versatility" when he heard the Arizona lawman-politician and the Ivy League athlete-physician "discussing Aryan root words together, and then sliding off into a review of the novels of Balzac. . . ."

As the May days swept by at sweltering Camp Wood, others of the western contingent came to Roosevelt's attention, men he remembered fondly to the end of his life: Ben Daniels of Dodge City; Sherman Bell, former deputy marshal of Cripple Creek, Colorado, and a former Wells Fargo stage driver; Tom Darnell of Denver, expert cowboy and horse breaker; William B. Proffit of North Carolina, a "sinewy, saturnine, fearless" son of a Confederate officer; Sam Rhodes, former deputy sheriff of Tonto Basin, Arizona, now a sergeant in O'Neill's A Troop; Charles Younger, a fireman out of Winslow, Arizona, and son of Bob Younger of Jesse James's gang; and Thomas Harbo "Tom" Rynning of Phoenix, thirty-two years old and a Norwegian by birth who had been a Texas bull whacker and cowboy before enlisting in the cavalry. He had fought with Leonard Wood in the Geronimo campaigns and later in the Sioux and Cheyenne wars. He received a commission as second lieutenant within days of the Rough Riders' first muster in San Antonio.

From Indian Territory came red-haired Tom Isbell, a cowboy who enlisted in Muskogee whom Roosevelt called "a half-breed Cherokee"; William Pollock of Oklahoma Territory, a full-blooded Pawnee, "a silent, solitary fellow," Roosevelt said, "and one of the gamest fighters and best soldiers in the regiment."

William "Little Billy" McGinty of Shipaupi, Indian Territory, also became a Roosevelt favorite. McGinty, born in Mercer County, Missouri, in 1870, stood five-foot-four-inches high, weighed 135 pounds and had been a cowboy and bronc buster since age fourteen. "He never had walked a hundred yards if by any possibility he could ride," Roosevelt wrote of him.

The tallest man in the regiment was Virginia-born Albert Wright, a thirty-nine-year-old cowboy out of Yuma, Arizona. He was six-foot-six, became guardian of the regimental colors and took his duty seriously.

Roosevelt took particular delight in the colorful nicknames of some of the Rough Riders' western contingent. There was "Grandma" Bill Greenwood of Prescott, Buckey O'Neill's Troop A sergeant; "Bronco George" Brown of Skull Valley, Arizona; "Dead Shot Jim" Simpson of Albuquerque; "Lariet Ned" Perkins of Colorado; and a number of men who seemed to have no identity other than their nicknames and what Roosevelt would subsequently say of them: "Tough Ike," a "brave but fastidious" eastern clubman; "Pork Chop"; "Metropolitan Bill"; "Sheeny Soloman" (a red-headed Irishman); "Hell-Roarer" (an "abnormally quiet and gentle" gambler); a particularly blasphemous trooper called "Prayerful James"; a joking trooper called "Weeping Dutchman"; a near-albino trooper called "Nigger"; and one who did not receive his name until the regiment reached Cuba. There, when he became known as the noisiest scout on the island, he was dubbed "Rubber Shoe Andy."

Camp Wood settled into routine. Emilio Cassi blew reveille at 5:30, a roll call followed, and at 6:10 stable call for feeding and rubbing down the horses. At 8:30, after breakfast, the horses and mules were led to the river for watering and preparation for morning mounted drills. (The first horseback drills with troopers firing blank shells in their Krags and Winchesters—to accustom the animals to gunfire—was held on May 23.) Dinner was at 1:30; foot-marching drills, rifle practice and inspections took up the early afternoon until stable call at four. Another roll call and a dress parade ended the day's work, with the troopers lined up in their blue shirts, khaki trousers, leggings, boots, slouch hats and navy blue-

and-white-polka-dotted neckerchiefs, first worn by Lieutenant Colonel Roosevelt, an added touch and an unofficial regimental symbol. The volunteers ate their evening meal in the Exposition building mess hall at seven, stood for a final roll call after tattoo, which sounded at precisely 8:30, and turned in at taps at nine.

Wood wrote his wife, "You would smile to see the New York swells sleeping on the ground and on the floor of the pavilion without blankets and doing kitchen police for a troop of New Mexico cowboys, all working together and chummy as can be."

The days snailed along. The San Antonio weather, incessantly hot and muggy, was bearable, the boredom wilting. "We were young and full of vinegar," Frank Brito of Troop H said, "and it was tough trying to fill twenty-four hours in camp with a war going on. We were sure it would be over while we were drilling out there at Camp Wood."

May 18 produced a break in the routine with the arrival in camp of two Colt rapid-firer guns costing ten thousand dollars each and capable of shooting five hundred bullets a minute. The weapons were a gift to the regiment from two of Roosevelt's wealthy New York friends, Woodbury Kane and William Tiffany, now K Troop volunteers.

The horseback drills, tedious to the Westerners especially, at least produced one of the best regimental tales—told often, with accumulating embellishments, in later years—and recorded by Roosevelt himself in his Rough Riders memoir.

Two days after he arrived at the camp, Roosevelt gathered the troops of the First and Second Squadrons, commanded by Majors Alex Brodie and Henry Hersey, and led them three miles from camp and back again in the baking sun. On the way back, the ever-solicitous Roosevelt called a halt at a beer garden near Riverside Park and announced that the troop captains "will let their men go in and drink all the beer they want, and I will pay for it."

After the beer-sated troopers filed back to camp, Wood learned of Roosevelt's largesse and notified him sternly in his customary poker-faced manner that it was against army regulations, not to mention common sense, for officers to supply alcoholic beverages to enlisted men, to drink with them or to encourage their drinking while on duty. Roosevelt visited Wood's command tent that evening, stood at attention and announced to the air above the colonel's head, "I wish to tell you that I took the troops out without thinking of this question of officers drinking with their men and gave them all a schooner of beer. I wish to say, sir, that I consider myself the damndest ass within ten miles of this camp. Good night."

Despite such momentary lapses, Roosevelt was having the time of his life. While Wood pored over maps, shuffled papers, and exchanged messages with the War Department and with General Shafter in Tampa, his second-in-command did the routine correspondence, took care of interviews with the newspapermen who made a second home near the camp command tents, supervised horseback and foot drills, made the inspections and parades and morale speeches.

One of Roosevelt's most onerous duties, now that the regiment had swelled to over one thousand men, was to turn down new applicants. A typical handling of this chore was his response to a letter he received on May 19 from a twenty-two-year-old veteran of the Seventh Cavalry who wrote from a remote ranch in Idaho, offering to come to San Antonio to enlist. "I wish I could take you in," Roosevelt wrote, "but I am afraid that the chances of our being over-enlisted forbid my bringing a man from such a distance." He signed the letter "Theodore Roosevelt, First Regt., U.S. Volunter Cavalry, In Camp near San Antonio, Texas," and sent it to Edgar Rice Burroughs of Pocatello, subsequently world famous as the creator of *Tarzan of the Apes.*

But one man who came a long distance did get sworn in. Jesse Langdon, the seventeen-year-old veterinarian's son who had hobo'd to Washington from Fargo, Dakota Territory, had the grit to brace Roosevelt on the stairs of the Navy Department and had thereby earned a ticket to San Antonio. Soon after the lieutenant colonel arrived at Camp Wood, Langdon reminded him of their encounter, was personally sworn in by Roosevelt and assigned to Troop K.

Roosevelt, who had no military experience beyond National Guard work, nonetheless had keen intuitive ideas on his role in the regiment. He felt, among other things, that it was his duty to instill in the men "a keen pride of the regiment, and a resolute purpose to do his whole duty uncomplainingly, and above all, to win glory by the way he handled himself in battle." He told the men these things when they took the oath, told them again when he felt it worth repeating.

Whatever frictions the stolid professional Leonard Wood and his ebullient dilettante lieutenant colonel had in commanding their weird amalgamation of volunteers, they managed to keep between themselves. Wood's practicality and Roosevelt's romanticism seem never to have created a serious breech in their relationship nor a problem in readying the regiment for war.

Roosevelt could look out at his beloved Westerners and say of them, "In all the world there could be no better material for soldiers than that afforded by these grim hunters of the mountains, these wild rough riders of the plains."

Wood looked out at them and admitted, "These men are wild. If we don't get them to Cuba quickly to fight the Spaniards there is great danger they'll be fighting themselves."

In free times, troopers lined up at the washtubs, took bars of soap and bathed in the river, saw to their horses and gear, wandered about camp smoking and talking, and wrote letters home.

George Hamner of F Troop, the former Western Union telegrapher who had come out of Wagon Mound to enlist with the New Mexico contingent, had regular letter-writing duty after he straightened up his bedroll and put his shelter-half in shape for the night's sleep. Hamner had a sweetheart in his hometown of Faber's Mill, Virginia, a Miss Blanche Stevens, who had her own ideas about his marching off to war. She had written him that she didn't think a war with Spain was necessary at all.

"So you think the war could have been averted, eh?" he wrote back with manly vigor in the glow of a kerosene lamp. "How about the *Maine,* dear? Do you think it would have been upholding the honor of the nation to let such an act of treachery as that pass unpunished? I am fighting, or going to fight, to avenge the *Maine.* And 'Remember the *Maine!*' is our war cry!"

3

"Let me git my pony."

Even Leonard Wood, privately horrified by the general un-military quality of his regiment, in particular Roosevelt's "grim hunters of the mountains" and "wild rough riders of the plains," could see the humor in laboring to make soldiers out of these ungovernable men.

David L. Hughes, a blacksmith from Tucson and a corporal in Jim McClintock's B Troop of Arizonans, left a vivid memoir of his experiences in the Rough Riders and told a story that illustrated the clash of the freewheeling cowboy with the formality, rules and protocol of the army and its officers—even the amateur ones such as Roosevelt.

Hughes told of his fellow B Trooper Bill Owens, a twenty-four-year-old Jerome, Arizona, cowpuncher and prospector who had enlisted in Globe and who earned the nickname "Smoke-'em-Up Bill" after he shot out several street lamps on the way from the San Antonio train station to Camp Wood.

Owens was on duty at the guardhouse when Roosevelt first came to the camp and when he asked, "Is the officer of the guard around?" Owens answered, "If you just holler out 'Officer of the Guard' two or three times, he'll come trottin' in."

He was one of the hardest-working of all the volunteers, Hughes said of Owens, but the cowboy never learned the military "niceties." He saluted everything that moved—buglers, corporals, sergeants, anybody with a stripe, and always greeted the officers, regardless of their rank, with a big grin and a friendly, "How are you, Captain?" Once, when Owens was on post near the officer's quarters, Lieutenant Thomas W. Hall, the regimental adjutant and a one-time West Pointer, came by. Owens, who had his Krag carbine on his shoulder, threw up his hand in a sort-of salute and said cheerily, "How are you, Captain?" Hall, a stiffly formal officer, barked, "PRE-sent ARMS!" Owens looked bewildered at this and Hall repeated the order even more sharply—"PRE-sent ARMS!" Owens, still puzzled, looked blankly at the lieutenant as Hall stepped forward to within two inches of "Smoke-'em-Up's" nose. *Can't you present arms?* Hall shouted up the trooper's nostrils. Owens, with an affable grin, took his carbine off his shoulder and extended it toward Hall, saying, "Here, take her, Captain, only she ain't loaded."

Owens, like all the Rough Riders, eventually learned to love "the Colonel," but during Camp Wood training days he was tentative about the "banty rooster with the funny eyeglasses." When Hughes asked him what he thought of Roosevelt, Owens said, "He looks as though he was there with the goods, only I don't like the way he skins his teeth back when he talks to a fellow."

Roosevelt had his own favorite stories of his unfettered troopers. On a hot night at the camp, when he and Wood were returning to their tents to escape the swarms of mosquitos that were blowing up from the nearby river bottom, they came across a sentry. This man, one of the western boys, had flung his rifle on the ground and was sitting by it vigorously slapping at the "skeeters" that had crawled under his shirt and trouser legs. The trooper, noting the two officers staring at him, nodded pleasantly at them, not missing a slap or scratch, and said with a grimace, "Ain't they *bad*?"

And everybody remembered "Little Billy" McGinty, the Shipaupi, Indian Territory, bronc buster, who presented the classic dilemma of the cowboy forced afoot. Despite his sweatily best efforts, McGinty could not keep in step on the parade ground and after being cussed and shouted at countless times, implored the drill sergeant, "Let me git my pony. I'm purty sure I can keep in step on horseback!"

On May 23, Wood received a telegram from the War Department inquiring when the regiment would be ready to leave for Tampa to join General Shafter's Fifth Corps. "AT ONCE," Wood replied.

Throughout the training days in San Antonio, daily scuttlebutt had passed from tent to tent on where the Rough Riders were heading, and when. One of the favorite rumors had the regiment shipping out directly to Havana to "take" the great Cuban port city, but now the official announcement was in hand—not about a specific ultimate destination, but at least about moving on to Tampa. And everyone knew about Tampa, the place where the big army was being gathered, the jumping-off place for Cuba.

With the departure of the regiment imminent, San Antonians, as represented by their mayor and city councilmen, decided to demonstrate their patriotism and general good will by staging a farewell band concert at Riverside Park. Professor Carl Beck, refulgent in his gold-braided uniform and wearing his medals from the Franco-Prussian War, led a program of martial tunes mixed with such general favorites as "Arkansas Traveler," "The Sweet Bye and Bye," "Good-bye, Dolly Gray," "Dixie," songs for the "Mexican boys" such as "La Paloma" and "Sobre las Olas," and, repeatedly, the adopted regimental anthem, which this night turned out to be prophetic, "There'll Be a Hot Time in the Old Town Tonight."

The concert was staged on the balmy, starry night of the 25th and drew an enormous crowd of townfolk. Everything moved along splendidly until Beck's rousing conclusion, a brassy "Cavalry Charge" punctuated on cue by the firing of a small ceremonial cannon situated on the outskirts of the crowd. With the first blank shot banging from the saluting cannon, a trooper seated near the bandstand jumped to his feet and shouted, "Help him out, boys!" Within seconds, several Rough Riders, in the words of New Mexico trooper Frank Brito, "slapped leather," and fired their six-shooters into the sky. One bullet clipped the only electric light wire in the park and men, women and children ran for cover, ducking under benches or stampeding into the dark.

The next day the *San Antonio Light,* in a story with the memorable heading, "Prof. Beck's Band Played the Cavalry Charge and the Rough Riders Played Hell," described the incident as "disgraceful," but reported no injuries from bullet or exodus.

On May 27, Wood received official orders to depart for Tampa and notified the Southern Pacific that he needed twenty-five day coaches, two Pullman cars, five baggage cars, eight boxcars and sixty livestock cars—space for the 1,060 officers and men plus 1,258 horses and mules, arms and equipage—to be readied at the Union Stockyards, three miles from Camp Wood.

Reveille sounded at three on the 29th and the heat rose almost as early as the regiment struck its tents and broke camp. The packing and boxing of the impedimenta of the camp, done the day before, had already been moved trackside and now the troopers—told they could take only what they could stuff in their knapsacks and blanket rolls—and the animals, were ready to move.

At eight, Major Alex Brodie and his First Squadron mounted up and marched to the stockyards. Roosevelt reflected on the moment with great satisfaction. The regiment had trained for barely three weeks and now, he felt, it was primed for whatever lay ahead:

"In their slouch hats, blue flannel shirts, brown trousers, leggings and boots, with handkerchiefs knotted loosely around their necks, they looked exactly as a body of cavalry should look."

It took all day for the loading of the regiment and its animals on the S-P cars. Among Brodie's officers of the First Squadron who had hurried up to wait were Captains Buckey O'Neill and Jim McClintock, who spent the day working with their Arizona troopers and horses and talking of the adventure that lay in wait for them. O'Neill, a cigarette addict who seemed always to have the Bull Durham "makin's" but never a light for them, was presented a gift by his nonsmoker friend. McClintock, who had heard O'Neill's "Jim, gimme a match" countless times over the twenty years they had been pals, presented Buckey with a black celluloid match case filled with wooden lucifers.

VIII

TAMPA

<hr>

1

"The rocking-chair period of the war"

"Instantly, all was joyful excitement," Roosevelt wrote of the War Department message ordering the Rough Riders to Tampa. "We had enjoyed San Antonio, and were glad that our regiment had been organized in the city where the Alamo commemorates the death fight of Crockett, Bowie, and their famous band of frontier heroes."

No man at Camp Wood was more joyful and excited—and worried—than the regiment's second-in-command. Roosevelt was haunted by the prospect that the war might be over before he could get into it, that the navy alone might fight all the battles and force the Spaniards to capitulate. He wrote to his sister from Tampa, "The navy has had all the fun so far; and I only hope that peace will not be declared without giving the army a chance at both Cuba and Porto Rico, as well as the Philippines."

In fact, the news out of Cuba while the Rough Riders were drilling at Riverside Park *was* all navy.

On May 11, with the blockade of the island in place, the

American torpedo boat *Winslow* had entered the harbor at Cárdenas, east of Havana, to sound the channel, and drew fire from
shore batteries and a Spanish gunboat lying at the wharf. The
Winslow's commander fell wounded, the ship's hull was riddled
and its steering gear shot away. An armed tug came in to tow the
disabled boat to safety but in this brave little action, a Spanish shell
exploded on the *Winslow,* killing an ensign and five sailors—the
first casualties of the war.

Meantime, the navy's search for the Spanish Cape Verde
Squadron under Admiral Cervera continued with the Spaniards
sighted at Puerto Rico; Fort de France, Martinique; Curaçao, off
Venezuela; in the Windward Passage, Haiti; and Cienfuegos off
the south coast of Cuba. On May 29, while the Rough Riders
were scurrying to load their horses and equipment on the Southern Pacific cars, the navy's commodore Winfield Scott Schley and
his "Flying Squadron" found Cervera's fleet. It lay, snugly anchored, the ships' awnings rolled out against the boiling heat, in
the fortified harbor of Santiago de Cuba in the far southeast quad-
rant of the island. With this critical intelligence in hand at last, the
navy responded. The first-class battleship *Oregon,* which had just
completed a flank-speed voyage around Cape Horn from dry-
dock in Bremerton, Washington, joined the other vessels of the
North Atlantic Fleet; Admiral Sampson established a blockade six
miles off the mouth of Santiago Harbor; and a small force of
sailors and marines was dispatched to establish a base at Guantánamo Bay, just east of Santiago.

Now the focus of the campaign shifted from Havana to Santiago de Cuba; the newspapers said the Spaniards were "bottled
up" there and that the war might be over before American land
forces could be transported to the island.

While this prospect loomed over them, the rush to get the
regiment underway and in Tampa in seventy-two hours stalled.
There were countless maddening logistical problems. The Southern Pacific train at the Union Stockyards was split into seven sec-

tions, the first three commanded by Wood, the last four by Roosevelt, but delays in loading were caused by the discovery that the S-P had no facilities for taking the horses and mules aboard and no feed and water for them. Makeshift ramps had to be jury-rigged, hay and water purchased and loaded in the stockcars, the work occupying all of that Sunday, May 29, the day of the planned departure.

Roosevelt marched his squadrons to the trainyard at dusk but passenger car loading continued to be balked and many troopers disappeared into the dark to find beer at what Roosevelt called "the vile drinking-booths around the stock-yards." Details were sent out to round up the drinkers, the trumpeter blew "Assembly," roll calls were repeatedly made among the milling, impatient, exhausted men, railroad cars were shunted, switched, added, deleted, and the Rough Rider train finally got underway before daybreak on the 30th.

The trip south took four days and for the most part was uneventful. There were frequent stops to replenish hay and water supplies, occasions which gave expert Rough Rider foragers time to raid a watermelon patch or accept a pie from a patriotic farm wife. Roosevelt opened his wallet to have buckets of coffee brought aboard the troop cars and attempted to keep order but Trooper Frank Brito of Pinos Altos, New Mexico Territory, called the trip a "nightmare." He remembered, "We had to stop ever so often to unload the animals to feed and water them, then load them up again. Those old coal-burners poured black smoke into both the stock cars and passenger cars and when we got a chance to get off, we all looked like we could play a minstrel show."

But there were the good moments, too. In Houston, New Orleans, Mobile, Tallahassee and towns large and small, crowds lined the tracks at every stop to greet the greatly publicized Rough Rider train, offering flowers and vegetables, jugs of coffee, pails of milk, pies, loaves of bread, baskets of fruit. Southern belles in crinolines and big sun hats waved and smiled and sometimes gave a ribbon and a mailing address to a grimy trooper; Confederate flags waved with the Stars and Stripes as old soldiers in old gray uniforms stood tearfully by, waving and saluting, and boys and men looked on enviously at the objects of all the celebration.

"The blood of the old men stirred to the distant breath of battle," Roosevelt mused, "the blood of the young men leaped hot with eager desire to accompany us."

During the long, hot journey south he passed the time reading the French revolutionary journalist Camille Desmoulins's *Supériorité des Anglo-Saxons* and contemplating the differences between American and European militarism.

The train reached Lakeland, Florida, thirty miles northeast of Tampa, at seven P.M. on June 1 and the next day moved to Tampa Heights—"Fifteen feet higher than Tampa itself," said Charles Johnson Post of the Seventy-first New York Regiment, "a veritable hill!"—where the main body of the Fifth U.S. Army Corps was bivouacked.

Whatever good feelings had been generated by the trip down from San Antonio evaporated that second day of June when the regiment caught its first glimpse of the bedlam spread in panoramic view before them from Tampa Heights.

The town of Tampa, population 26,000, lay on a piney sand flat at the terminus of a single-track railroad, the outskirts a depressing collection of derelict wooden shanties squatting in a sea of sawgrass and sand. Twenty thousand regular army troops had been billeted among the sand hummocks, pine and palmetto groves since May 10, a tent town on the dunes abuzz with clouds of mosquitos and bluebottle flies and crawling with centipedes and scorpions. On every point of the compass, soldiers—seventeen regiments of infantry, twelve artillery batteries, five regiments of regular cavalry—drilled and milled about in the sand and among mountains of fodder, ammunition stores, boxes and crates of clothing, harness, medicines, tinned beef and other foodstuffs, like armies of errant ants.

Into this boiling muddle came thirteen thousand volunteers, also in seventeen regiments, deployed from training camps in Mobile, New Orleans, Chickamauga Park and San Antonio. The Rough Riders, late in arriving on the Tampa anthill, were still early enough to become one of only three volunteer regiments— with the Seventy-first New York and Second Massachusetts, both infantry units—to take part in the coming campaign.

These regiments were thrown together, more or less, amidst the palmettos and saw grass south of Tampa town and there, in the June steambath of Florida's Gulf Coast, pegged down their tents and began the long wait for orders that would send them to Tampa Bay and out to sea. During the day, smoke from the cook-fires carried the fragrance of sowbelly and beans; at night, the glow of the fires could be seen for miles as the troopers hunkered down to talk, smoke, soak their hardtack to edible consistency, and boil their coffee.

When permitted, the men boarded a trolley or walked into town or made their way to Ybor City, named for a Cuban cigar factory entrepreneur, a wrong-side-of-the-tracks assortment of hovels, gambling hells, cribs and sidewalk vendors. Some even made their way nine miles south of Tampa proper to Tampa Bay, where stevedores, army and navy officers, merchant seamen, civilian sightseers, and newspaper correspondents picked their way along the mile-long wharf strewn with mountains of ammunition, fodder and supplies and where, in the bay, a shabby armada of merchant steamers bobbed at anchor.

Tampa itself, while poor and dreary, had paved streets, street-cars, electric street lamps, and a semblance of order despite the recent doubling of its population by the arrival of the army. The chief feature of the town was so remarkable it would have been the most gawked-about structure almost anywhere in America. The

Tampa Bay Hotel was an opulent, five-story, five hundred-room, vaguely Moorish confection with silver-tipped brick minarets, great balconies, verandas and piazzas, spacious halls filled with statuary, potted palms, high-backed, brass-studded, leather-upholstered chairs, and stuffed sofas. It sprawled over six acres of land, contained a golf course, casino, dining halls and ballrooms. There were rocking chairs on its porches; uniformed waiters serving bourbon, julips and iced tea; peacocks strutting around its grounds; and a hotel band which never seemed to rest from its playing of Strauss waltzes and fashionable tunes of the day—"The Sidewalks of New York" and "After the Ball" being particular favorites.

The bizarre structure had opened in 1891, the product of the eccentric imagination of Henry Bradley Plant, a wealthy seventy-nine-year-old visionary who believed in Tampa's destiny as a principal port city and who could afford to gamble on it: among his many enterprises, he owned a steamship line which included the *Olivette,* the popular Key West–to–Cuba steamer which had shuttled countless would-be filibusters, *insurrectos,* junta members and newspapermen to the island in the heyday of the revolution.

Two floors of Plant's hotel served as headquarters for General William Rufus Shafter's army and in May and June, the hotel and grounds swarmed with military men, visiting dignitaries, and the Fifth Corps' ubiquitous school of pilot-fish journalists diligently searching for news during a period of waiting for the "invasion" of Cuba to get underway.

Richard Harding Davis, ensconced in the Tampa Bay Hotel since May 3 with assignments to cover the war from *Scribner's,* the *New York Herald* and the *Times* of London, wandered about Henry Plant's sumptuous hostelry and grounds, sipped his drinks with the indolent officers lounging on the verandas and pronounced these languourous days "the rocking-chair period" of the war. In one letter home, he wrote that "one General counted today and forty enlisted men passed him without saluting. . . . We have a sentry here; he sits in a rocking chair."

Davis had been offered a captain's commission in the volunteer army but, after much agonizing, turned it down, convinced by friends that he would be far more "useful" as a correspondent than a paper shuffler behind the lines. Charles Johnson Post, who though now a New York infantry volunteer, had a cynical newspaperman's eye for such things, caught a glimpse of the *beau sabreur* of correspondents at the hotel. He wrote of Davis "conning his *Social Register* on the cool hotel porch, until he knew the elite of the Rough Riders from Teddy on up or down." Post, who clearly cared nothing about Davis's high-falutin' reputation, wrote that the lordly newsman was "keeping himself and his silk undies in perfect condition for the rigors of the coming campaign."

Davis was not the only celebrity wearing out the rocking chairs, wandering the piazzas and feeding the peacocks at the hotel. That other peacock, General of the Army Nelson Appleton Miles, blew in on June 1, braided and bemedalled and ready for action, and on the same day arrived Major General Joe Wheeler, "dashing about as cheerful as a cricket," a correspondent wrote. Clara Barton was there, together with many of her Red Cross volunteers, waiting to see if their services would be needed in Cuba; the renowned evangelist and hymn composer Ira D. Sankey came to pay a visit as did the "Message to García" hero Andrew Rowan, Count von Goetzen, Kaiser Wilhelm II's observer, and Edith Carow Roosevelt, come to visit her husband and see his beloved regiment.

Nor were all the correspondents as idle as Davis. Poultney Bigelow of *Harper's Weekly* scurried around the town, explored the encampments on the Tampa outskirts and teeming bayside and found much to write about. He was the son of a diplomat, reared in Berlin where he was a childhood friend of the future Kaiser Wilhelm II. He had given Frederick Remington his start as

DALE L. WALKER

a magazine illustrator and also knew Theodore Roosevelt, had attended law school with him and once characterized the ebullient Teddy as "an excellent specimen of *genus Americanus egotisticus.*"

In the May 28 issue of *Harper's,* Bigelow wrote, "Here we are thirty days after the declaration of war, and not one regiment is yet equipped with uniforms suitable for hot weather. The Cuban patriots and cigar-makers look happy in their big Panama hats and loose linen trousers, but the U.S. troops sit night and day in their cowhide boots, thick flannel shirts, and winter trousers."

He also wrote of the diet of "greasy pork and beans," the absence of fruit and vegetables and the onset of dysentery among the waiting troops.

While the army's officers fretted and paced among the potted palms of the Tampa Bay Hotel, the navy continued to fight the war and produce new heroes in those early June days. The latest name on everybody's lips was Lieutenant Richmond Pearson Hobson, a prodigy out of Greensboro, Alabama, who had entered Annapolis at age fifteen, graduated with the class of '89 and came to be considered an authority on ship construction. In the predawn hours of June 3 this studious loner, assigned to Admiral Sampson's flagship *New York,* undertook the most daring and dangerous mission of the war: attempting to scuttle a ship athwart the entrance to Santiago Harbor, thereby rendering the Spanish fleet *hors de combat* for the duration of the war. Hobson and his crew of seven sailors crept the old four-hundred-ton collier *Merrimac* into the channel by starlight on the third. Ten explosive mines, each containing three bags of gunpowder, were lashed twelve feet below the *Merrimac*'s waterline, to be triggered by an electric cable switch on the ship's bridge. An hour into the mission, with the collier just penetrating the channel entrance, Spanish shore batteries awoke suddenly and opened fire with artillery and small arms. The *Merrimac*'s rudder and anchor chains were shot away and while the ship managed to drift up the channel on the tide, only two of the mines could be triggered before an enemy shell struck the hold, blowing the *Merrimac* boilers skyward. The ship lurched, shuddered and sank in the mud, failing to block the channel but at least causing an impediment between the entrance and the harbor proper.

Miraculously, neither Hobson nor his crewmen were killed in the thirty-five-minute operation. All were flung over the side of the ship when the boilers blew, but all survived to be picked out of the water by Spanish gunboats and made prisoners of war.

Even one of Roosevelt's navy friends, with whom he had traded many letters on the war, got into the fighting while the Fifth Army Corps was stranded in Tampa. On June 10, Commander Bowman McCalla of the cruiser *Marblehead* directed the landing of 650 marines at Guantánamo Bay, forty miles east of Santiago. In the first land action of the war, the First Marine Battalion, aided by Cuban insurgents, chased the Spanish soldiers from the jungle surrounding Guantánamo in two days and secured it as a fueling and provisioning depot for Sampson's blockading fleet.

Roosevelt's Lantern Club acquaintance Stephen Crane witnessed the Guantánamo fighting and wrote lively accounts of it for *McClure's*.

The Rough Riders in their khaki uniforms, led by such public and publicized Washington figures as Leonard Wood and, especially, Theodore Roosevelt, were objects of intense curiosity throughout the camps around Tampa and the officers of the regiment were often visited and trailed by newspaper reporters.

The common trooper got little attention but none of them cared. They had drills, horse grooming and busywork to perform, and frequent passes to town where they could stroll around the big hotel or make a foray to notorious Ybor City. Private Frank Brito of H Troop, who was placed in charge of the Rough Riders' camp stockade outside Tampa, recalled a time when he and five or

six other New Mexico troopers found an opium den in Ybor City
and decided to give it a try. "We laid down on some cots," he said,
"and a Chinaman brought in a pipe about three feet long and
some black stuff that looked like coal-tar. He worked the stuff into
a ball and put it into the pipe and touched a candle flame to it
while we sucked on the mouthpiece. I took about four puffs and
that was enough. All of us were sick for a week."

Ybor City also had a shooting gallery that proved a popular
hangout for the Rough Riders, at least until they shot up the place
and were barred from it thereafter. Brito explained that in the
gallery there were cotton bales behind the targets to catch the .22-
caliber bullets from the rifles supplied to those who ante'd up the
twenty-five-cent admission fee. "We told the man we would use
our own six-shooters instead of the .22s, and when we all started
shooting, it scared hell out of everybody. People started jumping
the chicken-wire fence around the place and somebody called the
Tenth Georgia Cavalry to quiet us down. We took the pins off our
hats so nobody knew for a while that the trouble-makers were
Rough Riders. The Colonel—Colonel Roosevelt—found out
eventually, but by then it had all blown over."

2

"When will you sail?"

William R. Shafter, heaving his three hundred-pound bulk
around his headquarters rooms in the Tampa Bay Hotel, consulting his maps, holding interminable meetings with the senior officers of his army, suffered not only from gout, varicose veins and
prickly heat, but from a fusillade of urgent and impossible questions and instructions from the War Department. On May 29,
when the Spanish Fleet was discovered in Santiago Harbor, protected by a ring of shore batteries, War Secretary Alger cabled
Shafter in Tampa ordering him to load his transports and make

them ready for steaming. The order, which would have infuriated any man selected to command an invading army, even stipulated that the force of regulars and volunteers to invade Cuba, including two squadrons of cavalry, carry five hundred rounds of ammunition per man. Artillery, siege guns and howitzers were to be loaded up immediately together with two months' supplies for the army and a small number of horses and pack animals, and await steaming orders.

On the 30th the general received another order from Alger:

> You are directed to take your command on transports,
> proceed under convoy of the navy to the vicinity of Santiago
> de Cuba, land your force at such place east or west of that
> point as your judgment may dictate, under the protection
> of the navy . . . to capture or destroy the garrison there,
> and . . . with the aid of the navy capture or destroy the
> Spanish fleet now reported to be in Santiago harbor.

The cable ended, "When will you sail?"

"Pecos Bill" Shafter, famous for his choleric temper, smoldered. Sail? He had only just discovered his objective and had to shuffle through his maps and papers to find information on it. Intelligence reports said Santiago, capital of Oriente Province, had a population of about 45,000; was Cuba's third largest city; was not connected by rail to Havana—five hundred miles west on the opposite side of the island; had a fine harbor, second only to that of Havana; a deep, narrow bay; a garrison estimated at ten thousand Spanish soldiers.

Alger and other of President McKinley's military advisors wanted Shafter to assemble a force of 25,000 men to land on the coast in the vicinity of the entrance to Santiago Harbor. Once there, they were to assist the navy in silencing the gun batteries protecting the harbor and in the destruction of the Spanish Fleet. It was envisioned that after the fall of Santiago, Shafter's army would attack Puerto Rico and another force would steam from Mobile or New Orleans to take Havana.

But no matter how cogent this plan seemed in Washington, the sudden debarkation orders demonstrated a logistical ignorance that would plague the campaign from outset to end.

Shafter did not know when he could sail. Although he had arrived in Tampa on April 29, his actual command of the Fifth Corps was not given him until May 20, and by then things were in a state of staggering confusion. He had more than 25,000 men swarming about Tampa, but the army's supporting matériel—foodstuffs, uniforms, rifles and ammunition, tools, wagons, gun limbers, medical supplies—were scattered in three hundred unmarked boxcars all along the single-track railroad from Tampa Bay to Lakeland with no bills of lading to determine what was where. Moreover, volunteer regiments were still pouring into Tampa and, a critical matter, Shafter had too few transports to carry 25,000 men into the Caribbean. The steamers, most of them small, filthy, ramshackle veterans of the coastal trade, had been chartered by the army's Quartermaster Department from private shippers who, as Charles Johnson Post wrote, "to speed the war along, do his bit, and make, perhaps, a tidy profit," charged exorbitant fees for them. There were few bunks aboard, no stalls for animals, ventilation nonexistent except by opening side cargo ports and using canvas pipes to bring in outside air.

Nelson Miles came down to Tampa from Washington on June 1, surveyed the confusion and bemusedly reported to his superiors that there would necessarily be delays in getting the expedition underway. But even the general of the army and his personal inspection of the situation did not stem the flow of War Department cables: "When will you leave?" Alger asked the harried Shafter. The general gave June 4 as the debarkation date but when this proved impossible, notified Alger he needed more time. On the sixth, Alger messaged, "Since telegraphing you an hour since, the

President directs you to sail at once with what force you have ready."

Shafter hedged, saying it would take time to get steam up but that he would attempt to sail on June 7. Then, working from the veranda of the hotel, and later from a packing-crate desk at dock-side, personally directed the loading of the steamers with coal, water, food, forage, artillery pieces, wagons, and ammunition, while civilian carpenters furiously knocked together bunks for the men and stalls for horses and mules in the holds of the ships.

Early in the frantic efforts to get the expedition underway, a critical decision was made by the general commanding and his quartermaster officers. It was determined that the capacity of the motley collection of thirty-two transports was under twenty thousand men and so orders were issued that only eight troops of seventy men each could be taken from each regiment and all horses except for those for key officers and couriers were to be left behind in Tampa. This was devastating news.

Leonard Wood had reported to Shafter's headquarters in the Tampa Bay Hotel on June 2 and received camping space for the Rough Riders with General Joseph Wheeler's cavalry division. He told Shafter his regiment was poised and ready, but when the embarkation order reached the camp that he could send only eight of his twelve troops, Wood and Roosevelt had the depressing duty of announcing this to the regiment and selecting those who were to go and those who would stay behind.

"I had an awful morning . . . the four that are left behind feel fearfully," Roosevelt wrote to Cabot Lodge from the hotel, adding that the loss of the horses was almost as severe a blow. He urged Lodge to see Secretary Alger and "have him keep us in mind, and have the horses sent to us very early. It is a little bit rough to make us fight on foot with only two-thirds of our strength."

Since he was allowed only two squadrons, Wood selected Roosevelt and Major Alexander Brodie to command them, and with great reluctance, assigned Major Henry Hersey of the New Mexico contingent and Major George Dunn, the Maryland "master of hounds," to command Troops C, H, I and M, which were to remain in Tampa to care for the regiment's horses. Frank Brito of Troop H remembered that Wood tried to assure the stragglers that they would be coming along later, with the horses, and join their comrades in Cuba, but, Brito said, "We were too angry to hear him and if we had, I doubt we'd have believed him. We had come a long way together and being left out at the last minute was not something any of us had counted on."

Roosevelt later wrote, "The men who were left behind felt the most bitter heartburn. To the great bulk of them I think it will be a life-long sorrow. I saw more than one, both among the officers and privates, burst into tears. . . ."

Hersey was especially disappointed since he had brought to San Antonio the single largest number of volunteers, but he did not dispute the decision. One who did was Captain Maximiliano Luna of Las Lunas, New Mexico. He confronted Wood and argued that he was the only pure-blooded Spaniard in the regiment and must go to prove that his people, the Mexican Americans in the regiment, were as loyal to the cause as any other. Wood relented and Luna was given a place in Troop F.

The horseless Rough Riders now had a new nickname, one which K Trooper Jesse Langdon attributed to "some jealous wiseacre" in the Seventy-first New York Volunteers: "Wood's Weary Walkers."

Fortunately, it didn't stick.

3

"We are in a sewer."

The order passed along the waiting regiments that transports would be boarded at daybreak on June 8 and that the officers and troopers who were to board must make their way dockside to Port Tampa—nine miles from the town via the single-track railroad—by their own devices and ingenuity.

Wood and Roosevelt swung into action, intent on moving ahead of the other volunteer regiments. Squadron commanders were ordered to have their troops and gear trackside at midnight on the seventh, each man carrying his blanket in a roll slung over his shoulder plus rifle, cartridge belt and 125 Krag rounds, canteen and utensils, and a haversack containing rations.

While the troopers napped on their blanket rolls at the rail siding, Wood, Roosevelt and their officers wandered about buttonholing railroad men and other officials for information. "We were allowed to shove and hustle for ourselves as best we could, on much the same principles that had governed our preparations hitherto," Roosevelt recalled wryly.

Nobody knew anything; the train didn't show up. At three A.M., the regiment was moved to another part of the track but still could find no train to board. At six, some coal cars up from the bay slid to a stop near where the Rough Riders had gathered and, Roosevelt said, "these we seized." He convinced the engineer to back the coal cars down the nine miles to Port Tampa. En route, the soot-dusted troopers passed a line of flatcars carrying the Seventy-first New York Volunteers toward the single-track convergence that would carry all to the Tampa Bay wharf. Charles Johnson Post was among the New Yorkers and remembered "Colonel Theodore Roosevelt grinning. . . . His khaki uniform looked as if he had slept in it—as it always did."

The Rough Riders thus arrived pierside slapping coal dust from their khakis while they surveyed the mile-long wharf. There, occupying every square foot of it, milled a clamorous multitude of swearing, sweating, scurrying packers, stevedores, sailors, and merchant seamen; stamping horses and braying mules in noisome clots; a lunatic jumble of crates and boxes of supplies strewn like jackstraws dockside; and army officers frantically trying to find berths for their men on the Cuba-bound steamers.

Wood and Roosevelt spent an hour searching for the Fifth Corps's chief quartermaster, Lieutenant Colonel Charles F. Humphrey, and at last found the much-harried man. He consulted his papers and assigned the regiment the 420-foot *Yucatan,* then pointed toward midbay where the steamer swung at anchor awaiting room at the dock to take on its allotment of cargo and men.

Employing a favorite word to describe the desperate measures required to make progress in the Tampa asylum, Roosevelt said Wood "seized" a stray launch, made his way out to the *Yucatan* and boarded, telling the captain he was acting "by orders of General Shafter." Meantime, Roosevelt ran "at full speed back to our train" and "double-quicked the rest of the regiment up to the boat just in time to board her as she warped into the quay."

It turned out that two other regiments, the Second Infantry regulars and the Seventy-first New York Volunteers, had been assigned the *Yucatan* but Wood's ingenuity in boarding the transport gave the Rough Riders the upper hand. "There was a good deal of expostulation," Roosevelt said, "but we had possession." Room was made on the steamer for four companies of the Second Infantry and even two men from the Vitagraph Company who were desperate to take their motion picture equipment on board to photograph the war. But the New York volunteers were left at quayside. The colonel of that regiment, Wallace Downs, had his own initiative, however, and spying the transport *Vigilancia* in the bay, hired a launch and dispatched his lieutenant colonel and a party of twelve men to board the vessel and order its captain to bring it to the pier.

"Seizing" was spreading. There seemed to be no other way, at Tampa Bay in June 1898, at least, of embarking for war, than to put carpe diem into practice and not only for the day but for trains, boats and ships.

By late afternoon the Rough Riders—33 officers and eight

troops of 578 men—were aboard the *Yucatan* together with their supplies and weapons, including the Colt rapid-firers and a pneumatic dynamite gun.*

The officers' horses were loaded aboard another transport, Roosevelt's "Rain-in-the-Face" and "Texas" accompanied by his "colored body servant," Marshall, the old Ninth Cavalry soldier.

Most of the transports were crowded over their five-hundred-man capacity; the Rough Riders and the four companies of the Second Infantry brought the *Yucatan* complement to 43 officers and 773 men.

General Shafter boarded his headquarters transport, the *Segurança,* at two on the afternoon of June 8 and lay down for a nap. There were still men and supplies to board on the steamer-flotilla, but in a few hours he would be ready to sail.

Also on board the *Segurança* were several correspondents, among them novelist Frank Norris, representing *McClure's Magazine;* James F. J. Archibald of the *San Francisco Post;* Frederick Remington and Richard Harding Davis of the *New York Herald.* Davis, who had hired a catboat to get himself and his baggage out to the command ship, wrote in a letter home that he had spent the night of the 7th at the Tampa Bay wharf "watching troops arrive and lending a helping hand and a word of cheer to dispirited mules and men, also segars and cool drinks." None of the men boarding the transports, he said, had been fed for twenty-four hours, "the yellow Florida people having robbed them all day had shut up and wouldn't open their miserable shops."

Shafter was awakened from his nap that Wednesday afternoon by an aide delivering another message from Secretary Alger: "Wait until you get further orders before you sail. Answer quick," said

*This was a strange experimental weapon consisting of two long steel tubes with a superimposed barrel which fired a three-pound dynamite projectile by means of a gun-cotton explosion which forced compressed air into the breech. A bow hold of the *Yucatan* carried 3,500 pounds of dynamite ammunition for this gun.

the man who had pelted the general with "When can you sail?" messages.

Shafter and his seventeen-thousand-man army, conforming to the eternal habit of the military service, had hurried up to wait, the delay caused by what Roosevelt called "a blunder." Reports had reached Washington that a number of Spanish ships were sighted cruising in Nicholas Channel off the north coast of Cuba and directly in the sea path to be taken by Shafter's transports.

The reports were false but the expedition swung at anchor in the steam bath of Tampa Bay for a week before assurances came that it was safe to proceed, that all six of Cervera's warships were still anchored in Santiago Harbor. During the wait, the horses and pack animals had to be unloaded but there was little else to do. Some shore passes were granted but most of the officers and men were fearful that some sudden order to sail would leave them stranded on the beach. Some of the regiments, including the Rough Riders, were drilled by their officers aboard the transports; many sluiced off their accumulation of sweat and grime by taking a dip in the warm bay. The Westerners, many of whom had never seen a body of water larger than a lake, were awed to find the bay water too salty to drink.

On the *Yucatan* and every other troopship, card-playing, fishing, swimming and grousing were the round-the-clock pastimes, the ennui broken periodically when the band of the Second Infantry regulars played a tune of two, the favorite, which everybody learned to sing, being

> *Oh, I went to the animal fair,*
> *The birds and the beasts were there,*
> *The big baboon by the light of the moon*
> *Was combing his auburn hair . . .*

and, when the Rough Riders could talk them into it, "There'll Be a Hot Time in the Old Town Tonight."

THE BOYS OF '98

The travel rations issued to the men began running low a few days into the waiting, the tinned "fresh beef" found to be gristly, tasteless and topped by a slimy layer of grease. There were no fruits or vegetables on board, nor any ice; worse yet, the drinking water smelled fishy and had a tainted tang to it,

"We are in a sewer," Roosevelt wrote Cabot Lodge during this time aboard the *Yucatan*. "The steamer on which we are contains nearly one thousand men, there being room for about five hundred comfortably. We have given up the entire deck to the men, so that officers have to sit in the cabin, and even so several companies are down in the lower hold, which is unpleasantly suggestive of the Black Hole of Calcutta."

Early in the voyage one Rough Rider hung out a homemade "Standing Room Only" sign, to which another added, "And damn little of that!"

Finally, after five unnerving days listening to the creak of anchor chains and the slap of water against the hulls of their ships, the little bay tug *Captain Sam* steamed from ship during a heavy rain squall on the night of June 13, its skipper yelling through a megaphone, "Stand ready to sail at daylight!"

IX

DAIQUIRÍ

1

"Painted ships on a painted ocean"

The first transports weighed anchor in Tampa Bay at nine on the morning of June 14 and within an hour, three files of twelve ships each, funnels pluming black smoke into the radiant sky of the Gulf of Mexico, were plowing the sea toward Key West. Aboard the flotilla, "sardines standing in their cans," as Rough Rider Jesse Langdon described them, were 819 officers, 16,058 enlisted soldiers (fewer than 2,500 of them in volunteer regiments), 30 civilian clerks, 89 newspaper correspondents, 11 foreign military observers, and 272 teamsters. In the holds, with their water and fodder, about 1,000 horses and 1,300 mules were tethered in their makeshift stalls. Every other square foot along the rails, ladders, and bulkheads was chock-a-block with supplies, rations, guns and ammunition for eighteen regiments of regular infantry, two regiments of infantry volunteers, six regiments of cavalry, including one of volunteers, four field artillery batteries and a Gatling gun detachment.

The black-hulled transports carried sixteen pieces of light ar-

tillery and four seven-inch howitzers, plus field mortars, siege
guns, a Hotchkiss revolving cannon, a dynamite gun, four Gatling
guns, seven mule-drawn field ambulances and one observation
balloon and the paraphernalia to inflate and launch it. The expedition was led out of Tampa Bay by the battleship *Indiana* and
four smaller naval vessels, the escort increased in the Dry Tortugas by eleven additional ships. The transports were also trailed by
two water tenders, several small lighters and newspaper tugs.

The largest invading force ever to debark from the United
States had barely began its run south when it ran into trouble. The
Rough Riders' transport *Yucatan* steered out of its file momentarily and narrowly missed the *Mattewan*. The *Yucatan* with dynamite and guncotton in its bow storage compartments—slid by
the *Mattewan* with barely a yard to spare from collision. Other
problems followed. The towline of a water barge parted and the
wallowing, low-lying vessel nearly collided with the *Olivette;* a
strange small steamer entered the flotilla's sea-lane and a naval
torpedo boat was dispatched to investigate (it turned out to be a
friendly vessel); the ships traveled at uneven speeds, some developed engine problems, and the distances between them began to
open. Keeping the ships in some semblance of order slowed the
speed of all to below five knots average and the voyage to rendezvous with Admiral Sampson's blockading fleet, estimated to
take three-and-a-half days, took six.

Off Key West, the transports were intercepted by a naval escort
convoy, which guided the flotilla east toward the Bahama Channel in a calm, burning sea. On the *Yucatan,* Roosevelt wrote of
the "wonderful sapphire seas of the West Indies," of hailing the
Southern Cross and the new stars that bedecked the black canopy
overhead, and of holding daily "officer school," listening to Indian battle tales by the army regulars aboard and learning more
about his own officers. Allyn Capron, whose "training and temper fitted him to do great work in war," Roosevelt said, "looked
forward with eager confidence to what the future held, for he was

sure that for him it held either triumph or death." And he reflected at length on the man who was Capron's counterpart
among the western volunteers, Captain Buckey O'Neill. Roosevelt viewed the Prescott mayor in dime novel terms as "the iron-
nerved, iron-willed fighter from Arizona, the Sheriff whose name
was a by-word of terror to every wrong-doer, white or red, the
gambler who with unmoved face would stake and lose every dollar he had in the world." O'Neill often shared a place on the *Yucatan* rail with Roosevelt, the two men talking of the mysteries of
courage, fear and love. Buckey, "alone among his comrades was a
visionary, an articulate emotionalist" but he was no "mere
dreamer of dreams," indeed seemed a pragmatist in some matters.
"A stanchly loyal and generous friend," Roosevelt said, "he was
also exceedingly ambitious on his own account. If, by risking his
life, no matter how great the risk, he could gain high military distinction, he was bent on gaining it. He had taken so many chances
when death lay on the hazard, that he felt the odds were now
against him."

Leonard Wood, less effusive and more prosaic than Roosevelt,
also caught the evening breezes from the *Yucatan* deck and in a
letter to his wife described the Fifth Corp's flotilla as "Painted
ships on a painted ocean. . . . Simply a great peaceful, maritime
picture." He also mused on the historical significance of the voyage: "Hard it is to realize that this is the commencement of a new
policy and that this is the first great expedition our country has
ever sent overseas and marks the commencement of a new era in
our relations with the world."

Few of the troopers on the *Yucatan* were of a mind to reflect
on the ineffable beauty of the Southern Cross, the romance of the
West Indies, or the mysteries of life and death. Many were seasick
the entire six days. The hold of the ship was a fetid, sweltering
nightmare. The rickety bunks, tiered three high and knocked together by overpaid and underskilled carpenters at the last minute,
were soon crawling with lice. The water stank like a frog pond and

was not fit, some said, for shaving, let alone drinking. The tinned beef, a ration unfit for the tropics in any event, turned out to be a vile suppuration of grease, salt, fat and gristle which spoiled quickly when opened. (The bulk of this "embalmed beef," much of it tinned for use in the Sino-Japanese War of 1894, had to be jettisoned. Rough Rider George Hamner called it "shark poison.")

In the century that has passed since it fumbled its way to Cuba, the voyage of the Fifth Army Corps has stood the test of time as the greatest adventure in amateurism in American military annals. Even considering that at the time of it the United States had had no experience transporting troops to a foreign shore since the Mexican War fifty years past, there remains something forlorn and vaguely amusing, like a locally produced Gilbert and Sullivan operetta, about those days of June 14–20, 1898.

Richard Harding Davis, who fumed and seethed all the way to Cuba on Shafter's headquarters transport, gave a sense of the ridiculousness of it all when he wrote,

> We traveled at the rate of seven miles an hour, with long pauses for thought and consultation. Sometimes we moved at a rate of four miles an hour, and frequently we did not move at all. . . . We could not keep in line and we lost ourselves and each other, and the gunboats and torpedo boats were kept busy . . . giving us sharp, precise orders in passing through a megaphone, to which either nobody on board made any reply or everybody did.

No regular army officer or foreign military observer had to be reminded that the expedition was ignoring the fundamentals of the arts of war when the transports, lights ablaze in the inky night, moved into the St. Nicholas and Bahama Channels, traversing the enemy coastline where any number of Spanish gunboats might be lurking to challenge them and their escort vessels. And even the

most callow of volunteer officers must have sensed it odd that
their convoy, an uncoordinated collection of unarmed, snail-paced
merchant steamers, even with the protection of vigilant navy vessels, could churn past the enemy coast in the daylight with regimental bands gaily playing ragtime tunes while the men occupied
themselves by admiring the flying fish or dragging their shirts and
trousers on hooked lines behind their ships to rid them of lice.

"It was a most happy-go-lucky expedition," Davis wrote, "run
with real American optimism and readiness to take big chances,
and with the spirit of a people who recklessly trust that it will
come out all right in the end. . . ."

Shoehorned into his cabin on the *Segurança,* General Shafter,
gouty leg propped on his bunk, met with his senior officers,
pored over maps and spent the nights reading Edward Hale's
The Capture of Havana in 1762 by Forces of George III, which
contained an account of the failure, in 1741, by British forces to
capture Santiago via a march through the jungle from Guantánamo. He cut a ridiculous figure to Davis and his newspaper co-
horts, who saw him in his wrinkled, sweat-stained, tentlike
uniform and outsized pith helmet limping along the deck of his
headquarters ship, but Shafter was no fool. He was aware, and
worried, about landing his force on a barely reconnoitered enemy
shore. He had only primitive guesswork from Cuban rebels on
the resistence his troops might face from Spanish soldiery. And he
was facing a potentially deadlier foe than the Spaniards: the summer rainy season of the island and the horrors of malaria and,
especially, yellow fever, that rode the storms. Malaria could be
treated with quinine but "yellowjack" was a scourge whose origins were as yet unknown. Clara Barton of the Red Cross and
George Kennan of *Outlook* magazine had described its symptoms
during their time on the island in the aftermath of Weyler's *reconcentrado* program—chills, raging temperatures, swollen joints,
excruciating headaches, delirium—the progress of the disease

abated somewhat by quinine, calomel and sulphate of magnesia, but those stricken subject to fatal relapses.

Shafter, studying the history and geography of the island in his stifling cabin on the *Segurança,* had a simple goal for his army: to get to Santiago by the shortest possible route, surround the city on the east, north and south, and demand its surrender. He envisioned executing this plan in concert with the navy, which he imagined would penetrate Santiago Harbor, sink the Spanish Fleet at anchor there in a lightning Dewey-at-Manila-like strike, and threaten the city from the west. It would be an army plan with the navy making an important, but subordinate, contribution to its success.

In fact, only a few of the highest-ranking officers of the invading army knew the expedition's objective. Santiago was guessed at since the eastern provinces of the island were the home of the rebel forces and it was surmised that Calixto García and his insurgents would somehow assist the American invasion. But some officers felt sure they were heading for Havana; others were certain about Puerto Rico.

"It was very pleasant, sailing southward through the tropic seas toward the unknown," Roosevelt wrote. "We knew not whither we were bound, nor what we were to do; but we believed that the nearing future held for us many chances of death and hardship, of honor and renown."

The flotilla steamed along St. Nicholas Channel and past the Bahama Channel, the transports sometimes strung out in a ragged, wallowing line thirty-five miles or more long. On the fourth day at sea the ships plowed along the far southeastern limit of the Great Bahama Bank, between Ragged Island off the port bow and the Cuban coastal town of Gibara on the starboard. In these waters, 406 years ago, Columbus guided his three tiny caravels, his "Armada de India," to anchorage on an island where he said "Everything is green as April in Andalusia."

That Santiago was their destination became clear on the fifth day at sea, Sunday morning, June 19, when the leading transports spied Inaqua Island to the north and began a southward turn into the Windward Passage. The transports rounded Punta Maisí, the far eastern tip of Cuba, in the afternoon, and in the Monday dawn cruised past Guantánamo and its marine-held Camp McCalla, and joined the ships of Sampson's blockading squadron. Early in the afternoon the *Segurança* and other leading transports, with the stragglers arriving all afternoon, arrived off Santiago de Cuba, stopped their engines and dropped anchors.

To the north, above the jungle line, the peaks of the Sierra Maestras seemed painted against the cloudless sky; to the east and west of Santiago Channel could be seen white beach and green jungle and little else.

2

"Stop that goddamned animal torture!"

Admiral Sampson, his aides and key officers, came to the *Segurança* by gig from his flagship and spent a day with Shafter working on the problem of where to land the army. Sampson had the answer before he came aboard: disembark on the beach and rocks under the Morro Castle (a hundred years older but similar to the one guarding the entrance to Havana Harbor) on the east side of Santiago Channel, and assault it while the navy swept the channel of mines, steamed into the harbor and destroyed Cervera's fleet.

This plan did not appeal in the slightest to Shafter who had no intention serving as a support force for the navy. In any event, the rock-ribbed Morro fort stood 100 feet high on a 130-foot-high bluff, an impossible objective for an army approaching it via a toe-hold on its seaward cliffs. Moreover, he had no big artillery to reduce its walls, gun embrasures and battlements. Shafter intended landing somewhere close to Santiago, make a short march inland, surround the city, and demand its surrender. He saw the navy's role as helping disembark his army, bombarding the city from off-shore while his troops made their way to its perimeter. He expected the navy to sweep Santiago Channel of its mines, penetrate the harbor, destroy its defenses and Cervera's warships, and lay siege to the city timed with his army's landward stranglehold.

While Sampson was explaining the difficulty of clearing the mined channel, the *Segurança* explored the coast between Guantánamo Bay and Santiago, looking for likely landing spots. Although Guantánamo had been captured by the navy and marines and would thus be secure for the landing, Shafter did not consider it an option. It was forty-five miles east of Santiago and the general had read up on the expedition of 1741 in which Lord Vernon landed five thousand men there and attempted to move them west to capture Santiago. The British force had to abandon their march sixteen miles short of their goal when the summer rains, heat and fevers threatened to kill them all.

There were several coastal villages east of Santiago Channel that seemed practicable. Siboney lay eleven miles east, Daiquirí seventeen miles east, and Aguadores, at the mouth of the San Juan River, lay just west of the channel, as did Cabañas, on a small, shallow bay by that name.

The landing site question was not settled until Shafter, Sampson and their party went ashore later in the day. They were taken by a navy launch to the fishing village of Aserraderos, twenty miles west of Santiago, then inland on horse and muleback. In a thatched hut under a palm tree they rendezvoused with the man whose name had been synonymous with the revolution since the Ten Years' War.

Calixto García impressed all who met him—including Lieutenant Andrew Rowan, who had delivered the celebrated "message" to him on May 1 past. While he was frail and elderly, he still exuded power, standing six-foot-four in his white linen suit, a gravely serious white-haired man with a deep cleft in his forehead, a reminder of the time many years before when in a moment of despair he'd attempted suicide by a pistol shot.

García, who spoke English, talked solemnly with the Americans, his aide, General Rabi, a Carib Indian, standing at his chief's side. The old warrior consulted Shafter's maps and said that Daiquirí was the best and safest spot, since it was virtually undefended, to disembark the American army. It had an adequate beach, a pier, and one other very important feature—a road that ran west to Siboney and then turned inland toward Santiago.

Back aboard the *Segurança,* Shafter, Sampson, and their officers worked out the basic landing plan: the navy would bombard Daiquirí and, as a feint, other nearby coastal villages, while five hundred of García's insurgents made an attack on Cabañas Bay. After the bombardment, a naval officer and beachmaster would go ashore at Daiquirí and direct the army's debarkation, the troops to be conveyed to the pier by steam lighters and launches, tugs, gigs and longboats.

Before daybreak on June 22 the navy began its bombardment along a twenty-mile stretch of the Cuban coast between Aguadores on the west to Daiquirí and Siboney on the east, a grand display of fire power, and a gay one since it was accompanied by a band aboard one of the transports playing a brassy version of that most requested of tunes, "There'll Be a Hot Time in the Old Town Tonight."

A reconnoitering of Daiquirí did not reveal the presence of the enemy but did provide some other valuable details. It was a squalid, fly-blown little village fronting on a small strip of bald beach. An American iron mining company had built a large iron pier there for loading ore into small steam barges and while the pier extended a sufficient distance from the shore, it rose too high out of the water to be of use in landing troops—wooden boats rising on swells would be smashed to kindling against its rusty supports. Alongside it, however, stood a twenty-five-foot-wide wooden jetty extending sixty feet into the water and low enough for use in the debarkation.

Ashore, wisps of black smoke rose from a number of palm-thatched shacks and zinc-roofed machine shops which had been set afire some time recently; rusted machinery and long-abandoned ore cars littered the ground, and on a steep hill behind the village a blockhouse commanded a view of Daiquirí's seaward approaches. This sturdy little fortress could have provided a serious problem for the Americans had it been occupied by even a handful of Spanish sharpshooters, but it, and the village, appeared to be deserted.

With the reconnaissance done, the landing of the army at Daiquirí proceeded in the by-now-familiar farcical chaos, a seagoing version of the Tampa transport-loading madness.

At six on the morning of June 22, the navy's steam launches and tugs began drawing alongside the transports to guide them closer to shore and immediately ran into trouble: the civilian captains of the troopships refused to approach closer than four or five miles of the beach and some of the steamers had strayed so far out to sea that the navy had to dispatch launches to locate them and bring them forward.

On the *Yucatan*, Roosevelt hailed the converted steam yacht *Vixen*, commanded by a Lieutenant Sharp who had served as a Navy Department aide, and Sharp took Roosevelt and Wood aboard and offered to pilot the *Yucatan* to a berth a few hundred yards from shore. Elsewhere, troops jumped and tumbled into the navy landing craft in a haphazard scramble and were towed toward shore by the steam launches. By midmorning the swelling seas facing Daiquirí village were strewn with bobbing boats, their gunwales awash from overloading with green-gilled landlubbers and navy coxswains shouting unintelligible words through megaphones.

On the *Segurança*, Dick Davis, decked out in khakis and a

pith helmet with a white puggaree to keep the sun off his neck, peered around the landing zone through his binoculars. "Soon the sea was dotted with rows of white boats filled with men bound about with blanket rolls and with muskets at all angles," he wrote. "The scene was strangely suggestive of a boat race, and one almost waited for the starting gun."

Leonard Wood was also aware of the Sunday-afternoon-on-Coney-Island atmosphere of the debarkation scene, writing later to his wife, "Somehow everything seems to go in a happy-go-lucky way." He said the army was very fortunate to be going to war "with a broken-down power, for we would surely have had a deuced hard time with any other."

And Frederick Remington, who like Davis watched the weird proceedings from the *Segurança*, scribbled a note: "We held our breath. We expected a most desperate fight for the landing."

Shafter's plan called for the Second Infantry regulars to be first unit ashore, followed by the battery of four Gatling guns, then by Brigadier General Gates's detached brigade and Major General Joe Wheeler's dismounted cavalry, including the Rough Riders. The other regiments, regular and volunteer, plus the artillery units, stores and matériel, would follow throughout the day.

The first boats reached Daiquirí beach at ten-thirty and in a perilous choreography danced with the slimy, sea-rotted, wooden pier, the gunwales of the landing craft slamming against the pilings as the troopers timed the boats' rise on the swells until nearly level with the platform, then leaping onto it pell-mell, grabbing at the slick piles and stringpieces, heaving themselves up and pulling others up when the next boat rose on the next wave crest.

Meantime, with the transports still at anchor four to six miles offshore, the animals—horses reserved for top officers and staff, orderlies and messengers, and mules for hauling transport wagons and ambulances—were landed by the simple expediency of opening cargo ports, lowering the animals to the sea in slings, or by pushing them into the water, for them to swim ashore. Many of the terrified animals swam in the wrong direction—toward Haiti—and drowned, others were strung together by their halters and towed toward shore. Roosevelt, witnessing this scene on the steam-launch *Vixen* as it guided the *Yucatan* to a landing berth, exploded in a rare fury and a lapse into language he had found offensive in the Dakota cattle camps. One of the Vitagraph cameramen he had invited aboard the *Yucatan* said the colonel "snorted like a bull" and "split the air with one blasphemy after another," stamped his feet, shook his fists at the transport captains and shouted, "Stop that goddamned animal torture!"

But while Roosevelt's big roan Little Texas swam bravely and miraculously made it safely to the Daiquirí beach, his other horse purchased in San Antonio was not so lucky. Rain-in-the-Face was lowered from the horse transport by bellyband just as a huge wave smacked the hull of the ship and carried the horse to its death.

As the day wore on, Dick Davis, pacing the deck of the *Segurança,* grew weary of waiting to get ashore. He sought out Shafter on the deck and announced, "General, I see the order for disembarkation directs that none but fighting men may be allowed in the boats of the first landing party. This will keep back reporters."

Shafter allowed that this was true. For all he knew, he said, the sand hills, blockhouse, brush and jungle might be swarming with Spanish snipers and he needed to get every soldier ashore to secure the village.

The unassailable logic of this explanation did not register, or impress, Davis. He countered weakly that he was no mere reporter but "a descriptive writer" with an important job to do. Shafter, whose choler had left scars from San Francisco to the Texas frontier, had no time for an intellectual discussion, least of all with a journalist, while trying to direct a beachhead where an enemy likely lurked. The general, who shared the view expressed by England's greatest colonial soldier, Lord Garnet Wolseley, that correspondents were "the curse of modern armies," looked Davis in the eye and snapped, "I do not give a damn what you are." He added, referring to all the reporters accompanying his army, "I'll treat you all alike."

Davis was sorely offended by Shafter's response and, according to the general's assistant adjutant general, E. J. McClernand, who recorded the incident, the descriptive writer went below decks to sulk in the cabin *Scribner's Magazine* had arranged for him.

"So far as I know," McClernand said, "Mr. Davis never said a kindly word about General Shafter afterward."

By dusk on the 22nd, six thousand men had been landed at Daiquirí and, miraculously, only two men were lost in the muddled operation. The casualties were Corporal Edward Cobb of Richmond, Virginia, and Private John English of Chattanooga, Tennessee, both Tenth (Negro) Cavalry troopers who were knocked overboard when their landing boat capsized. Stephen Crane of the *New York World* witnessed the incident and reported that the two men, "tied in blanket rolls and weighty cartridge belts . . . clasped in the arms of their heavy accoutrements," went to the bottom when their boat bellied over at the pier head. Roosevelt, now ashore and in his yellow rain slicker directing the landings on the wooden jetty with Captain Buckey O'Neill of the Arizona volunteers, recorded that O'Neill plunged into the water in full uniform in a vain attempt to rescue the two men.

The advance parties ashore discovered the village was deserted. Shafter later learned that General Arsenio Linares, in command of Spanish forces in Oriente Province, had at least 36,000 troops in his command, nearly 10,000 of them scattered in garrisons around Santiago as far east as Guantánamo Bay. He had originally planned to hold Daiquirí but later, perhaps seeking a better defensive position, decided to burn and evacuate the village, pulling his force out on the morning of the American bombardment and moving a portion of it upcoast toward Siboney.

The only "inhabitants" of the village, Roosevelt noted, were Calixto García's band of rebels, "a crew of as utter tatter-demalions as human eyes ever looked upon . . . armed with every kind of rifle in all stages of dilapidation." He determined that these men were not going to be "useful" in the fighting, or even, in his opinion, as scouts.

The Rough Riders made their way ashore that afternoon. They had been awake twelve hours, wrapped in their sopping gear, carrying one hundred rounds of Krag ammunition, their knapsacks stuffed with three days' rations: bacon sheathed in sacking, hard-tack, socks filled with beans—green unroasted beans for coffee, dried beans to be boiled with the fatback.

Before the landing, Roosevelt had a chore delegated to him. One of the Rough Riders had been placed under arrest during the voyage for refusing an order from a regular army officer and threatening to punch the officer in the jaw. This trooper, William G. Shields of Santa Fe, whom Roosevelt described as "an ex-cow puncher and former roundup cook, a very good shot and rider," had been hauled before a summary court-martial, found guilty and sentenced to a year's imprisonment for his impertinence and flouting of the Articles of War. Off Daiquirí, the man accosted Roosevelt and said, "Colonel, they say that you're going to leave me with the baggage when the fight is on . . . if you will let me go to the front, I promise I will obey any one you say." Said the colonel, "Shields, there is no one in this regiment more entitled to be shot than you are, and you shall go to the front." The trooper, Roosevelt said, "behaved extremely well in both fights, and after the second one I had him formally before me and re-mitted his sentence—something which of course I had not the slightest power to do, although at the time it seemed natural and proper to me."

* * *

Some casks of a winelike spirit were found at Daiquirí, discovered by an enterprising scrounger, Burr McIntosh, photographer-correspondent for *Leslie's Weekly*. He shared the wine with his fellow reporters, with Roosevelt and other Rough Rider officers, providing them a bizarre aperitif to go with their hardtack, bacon and beans.

Late in the afternoon, after Joe Wheeler came ashore, and acting on a suggestion by Edward Marshall, the *New York Journal* correspondent, three Rough Riders were dispatched to the blockhouse on the hill behind Daiquirí called Mount Losiltires. The party took along the flag handmade by the Women's Relief Corps of Prescott and Color Sergeant Albert Wright of Yuma, Arizona Territory, fixed it to the blockhouse staff. For fifteen minutes after the flag was spotted fluttering from the Spanish fort, the transports offshore saluted it with steam whistles and foghorns as the band aboard the *Mattewan* struck up the "Star-Spangled Banner."

The landing of the Fifth Corps, men and matériel, continued through the night of the 22nd under searchlights from the transports and navy escort vessels. Richard Harding Davis, who had managed to get ashore in the afternoon, provided a vivid, descriptive writer's word picture of the tableau:

> It was one of the most weird and remarkable scenes of the war, probably of any war. An army was being landed on an enemy's coast at the dead of night, but with the same cheers and shrieks and laughter that rise from the bathers at Coney Island on a hot Sunday. It was a pandemonium of noises. The men still to be landed from the 'prison hulks,' as they called the transports, were dancing naked around the campfires on the beach, or shouting with delight as they plunged into the first bath that had offered in seven days, and those in the

launches as they were pitched head-first at the soil of Cuba, signalized their arrival by howls of triumph. On either side rose black overhanging ridges, in the lowland between were white tents and burning fires, and from the ocean came the blazing, dazzling eyes of the searchlights shaming the quiet moonlight.

Shafter was determined to push on toward Santiago at the earliest possible moment and so, with troops still debarking but a sizeable force already ashore, he ordered Brigadier General Henry Lawton's division forward to Siboney with Wheeler and his horseless cavalry to bring up the rear. The march was unopposed and the vanguard of the army reached the coastal village at mid-morning on the 23rd. Lawton's troops found the place deserted, the inhabitants leaving behind thirty barrels of wine and whiskey and little else. After establishing a perimeter around the position and a guard over the spirits, he sent a courier to Shafter notifying him that Siboney had been secured.

(Shafter's choice of Henry Ware Lawton to lead the march toward Santiago was a shrewd and pivotally important decision. He was an expert field commander and organizer, the veteran of twenty of the worst Civil War battles—including Shiloh, Stone's River, Chickamauga, Franklin and Nashville—and an Apache fighter who became one of the two non–West Pointers promoted in the field for service in the Geronimo campaign [Leonard Wood was the other]. He was an imposing six-foot-four 200-pound "soldier's soldier," a heavy drinker but a stern, cool, deliberate, and utterly professional officer.)

With the Sierra Maestras looming behind them, and a thicket of bamboo, palms and mangroves at their back, the Rough Riders bivouacked along the Siboney trail the night of the 22nd and settled down to cook and rest. The naps were fitful: the jungle was alive with screeching birds, clouds of mosquitos harassed them, and from the edge of the brush tarantulas and huge scuttling land crabs emerged to investigate the newcomers. The hideous orchid-colored crabs gave the Westerners, who would have thought a carp a strange life-form, a nightmare they never forgot, and even the New Englanders, such as trooper Charles Johnson Post, whose Seventy-first New York volunteers were camped near the Rough Riders, had never seen such a creature. Sixty years after watching them at the Daiquirí camp, Post shuddered at the memory when he wrote, "He is an armored spider surrounded by legs; the hub of these legs is a globular turret in the center of which is a pair of eyes on stems, like two periscopes. His total complexion matches the withered vegetation he travels on. . . . He moves in vast hordes that crackle through the underbrush. . . ."

3

"A regular gamecock"

With Wood in conference with Wheeler and the regimental commanders, Roosevelt, in the Rough Riders' makeshift camp on the Siboney road, spent a nervous first night in enemy territory. He passed much of the muggy evening hunkered at the campfire talking with the officers and men of Troop L—Captain Allyn Capron, Lieutenants Richard C. Day and John R. Thomas of Indian Territory, trooper Elliot Cowdin, once a member of Roosevelt's Oyster Bay polo team, and New Yorker Hamilton Fish, whom Roosevelt described as "a huge fellow of enormous strength and endurance and dauntless courage.

"As we stood around the flickering blaze that night," Roosevelt, in a spasm of manly, romantic prose, recalled, "I caught myself admiring the splendid bodily vigor of Capron and Fish—the captain and the sergeant. Their frames seemed of steel, to withstand all fatigue; they were flushed with health, in their eyes shone high resolve and fiery desire. Two finer types of the fighting man, two better representatives of the American soldier, there were not in the whole army."

Siboney, a scattering of rickety fishing shacks on the edge of a swampy, mosquito-infested creek, became Shafter's temporary headquarters during much of the three-day, seventeen-thousand-man landing operation, and General Henry Lawton had been assigned to reconnoiter the area and determine the whereabouts of the Spanish rearguard which had moved upcoast after abandoning Daiquirí.

During the reconnaissance, Shafter kept Wheeler's dismounted cavalry division well back in the rear on the Daiquirí-Siboney road but during the afternoon of June 23, Wood and Roosevelt, on horseback, moved the Rough Riders northwest toward Siboney. It was a leisurely march with the sun punishing them every step, and made worse by the apprehension that the enemy might be laying in wait to ambush them from the heavy jungle cover.

"The heat was intense," Roosevelt wrote of the men trudging along the rutted trail, "and their burdens very heavy. Whenever we halted they instantly took off their packs and threw themselves on their backs. Then at a word to start they would spring into place again." He marched with Captain William H. H. Llewellyn, the Las Cruces, New Mexico, attorney in command of Troop G, and Lieutenant John C. "Jack" Greenway of Hot Springs, Arkansas. He admired Llewellyn for the firm and caring hand he had on his troop and the devotion his men returned to him; as for Greenway, Roosevelt said, "the entire march was nothing but an enjoyable outing, the chance of a fight on the morrow simply adding spice to the excitement."

Just after dark on the 23rd, Wood and Roosevelt, accompanied by Richard Harding Davis, rode into Siboney. There, under the glare of offshore searchlights, Brigadier General Jacob Kent's division was making its landing. Henry Lawton was absent, in conference with Shafter and awaiting orders to pursue the Spanish rearguard northwest toward Santiago. Joe Wheeler, technically Lawton's superior officer, had decided, without Shafter's knowledge or sanction, to conduct his own reconnaissance out of Siboney, take the initiative in pursuing the enemy and perhaps lead the first clash with the Spaniards. It was a reckless notion and one which Wheeler himself would never have countenanced in his cavalry commands in the Civil War, but Roosevelt saw it as an admirably daring thing. "General Wheeler, a regular gamecock," he wrote, "was as anxious as Lawton to get first blood, and he was bent on putting the cavalry division to the front as quickly as possible."

General Demetrio Castillo, in command of Calixto García's rebel force at Siboney, told Wheeler that the enemy force, perhaps six hundred men (later determined to be over one thousand five hundred) had retired to an entrenched position two or three miles north on the road out of Siboney toward Santiago. The place was called Las Guásimas and there was a crude wagon road that led near to it.

X

LAS GUÁSIMAS

1
"When the wolf rises in the heart"

The indefatigable Joe Wheeler, a gray-whiskered pocket dynamo in a baggy uniform darting around the Siboney camp, put his force together in the evening of the 23rd, gathering his officers, consulting the maps, issuing orders, and questioning the rebel General Castillo on the lay of the land.

They would advance at dawn: the eight troops of the First Volunteer Cavalry under Wood and Roosevelt, a two-hundred-man squadron of the First Regular Cavalry and another from the Tenth. They would take with them a pair of Hotchkiss mountain cannon and the Rough Riders' two Colt rapid-firers. Wheeler would be in overall command of the 964-man force with Brigadier General S. B. M. Young his second-in-command. Samuel Baldwin Marks Young was a veteran regular army officer and among the most respected in Shafter's army. A fifty-eight-year-old native of Forest Grove, Pennsylvania, he had fought in the Peninsula campaign—coincidentally in the Fifth Army Corps—and had a distinguished record at Antietam, Brandy Station and Appomattox.

He had served in Indian campaigns in Arizona and Texas, and during a brief assignment as superintendent of Yellowstone National Park met and became a friend of Theodore Roosevelt's. He was known as a "fire-eater," an aggressive officer much in the "Fighting Joe" Wheeler mode.

Wheeler's plan called for a small force of Castillo's insurgents to accompany the Americans on the road north out of Siboney. Stephen Crane of the *World* said, in a typically harsh reference to the rebels, that these shabby soldiers "looked like a collection of real tropic savages at whom some philanthropist had flung a bundle of rags; some of the rags had stuck here and there."

Crane was a last minute arrival among the correspondents who were camped with the Rough Riders and accompanying Wheeler's sortie. Richard Harding Davis was there, in khaki jodhpurs, tall boots and jaunty hat-with-puggaree, animatedly chatting with Roosevelt and avoiding the hoi polloi of common reporters in Siboney camp. He was suffering from sciatica and had a mule assigned to him to ride into battle. The correspondents traveling by shank's mare were Kennett Harris of the *Chicago Record*, who had followed the Rough Riders since their San Antonio training days, Edward Marshall of Hearst's *New York Journal*, John Dunning of the Associated Press, John Fox, Jr. and Caspar Whitney of *Harper's Weekly*.

The Rough Riders spent the night of the 23rd in a grove of coconut trees beyond Siboney. Dark clouds lowered over their camp at dusk and no sooner had they built their fires to cook their coffee, pork and presoaked hardtack, than a downpour extinguished the fires. When it abated after two hours, the troopers rebuilt their fires and dried out their clothing as best they could before curling up in their blankets for a few hours of sleep.

Wood spent much of the evening talking with General Sam Young on the plans to pursue the Spaniards at daybreak. The enemy rearguard was believed to be entrenched a few miles to the northwest but the terrain ahead was unknown; the deployment of the Spanish defenders was unknown; their number and armaments were unknown.

At 5:40 on June 24, the eight troops of Rough Riders and the four troops each of the First and Tenth Cavalry regulars were rousted from their blankets and roughly organized to begin the march. Wheeler and Young led the regulars along the grandiosely named *Camino Real* (Royal Road), a rutted, mud-soupy wagon track that cut through the brush and jungle north out of Siboney; Wood and Roosevelt led the Rough Riders along a second, even more primitive, trail to the left of the main road which reconverged with the Royal Road about four miles north. The two generals, together with Wood, Roosevelt, Major Alex Brodie and Wheeler's aide-de-camp, Captain William D. Beach, were on horse or muleback; Dick Davis, his back pains not helped by it, rode a mule; all others were afoot.

The correspondents tagged along with the Rough Riders. Stephen Crane, who had landed at Siboney in a dispatch boat just as Wheeler's troopers were heading out, found a spot in the rear with Brodie's squadron and the mules carrying the awkward and heavy Colt automatic guns. He wrote of the men he called "Teddy's Terrors" and their advance: "They wound along this narrow winding path, babbling joyously, arguing, recounting, and laughing; making more noise than a train going through a tunnel."

The noise bothered Wood and after a mile or two progress he told Roosevelt, "Pass the word back to keep silence in the ranks."

The trail the Rough Riders followed cut such a narrow swath through the brush that the troopers had to walk single file. Although scouts were sent ahead, no flankers were placed since the dense foliage alongside the trail made it impossible for them to maneuver. The rising sun in the cloudless sky beat down on them as they slogged along between great stands of palms, thorny, flat-topped acacias and patches of wild flowers, and hats were soon removed for fanning faces and the cumbersome packs, which bit deep into shoulder and backbone, were stripped off and tossed by the trail.

On the main trail at about 7:30, Wheeler's Cuban insurgent scouts found the Spaniards. They were well-hidden in rifle pits, stone breastworks and under jungly cover on a 250-foot-high ridge to the right of the Santiago road and directly in front of the spot toward which the Rough Riders were advancing on the alternate trail. The convergence was called Las Guásimas, named after the *guácimo*—hog-nut—trees in the region. Richard Harding Davis said of the place, "Guásimas is not a village, nor even a collection of houses; it is a meeting place of two trails which join at the apex of a V, three miles from the seaport town of Siboney, and which continue to merge in a single trail to Santiago."

General Young ordered the Hotchkiss one-pounder cannon moved forward and set up behind a screen of brush about nine hundred yards from the enemy position, and deployed his regulars in a skirmish line along each side of the road. He left the Tenth Cavalry behind as a reserve force and sent a messenger down the alternate trail to find Wood and the Rough Riders and bring them up. Wheeler meantime arrived on the scene, approved the deployment and gave Young a free hand to conduct the battle.

The opening shot of the Santiago Campaign occurred at about 8:15 when Young's skirmishers fired a few shots toward the enemy breastworks and brought a volley of Mauser fire in return, the smokeless powder giving no clue as to where, precisely, the enemy volley originated.

The Rough Riders were by now nearing the apex of the V with Captain Allyn Capron and his L Troop in the vanguard. Capron, whose twenty-seventh birthday fell on that day of Las Guásimas, had asked for the dangerous front position and it had been granted it to him. "He wanted it and I wanted him to have it," Wood said later. "I had known him from a boy, seen him win promotion from the ranks, and knew that in his hands the advance was as safe as in the hands of any man living."

Another who had asked for a front-line assignment was Sergeant Hamilton Fish, the grandson of Grant's secretary of state, the former captain of the Columbia University rowing team. With Capron's permission, Fish took a four-man squad and two of General Castillo's scouts to serve as "point" for the advancing Rough Rider column.

After Fish and his men, and Capron and his sixty troopers, moved up, Wood and Roosevelt followed at the head of three troops and Alex Brodie's squadron brought up the rear, together with the mules carrying Sergeant William Tiffany's Colt automatic guns. Correspondents Dick Davis and Edward Marshall accompanied Roosevelt's troops—"two men who did not run away," he called them, "who, though non-combatants . . . showed as much gallantry as any soldier in the field."

Not long after the first shots were exchanged by Young's force on the Santiago road, the Cuban scouts with Hamilton Fish's squad found enemy outposts on the converging trail and the word was passed back. As Capron's troopers took positions along the trail, Wood rode forward for his own reconnoitering, then returned to the main body of Rough Riders, joined Roosevelt, and brought five troops forward, deploying them in the thick brush on both sides of the roadway.

With Fish and Capron uptrail and the Rough Riders still out of contact with Sam Young's regular cavalry force, the small-arms fire began, the Spanish soldiery, located athwart the road, sending volley after volley into the American position. The Mauser bullets—"singing through the trees over our heads, making a noise like the humming of telephone wires," Roosevelt said—came in sheets, whining through the trees, clipping showers of leaves and thudding into the palm trunks. Stephen Crane found himself suddenly living the experiences he had described in *The Red Badge of*

Courage three years before: "Bullets began to whistle among the branches and nip at the trees. Twigs and leaves came sailing down. It was as if a thousand axes, wee and invisible, were being wielded."

At first the enemy fire was aimed high, but it soon began finding its mark. The Rough Riders returned the fire, their Krags heating from the effort, but the smokeless powder used by the Spanish snipers made finding an enemy target difficult and much of the firing was directed toward imaginary targets—a gap in the foliage or a place where something moved.

Early in the fight, Roosevelt was standing near a tree which was struck by a Mauser bullet, the impact throwing a shower of splinters in his face. He talked about it later, but at the time gave it no attention. He was under fire, leading men, shooting at the enemy and being shot at. He would remember this time with a surge of pride the rest of his life and say of it, "All men who feel any power of joy in battle, know what it is like when the wolf rises in the heart."

2

"Don't swear—shoot!"

"It was a very warm engagement," trooper Jesse Langdon said of the opening minutes of the Las Guásimas fight, "very warm. These were the first shots fired in anger that most of us had ever heard, and so were the ones we fired back."

Langdon's troop, commanded by Captain Woodbury Kane of New York, was among three Roosevelt deployed to the right side of the trail after Wood's order came back. Brodie's squadron took positions on the left while Roosevelt, Kane and Captain William H. H. Llewellyn of Troop G studied the jungle ahead through field glasses, trying futilely to locate the enemy positions. Mauser bullets continued to zing and whine around them and ahead they could hear, faintly, the reports of the Hotchkiss cannon from Young's position and the reply of the Spanish guns.

The Mauser fire began finding its mark among the crouching Rough Riders. Men began to crumple, a few left the skirmish line and began drifting back on the trail. "There was unlimited opportunity for dropping out without attracting notice," Roosevelt said, "while it was peculiarly hard to be exposed to the fire of an unseen foe, and to see men dropping under it, and yet to be, for some time, unable to return it, and also to be entirely ignorant of what was going on in any other part of the field."

Roosevelt, who abandoned his saber after it got tangled in his legs, and Brodie, led their men forward cautiously under the withering fire, stopping occasionally for a volley toward the imagined enemy positions in the brush ahead. Richard Harding Davis, who stuck closely to Roosevelt, said, "The advances were made in quick, desperate rushes—sometimes the ground gained was no more than a man covers in sliding for a base. At other times half a troop would rise and race forward and then burrow deep in the hot grass and fire."

Roosevelt credited Davis with being the first to actually locate the enemy, crouched in a line of trenches dug across the trail some five hundred yards ahead, giving the Rough Riders "our first opportunity to shoot back with effect." According to Roosevelt, Davis was "behaving precisely like my officers, being in the extreme front of the line," when he suddenly shouted, "There they are, Colonel; look over there; I can see their hats near that glade." Roosevelt looked, made out the hats and brought three or four of the regiment's best sharpshooters forward. The range was estimated and the men sighted their Krags on the bobbing hats in the distance while more men were brought up to the firing line. At first the Krags seemed to have no effect, but after the range was raised, Roosevelt said, "the Spaniards suddenly sprang out of the cover through which we had seen their hats, and ran to another spot; and we could now make out a large number of them."

The Rough Riders rushed forward to pursue the fleeing snipers and spotted a large body of men pouring out of a glade ahead. Roosevelt hesitated and called a cease-fire, believing these men to be among Castillo's rebel soldiers who were supposed to have accompanied Young's force on the main Santiago road. "It was impossible to tell the Cubans from the Spaniards," he said. He learned later that the fleeing men were Spanish, not rebel, soldiers. Castillo, according to Roosevelt, had promised Young that eight hundred of his rebels would join him in the advance toward Santiago. "This promised Cuban aid did not, however, materialize," he said, adding sourly that Cubans did not show up on the firing line until the battle was over.

The Spaniards occupying the trenches across the trail represented only a fraction of the enemy force engaging Young on the main road but the fraction was taking its toll among the Americans. The dead and wounded had to be left where they fell—"It was hard to leave them there in the jungle," Roosevelt said, "where they might not be found again until the vultures and landcrabs came, but war is a grim game and there was no choice."

One who fell near him was Henry Haefner of Llewellyn's troop, a twenty-three-year-old Gallup, New Mexico, miner who had joined the regiment with his brother George, also a G trooper in the Las Guásimas fight. Haefner, shot through the hips, "fell without uttering a sound," Roosevelt said, and was dragged under a tree by two men. He propped himself up, asked for his canteen and rifle, and was last seen firing his Krag as the Rough Riders continued their move forward. (Haefner died under the tree; his body was recovered after the fight.) Another of Llewellyn's men who impressed Roosevelt was George Roland, a Deming, New Mexico, cowboy. Roland, Lieutenant John Greenway of Troop A and Marcus D. Russell, a Troy, New York, sergeant in G Troop, had been sent back along the line to make contact with the right wing of the skirmish line. Russell was killed during the mission but Greenway and Roland returned and reported the positions of

Buckey O'Neill's troopers and the remnant of Troop K being led by Major Micah Jenkins, the West Point graduate and former Fourth Cavalry regular out of South Carolina. When Roland returned to the front, Roosevelt noticed blood on the trooper's blue shirt and asked about it. Roland said it was a minor wound, that a Mauser bullet had broken a rib. He was ordered to the rear to find an ambulance and, "After some grumbling," Roosevelt recalled with pride, "he went, but fifteen minutes later he was back on the firing-line again and said he could not find the hospital—which I doubted." Roland worked his Krag to the end of the battle.

Roosevelt had not seen Wood since the opening of the Las Guási-mas engagement and did not know the fate of the men ahead of his position or, least of all, what was happening to Young and Wheeler's force on the Santiago road. In fact, the Rough Riders fought in isolated pockets, singly or in small clots of troopers, not only out of touch with the main force, but often out of touch with their own officers and troop members. "I don't suppose Wood, out of the five hundred men [Rough Riders] engaged, saw more than thirty of his men at any one time," Richard Harding Davis wrote. Moreover, Wood and Roosevelt, and on the main road, Wheeler and Young, were ignorant of the enemy strength and its deployment. Roosevelt, now commanding the main force of Rough Riders, recalled his own dilemma at this critical juncture: "I was in a mood to cordially welcome guidance, for it was most bewildering to fight an enemy whom one so rarely saw."

There came a lull in the enemy fire on Roosevelt's troops after the Spanish riflemen were driven from their trenches, but the rat-tle of Mauser and Krag was still heavy on other parts of the line. Across a ravine not far from the recently abandoned trenches, some American uniforms were sighted and Roosevelt sent a man to climb a tree and wave a troop guidon to attract the attention of the distant men. They waved back. They were regulars from

Wheeler and Young's force and the Rough Riders were relieved to join them. "I was still very much in the dark as to where the main body of the Spanish forces were," Roosevelt said, "or exactly what lines the battle was following." He hoped to find Wood and receive orders on what, precisely, he should be doing. He knew instinctively, he said, "it would not be wrong to go forward," so he went forward in the direction of Young's regulars—and found his man.

Wood had been in the thick of the fight from the outset but far in advance of Roosevelt's troops and thus out of sight and contact. While others were hunkered down seeking whatever cover the jungle-side brush could afford, Wood—in the admired fashion of combat officers of the day—stood beside his horse in the high grass, "with absolute indifference," it was said, searching enemy positions through his binoculars and snapping orders. Once, with bullets whining around him, he sensed a stinging on his wrist and found that a bullet had shattered a cuff link and scorched his arm. When the pop and crackle of enemy fire intensified to the sound of a tearing of a giant strip of canvas, and the troopers began kissing the ground and cursing, Wood strode along the trail leading his horse and yelling, "Don't swear— shoot!" Roosevelt observed this and said, "How Wood escaped being hit, I do not see, and still less how his horse escaped."

Standing near Wood, Major Alex Brodie took a bullet in the arm, the impact spinning him around in a blood-spraying pirouette. Brodie at first refused to go to the rear but when he grew faint from the pain, agreed and left the battlefield. Wood later told correspondent Edward Marshall that "Brodie had not the least idea that he could be hit by a mere Spaniard. I shall never forget his expression of amazement and anger as he hopped down the hill. . . . He came toward me shouting, 'Great Scott, Colonel, they've *hit* me!' "

Albert Wright, the tall color sergeant from Yuma, Arizona, who had raised the flag on Mount Losiltires at Daiquirí, was slightly wounded by Mauser fire at the same time as Brodie. Wright was nicked three times in the head and neck and four Mauser bullets holed the regimental flag he carried.

L trooper Tom Isbell of Hamilton Fish's advance squad, a red-haired cowboy out of Fort Gibson, Indian Territory, whom Roosevelt described as "a half-breed Cherokee," peered through the brush and found a Spaniard in his Krag sights. He pulled the trigger and the man fell. Instantly a fusillade of Mauser bullets rained on him and within minutes he had suffered seven wounds—head, neck, thumb, hand, hip—and had to retire to the rear in his bloody dressings.

Lieutenant John R. Thomas of Muskogee, Oklahoma Territory, also of L Troop, took a serious wound in his upper thigh and Dick Davis, scurrying down the trail after Roosevelt, found the officer lying on a litter, his bloodied leg bound with tourniquets. Thomas rose up on his elbows and shouted at Davis, "You're taking me to the front aren't you? . . . They've killed my captain! Do you understand?" He then fainted. It was as if a scene had been lifted whole and unrevised from Crane's *Red Badge:* "The captain of the youth's company had been killed in an early part of the action. His body had been stretched out in the position of a tired man resting, but upon his face there was an astonished and sorrowful look, as if he thought some friend had done him an ill turn."

Lieutenant Thomas's captain was Allyn Capron, Jr., the Seventh Cavalry veteran who had begged Wood to be allowed to lead the Rough Rider advance, and Davis found him, lying dead, his body propped against the knee of the regimental surgeon, Lieutenant Rob Church, who had comforted the officer as he died. Davis wrote:

Capron was always a handsome, soldierly looking man . . . and as I saw him then death had given him a great dignity and nobleness. . . . His breast and shoulders were bare, and, as the surgeon cut the tunic from him the sight of his great chest and the skin, as white as a girl's, and the black open wound against it made the yellow stripes and the brass insignia on the tunic strangely mean and tawdry.

Nearby, Davis saw the body of Sergeant Hamilton Fish, who had fallen with a bullet in his heart at Capron's feet. He lay in a welter of discarded backpacks, rolled blankets and equipage, his fists clenched, jaw set. "And so Hamilton Fish died," Davis wrote,

as he had lived—defiantly, running into the very face of the enemy, standing squarely upright on his legs instead of crouching, as the others called to him to do, until he fell like a column across the trail. "God gives," was the motto on the watch I took from his blouse, and God could not have given him a nobler end; to die in the fore-front of the first fight of the war, quickly, painlessly, with a bullet through the heart, with his regiment behind him, and facing the enemies of his country.

Davis also found a "boy" dying behind a rock off the trail, breathing stertorously, a bullet wound between his eyes. The correspondent tried to feed the young trooper some water from his canteen but it was no use. Davis found a New Testament in the soldier's blouse identifying him. An L Troop private, Tilden Dawson, of Nevada, Missouri, was twenty-two, a brickmaker working in Vinita, Indian Territory, when he enlisted.

With Capron dead, command of the Indian Territory troop devolved upon Lieutenant Thomas, who, like Capron, was the fifth generation of his family to fight in America's wars. After Thomas suffered his thigh wound, Lieutenant Richard Cushing Day took command of the ill-fated troop and, Roosevelt said, "brought them steadily forward," as Captain James McClintock came up in relief with his Arizonans. McClintock also became a Mauser bullet casualty—another leg wound—and was replaced by Lieutenant George B. Wilcox, one of Buckey O'Neill's Prescott friends.

With Brodie out of the action, Roosevelt took command of the squadron consisting of New Mexico Troops E and F under Captains Frederick Muller and Maximiliano Luna, both of Santa Fe, and Captain Robert B. Huston's D Troop of Oklahomans, and began moving them forward, "well spread out, through the high grass of a rather open forest." The enemy fire on them was severe but they escaped being hit—the Spaniards, Roosevelt guessed, were firing high again. He found what he thought was the source of the enemy volleys, some red-tiled buildings of an abandoned ranch about five hundred yards in front, and moved his troopers toward these sniper posts. He had meantime lost contact with Wood again, but hearing shouts and cheering on the right side of his hunkered troopers, thought Wood might be leading an assault on the ranch buildings and sprang up to lead his troopers in the rush ahead.

"They went forward with a will," he said, under a momentary bullet-blizzard, fired over their heads. The Spanish volleys ended suddenly and Roosevelt led his men into the outbuildings. "I had not the faintest idea what had happened," he wrote, "whether the fight was over; or whether this was merely a lull in the fight; or where the Spaniards were; or whether we might be attacked again; or whether we ought ourselves to attack somebody somewhere else."

The enemy had disappeared, as if vaporizing after their last desperate volley. Inside the ranch buildings, one of them a former distillery, the Rough Riders found heaps of spent cartridge shells and the bodies of two Spanish soldiers, each shot through the head.

3

"We've got the damn Yankees on the run."

He had held up well. Roosevelt, the amateur soldier among amateur soldiers, had been blooded. He had fired his pistol at the enemy, been fired at, and had led men into battle. He had seen blood fly, witnessed the deaths and wounds of his men, experienced the exhaustion of battle-tensed muscles, nerves and senses. This was a far more serious business than hunting game or arresting thieves in the Badlands but he had adapted to it with extraordinary quickness—two months and two days had passed since Congress had declared the "state of war"—and he had a peculiar zest for it. He was saddened by the misery and pain of war as evident even in such a small arena as Las Guásimas, but the misery and pain did not diminish his romantic ideas of military glory. Through his pince-nez, as if viewing patriotic scenes through a stereopticon, he saw great deeds of "valor," "fortitude," "coolness and courage," and "conspicuous gallantry," in much finer resolution than the horrors of the battlefield. What his men had gone through in their baptism of fire was "heartbreaking," he said, but he took pride in his casualties.

In the captured buildings, Roosevelt ordered his men to reload and refill their canteens from the captured water casks, and sent details down trail to bring in the wounded and those suffering from heat exhaustion. The firing had all but ceased and the unnatural silence puzzled Roosevelt. "I was still entirely uncertain as to exactly what had happened," he said. "I did not know whether the enemy had been driven back or whether it was merely a lull in the fight, and we might be attacked again; nor did I know what had happened in any other part of the line, while as I was occupied on the extreme left, I was not sure whether or not my flank was in danger."

One thing chilled him momentarily: a trooper reported a rumor that Wood had been killed. Roosevelt could not credit the news but had no time to think about it as he scurried to reform his battered troopers in a skirmish line across the road and make contact with the main force under Wheeler and Young. Within a quarter-hour of hearing the rumor, Roosevelt was relieved to find Wood alive and actively in command of the center of the American position.

While the Rough Riders were engaged on the left of the advance, unaware that they had pushed back the Spanish forward flank, Wood, in the center of the line and Young's 470 regulars on the right—with Joe Wheeler in their midst—were chasing the enemy off its entrenchments along the hogback ridge to the east of the Santiago road. Only minutes earlier, during the hottest exchange of fire, Wheeler's chief cavalry engineer, Major William D. Beach, suggested, "General, we have nine regiments of infantry only a few miles back on the road. Let me send to General Lawton for one of them and close this action up." Wheeler assented and a scrawled message was sent by courier back toward Siboney. Lawton dispatched the regiment on the double, the leading brigade commanded by Brigadier General Adna R. Chaffee, a tough fifty-six-year-old Civil War veteran, Comanche and Apache fighter out of Ohio.

But by the time the reinforcing division reached Las Guásimas, the fighting was over. The combined regulars and volunteers— over nine hundred men, assisted by the Hotchkiss cannon—had placed a lethal screen of rifle fire on the ridge and its stone emplacements and by nine that morning of June 24, witnessed the defenders, over a thousand Spanish soldiers, erupting from the trenches and fortifications and withdrawing toward Santiago.

Major Beach, standing next to Joe Wheeler, watched the departure and Wheeler, forgetting in the heat of the moment which war he was fighting, said, "We've got the damn Yankees on the run!"

It was now 9:20. The Las Guásimas engagement had lasted under two hours although those who fought in would have guessed three times that. In surveying the enemy trenches, Roosevelt, who walked the battlefield with Captain Buckey O'Neill, counted eleven enemy dead left behind, an untold number of dead and wounded taken away by the retiring force. The army gave forty-two as the number of enemy dead on the battlefield.

The American casualties were 16 dead and 52 wounded out of 964 men engaged; the Rough Riders accounted for half the dead—8 men—and sixty percent—31—of the wounded. The Rough Riders killed at Las Guásimas were: Allyn Capron and Hamilton Fish; Tilden W. Dawson, the Nevada, Missouri, brick-maker of L Troop; George W. Haefner of Gallup, New Mexico, an Illinoisian and miner in Troop G; Marcus D. Russell of Troy, New York, of G Troop; George H. Doherty, a carpenter from Jerome, Indian Territory, and a corporal in A Troop, age thirty; Edward Liggett of Jerome, Arizona, a teamster, also of A Troop; and William T. Erwin of Austin, Texas, a baker and an F Troop private.

One Rough Rider casualty not counted among the troopers was *New York Journal* correspondent Edward Marshall, who had followed the regiment from its San Antonio training to Tampa, Daiquirí, Siboney and Las Guásimas, positioning himself close to Roosevelt, for whom he had a high regard. Marshall had been shot through the spine and partially paralyzed early in the action and by the time he was taken to Siboney on a litter, was alternately still as death, convulsing in agony, smoking a cigarette and deliri-ously singing "On the Banks of the Wabash Far Away." A medic who examined him in Siboney told the correspondent if he had any messages to send to relatives, "You better write 'em and be quick." Roosevelt visited him and later wrote that Marshall "showed as much heroism as any soldier in the whole army." Leonard Wood came by and gave Marshall a sip of whiskey from a flask. Stephen Crane, a close friend from the days when Marshall, then an editor at the *New York Post*, gave him freelance work, thought his friend's wound was mortal. When Marshall asked him to telegraph his dispatches to the *Journal*, Crane did so, thinking they were the last writings of a dead man. The last Crane saw of him in Cuba was when he was taken out to the transport *Olivette*, which was serving as a hospital ship.

(Marshall miraculously survived. Burr McIntosh said he lost a leg to amputation, but he walked again and wrote a book about his experiences with the Rough Riders in which he described the bullet that hit him: "The noise of the Mauser bullet is not impressive enough to be really terrifying until you have seen what it does when it strikes. It is a nasty, malicious little noise, like the soul of a very petty and mean person turned into sound.")

With the battle information and casualty reports in hand, Shafter, on the *Segurança,* anchored off Siboney, sent a congratulatory message on the "gallant action." To Wheeler, author of the stolen march on Henry Lawton and instigator of the skirmish, Shafter offered a reluctant thanks for the success of the fight but ordered his cavalry commander, "Get your men in hand, but make no forward movement."

Everybody except Lawton, still furious at Wheeler's action, congratulated everybody: Secretary of War Alger wired Shafter, "The President directs me to send his thanks to you and your army for the gallant action of yesterday"; Shafter gave credit to his commanders and their men, saying, "The engagement had an inspiring effect on our men and doubtless correspondingly depressed the enemy"; Wood congratulated Roosevelt, Roosevelt congratulated Wood, each congratulated Young and Wheeler.

While the Rough Riders made camp west of Las Guásimas, on the Santiago road near the village of Sevilla, the regimental surgeon, Lieutenant Church, worked furiously to tend to the casualties, preparing the seriously wounded for transfer to offshore hospital ships and tending to the ambulatory who made their own way to the little field hospital he had set up near the new camp.

Rob Church became everybody's Rough Rider hero. Richard Harding Davis spoke of him as "a friend of mine from Princeton, who is quite the most cheerful soul and the funniest I ever met,"

and wrote eloquently of the "tall, gaunt young man with a cross
on his arm" trudging back along the trail from the battlefield,
head bent, soaked with blood and sweat, carrying wounded men
across his shoulders to a makeshift dressing station with the bullets whizzing around him. "He carried four men from the firing
line the other day back half a mile to the hospital tent," Davis
wrote.*

The search for the wounded along the jungle paths and dense
brush continued for some hours after the fight and it was hated
work. Roosevelt wrote of finding one of his troopers and several
of the Spanish dead with their eyes eaten out by vultures, and remarked on the repulsive land crabs "gathered in a gruesome ring,
waiting for life to be extinct." He and Buckey O'Neill at one
point stood over the corpse of one of O'Neill's Arizona troopers,
already discovered by the carrion birds wheeling overhead.
"Colonel," O'Neill asked, "isn't it Whitman who said of the vultures that 'they pluck the eyes of princes and tear the flesh of
kings'?" Roosevelt later concluded that the Arizonan was thinking
of Ezekiel 39—"Speak unto every feathered fowl. . . . Ye shall eat
the flesh of the mighty and drink the blood of the princes of the
earth."

In the respite after Las Guásimas, while Shafter and his divisional and regimental officers were laying plans for the advance on
Santiago, there was ample time to reflect on what had happened
in those two hours of confusion on the morning of June 24. Roosevelt spent his time in devising ways to feed his men—comman-
deering beans, salt pork, coffee, sugar and vegetables, sending
foragers out to pick mangoes. He complained in letters home of

---

*On January 10, 1906, Church was awarded the Medal of Honor for his work
at Las Guásimas. The citation accompanying the medal said, "In addition to per-
forming gallantly the duties pertaining to his position, voluntarily and unaided
carried several seriously wounded men from the firing line to a secure position in
the rear, in each instance being subjected to a heavy fire and great exposure and
danger."

the clothing issue which he said "was fitter for the Klondyke than for Cuba"—and railed at the Army Commissary Department, Shafter, the smokeless powder of the "unseen foe" and the entire lack of preparedness that had now become a fulfilled prophecy. "Our regiment has been in the first fight on land and has done well," he wrote Henry Cabot Lodge. "Our regiment furnished over half the men and over half the loss. . . . The smokeless powder made it very hard to place the men who were shooting at us. . . . Shafter was not even ashore! The mismanagement has been maddening. We have had very little to eat. But we care nothing for that as long as we got into the fight."

One development took the edge off Roosevelt's postbattle ire: General Sam Young was struck down with a fever and had to retire from the field to recuperate. Leonard Wood took over Young's brigade and as a result Roosevelt was advanced to a colonelcy and "command of the regiment, of which I was very glad," he said, "for such experience as we had had is a quick teacher."

The *New York World* agreed. In a story—perhaps by Stephen Crane—which ran on May 26, two days after the Las Guásimas fight, the *World* opined:

> In many ways the regiment is an elaborate photograph of the character of its founder, Theodore Roosevelt. At odd times he is a ranchman, hunter, politician, reformer, society man, athlete, littérateur and statesman. Only in his complex brain, with its intense versatility, could the idea of forming such a regiment have been born. But its wide knowledge of the ramifications of the social scale told him that the men he wanted were working upon every round of the ladder from the bottom to the top.

He knew that the Fifth Avenue clubmen
had the genuine fighting stuff, as well as
the plainsman who carried a dozen
notches on his gun. It only needed opportunity to bring it out.

On the morning of the 25th, with vultures sailing the hot cur-
rents overhead, the Rough Rider dead were buried in a mass grave
in a clearing off the Santiago road. Chaplain Henry A. Brown of
Prescott, Arizona Territory, conducted the service and led the
singing of "Rock of Ages."

Roosevelt said, "There could be no more honorable burial
than that of these men in a common grave—Indian and cowboy,
miner, packer, and college athlete—the man of unknown ancestry from the lonely western plains, and the man who carried on his
watch the crests of the Stuyvesants and the Fishes, one in the way
they had met death, just as during life they had been one in their
daring and their loyalty."

XI

EL POZO

1

"As fireworks it was a fizzle."

After the Las Guásimas skirmish, the troops ashore settled down in their muddy encampments, awaiting the rest of the army—and food stores, equipment, wagons and the draft mules and horses to pull them—to be landed at Daiquirí and Siboney. Medical supplies, desperately needed after the fight, had to be located and rushed to the beaches, and even simple tools were missing. Joe Wheeler, as late as June 29, was sending couriers to Shafter's adjutant general asking for a supply of wire cutters, which were still afloat in the hold of a tranport.

Communications were improved, at least, when the Signal Corps established a telegraph line from Siboney to Playa del Este, a village at the mouth of Guantánamo Bay, connecting Shafter's headquarters directly to the War Department. And, although of no interest to Shafter, the correspondents were now in touch with their editors: A telegraph station was rigged up at Siboney, enabling Stephen Crane to send Edward Marshall's dispatch to the *Herald,* his own to the *World,* and Dick Davis and all the others to keep their war news–hungry readers happy and the army commanders uneasy.

The action at Las Guásimas, unplanned, unprofessional and chaotic, did have the effect of giving the Americans a new staging area five miles closer to their objective. General Henry W. Lawton, commanding the Second Division, and General Joseph Wheeler, the venerable cavalry leader who had usurped Lawton's authority, could now look westward from the abandoned Las Guásimas ridge toward the broad basinlike valley that separated them from the housetops of Santiago de Cuba.

Three miles into the valley, a mile east of the city, lay a series of low ridges, the San Juan Heights, which had to be crossed to reach the outer defenses of Santiago. This complex of hills, with the shallow San Juan and Las Guamas creeks in front of them, was strongly defended and the trail approaching them laced with wire-protected entrenchments enclosed in heavy brush, providing the defenders the opportunity for enfilading fire against any approaching enemy.

The trail, the so-called "Royal Road," from Siboney to Santiago, which crossed and recrossed the sluggish Aguadores River, was so narrow at times that two wagons could not pass one another, and rains—sudden, violent squalls—turned it into a bog and rendered the road indistinguishable from the river.

The six-day respite following Las Guásimas provided time for the balance of the men and matériel to be landed on Siboney beach, for the wounded to be moved to the hospital transports, for the dead to be buried, the men to be reprovisioned, the mules and horses to be gathered and inspected and their mountain of fodder moved ashore. The week also gave Shafter and his commanders the opportunity to study the lay of the land, make plans for the advance, and, it was hoped, to capture the San Juan Heights and

Santiago in one sweeping attack and end the campaign before the rainy season fevers decimated his army.

That week before July 1 had another, and to the army, less salubrious effect: It gave the correspondent corps, strung out from Daiquirí to the front, time to write and rewrite their accounts of the fight of June 24 and, when repetition of the facts became tedious, to fall back on their habitual role of tent-stool tactician, taking up the universal question of postbattle strategists everywhere: What went wrong?

And the answer spreading among the newspaper and magazine writers behind Santiago was a single sensational word: ambush.

The word seems to have begun its rounds soon after Edward Marshall of the *New York Journal* was shot in the spine early in the battle. But the bad news messenger was not Stephen Crane or Richard Harding Davis, or any of the other correspondents; it was carried by a Rough Rider.

Lieutenant Thomas W. Hall, the West Pointer and regular army veteran from New Jersey who was serving as regimental adjutant, was the culprit. This officer, the one who had upbraided "Smoke-'em-Up Bill" Owens for not understanding the meaning of "Present arms!", had earned a wide-spread enmity among the Rough Riders for his persnickity "by-the-book" rules on granting passes to the troopers in San Antonio.

Early in the Las Guásimas fight, Hall witnessed Edward Marshall crumple to the ground after being shot through the back by a Spanish sniper and since Leonard Wood had been standing in the exact spot a few minutes before, Hall apparently concluded that it was Wood who had been shot. Hall bolted, saying he was going back for reinforcements. He grabbed a mule and kicked it down trail to Siboney, where he told the story that Wood was dead and that the Rough Riders had walked into an ambush. The Wood part of the rumor made its way back up trail in a hurry—Roosevelt learned of it after entering the abandoned ranch buildings toward the end of the fight—and was quickly put to rest, but the ambush notion had staying power.

Hall's panic had widespread consequences. Regular army officers, dubious to begin with of the worth of the volunteers and especially such upstart commanders as Roosevelt, took the ambush rumor as gospel and expressed no surprise that even Joe Wheeler, whose last war was over thirty years past, could lead men into such a trap. Henry Lawton, still smarting over being superceded by Wheeler, felt vindicated. And the correspondents, including Edward Marshall and especially Stephen Crane, had the answer to what-went-wrong?

Tom Hall's fighting days, such as they were, were over. When his ride to Siboney in the heat of the battle, and his rumor-mongering, became known, there was instant agitation for his removal from the regiment and court-martial. Captain William Llewellyn, the New Mexico lawyer and bullet-scarred former lawman, personally made the case against Hall to Wood and Roosevelt, but Wood wished to keep the matter quiet.

A significant account of Hall's role in the rumors was written by the poet, novelist and biographer Hermann Hagedorn, a personal friend of both Wood and Roosevelt and author of books on each man. Hagedorn wrote of the incident in a novel but clearly got the story from primary sources. Hall, his name changed to "Adjutant Blair Fisker" in the novel, is depicted as having reported to Llewellyn that Wood had been killed, the regiment "cut to pieces, annihilated, and he was going for reinforcements." Later, Hagedorn has Fisker/Hall returning to the regiment, "pale, humble, with many sidelong glances to right and left, as though he were aware of hidden perils." Then, a passage with such detail that it could only have come from Wood or Roosevelt, most likely both:

> Wood insisted on seeing him alone in front of the square of
> stretched canvas, which was the regimental headquarters,

refusing even to let Roosevelt be present. Officers and men, listening with a kind of ferocious curiosity all over the camp, heard nothing melodramatic float through the hot tropical air, and were disappointed. They had confidently expected a fierce denunication and a court-martial; Roosevelt had stated with customary emphasis and with no pretence of reticence that Mr. Fisker deserved to be hanged, drawn and quartered. . . . The sentry, pacing up and down near the headquarters, heard a hum of low voices under perfect control and in the moonlight saw Mr. Fisker salute and say, in a low voice that quavered, "I'll try to deserve your consideration, sir." And that was all there was; as fireworks it was a fizzle.

Hagedorn portrayed Wood emerging from the tent to announce that he has removed Fisker/Hall as adjutant, "But he will remain with the regiment. . . . He says he lost his head. He evidently saw Inglis [Edward Marshall], the war correspondent, go down and thought it was myself. . . . He has begged me to give him another chance, and I have told him I would."

What, precisely, Wood said and did is not known, but it is likely that Hagedorn's scenario is close to the facts. Whatever transpired in Wood's command tent, after a brief appearance during the advance toward the San Juan Heights, Hall resigned from the regiment and was shipped home.

2

"It was simply a gallant blunder."

Whether or not Tom Hall was responsible for launching the ambush rumor after his mule ride to Siboney, the correspondents, some of them actually present during the fight, did not need Hall to tell them what had happened at Las Guásimas. They knew an ambush when they saw one and wrote of it with a will.

In the dispatch he entrusted to Stephen Crane, Edward Mar-

shall resorted to euphemism in telling *New York Journal* readers
that the American force had "met the Spanish before they expected to," but, among others, Davis and Crane had no such
compunctions. Davis telegraphed the *New York Herald* that the
Rough Riders were "ambushed by receding Spaniards with the advantage all on the side of the enemy" and wrote privately to his
family after the fight that "We were caught in a clear case of ambush. Every precaution had been taken, but the natives knew the
ground and our men did not. It was the hottest, nastiest fight I
ever imagined. We never saw the enemy except glimpses."

Davis, sounding peculiarly more like a Rough Rider than a
"creative writer," took a dim view of General Castillo's rebels
("worthless in every way"), who were supposed to have reconnoitered the roads to Las Guásimas, and said, "No one knew we
were near the Spaniards until both columns were on the place
where the two trails meet. . . . The ground was covered with high
grass and cactus and vines so that you could not see twenty feet
ahead, the men had to beat the vines to get through them."

Nor did he avoid telling of his own intrepidity:

> We had not run fifty yards through the jungle before they
> opened on us with a quick firing gun at a hundred yards. I
> saw the enemy on the hill across the valley and got six sharp
> shooters and began on them, then the fire got so hot that we
> had to lie on our faces and crawl back to the rear. I had a
> wounded man to carry and was in a very bad way because I
> had sciatica. Two of his men took him off while I stopped to
> help a worse wounded trooper, but I found he was dead.
> When I came back for him in an hour, the vultures had eaten
> out his eyes and lips.

"It was as fast as a hard football match," he said. "It was like
playing blindman's bluff and you were it."

The ambush idea Davis later softened, then abandoned. For

Scribner's, two months after the war ended, he seemed to acknowledge that the Americans had indeed been "caught in a clear case of ambush," but he provided a rationale for it: that the Spaniards "would be fools to fight us in any other way." And when he reminisced on the battle in his *Notes of a War Correspondent* thirteen years later, he wrote, in somewhat awkward and halting prose, "It has been stated that at Guásimas, the Rough Riders were trapped in an ambush, but, as the plan was discussed while I was present, I know that so far from any one's running into an ambush, every one of the officers concerned had a full knowledge of where he would find the enemy, and what he was to do when he found him."

By then Davis shared Roosevelt's assertion that "we struck the Spaniards exactly where we expected," and that each officer "had full knowledge of where he would find the enemy" (although this was considerably at odds with Roosevelt's subsequent statement that "we strolled into the fight with no definite idea on the part of any one as to what we were to do or what would happen.").

Davis, who owed a great deal to the Rough Riders and especially to Roosevelt, who had mentioned him in his official battle report, perhaps revised his original views of the battle after talking to Wood and Roosevelt. Two days after the fight he wrote in a letter home that John Fox, Caspar Whitney and he "are living on Wood's rough riders. We are very welcome and Roosevelt had us at Headquarters. . . . Whitney and I were the only correspondents that saw the fight at Guásimas. He was with the regulars but I had the luck to be with Roosevelt."

Charles Johnson Post, who fought at Las Guásimas with the New York infantry volunteers, was not surprised at the correspondent's change of heart. He had little use for Davis, calling him "a brilliant and superficial writer to whom glamour was always gold," and saying acerbically that in Tampa the correspondent was "keeping himself and his silk undies in perfect condition for the rigors of the coming campaign." Of Davis's almost symbiotic relationship with the celebrated regiment, Post wrote in his memoir of the Santiago campaign:

> The Rough Riders were the supreme of the elite; no regiment has ever received the newspaper space that was devoted to them. They were good men—make no mistake about that, even if some did admit it easily—and they could man the trenches or a cotillion with intrepidity. In addition to having Teddy as its second in command, this regiment had its own press agent in Richard Harding Davis, to whom the human beings not listed in the *Social Register* were merely varied forms of pollution.

Stephen Crane of the *World*, despite not appearing on Dick Davis's list of those who "saw the fight at Guásimas," was there. He had been late getting ashore at Siboney and had to tag along at the rear of the Rough Riders with Tiffany's gun mules, but he saw the fight. Moreover, he had no Davis-like obligations to the Rough Riders or the regiment's commanders. Roosevelt, in his New York police commissioner days had met Crane and admired *The Red Badge of Courage,* but after Crane wrote a police harassment scandal story for the *New York Journal* in 1896, Roosevelt conceived a distaste for the fervent writer, an attitude not improved by Crane's dispatch to his newspaper on the fight at Las Guásimas.

Sent by telegraph from the Playa del Este station and dated the day of the battle, Crane's initial story was clear and concise, a model of word efficiency:

> Lt. Col. Roosevelt's Rough Riders, who were ambushed yesterday, advanced at daylight without any particular plan of action as to how to strike the enemy.

The men marched noisily through the narrow road in the woods, talking volubly, when suddenly they struck the Spanish lines.

Fierce fire was poured into their ranks and there began a great fight in the thickets.

Nothing of the enemy was visible to our men, who displayed much gallantry. In fact, their bearing was superb and couldn't have been finer.

They suffered a heavy loss, however, due to the remarkably wrong idea of how the Spanish bushwhack.

It was simply a gallant blunder.

Crane's bald assertion was supported by Stephen Bonsal, the *McClure's* reporter, who was not present during the fight, and Burr McIntosh, the photographer-correspondent for *Leslie's Weekly,* who arrived on the battlefield after the fight but who took pictures of the dead and wounded and talked to many of the participants. He wrote a heated story for his magazine criticizing Joe Wheeler for the rash plunge into the jungle in which, McIntosh said, "There was no vital end to be gained." He later wrote: "A thorough investigation of the battlefield proved conclusively that, whether or not the Rough Riders had been ambushed, it was at least a very patent fact that such a thing could easily have happened, judging from the positions of both the Spaniards and the Rough Riders during the fight. . . . There was no question in the mind of anybody whom I saw that day, but that they had been ambushed."

3

"Among the signal days of my life"

Two days after the battle, Clara Barton and her Red Cross volunteers arrived on the *State of Texas* hospital ship and anchored off Siboney, sending a team of medical officers, nurses and supplies ashore to give some relief to the beleaguered Dr. Rob Church and his medics.

Also on May 26, as the last of his troops and matériel were being landed, General Shafter came ashore from the *Segurança*. He was still suffering from a gouty leg, his pain exacerbated by riding in a buckboard and on a very stout mule along the *Camino Real* to survey the route, a sixteen-mile stretch of jungle and brush, from Siboney to Santiago.

Shafter's officers had discovered a fine lookout just off the Santiago road, a hill called El Pozo, with the meandering Aguadores River running at its front. This vantage point, fewer than five miles east of Santiago, provided a panoramic view of the rough country the army would have to negotiate to reach the outskirts of the capital and its formidable defenses. Through his field glasses, Shafter could see details of the hills and ridges rising up on the flanks of the road and the big blockhouse dominating the San Juan Heights, which Dick Davis, who surveyed the countryside on horseback from El Pozo, said "looked like a Chinese Pagoda." Through his binoculars, the hills looked to Davis "so quiet and sunny and well kept that they reminded one of a New England orchard," and in the shade of the blockhouse, he saw "Spaniards strolling leisurely about or riding forth on little white ponies to scamper over the hills."

The military men peering out toward Santiago saw other things: the barbed wire that encircled the city, the impediments to reaching the San Juan Heights—the river and a wide, grassy savanna that had to be crossed to reach the foothills; ugly rifle pits along the heights, and, a mile beyond the blockhouse, the dim, tantalizing outline of the Reina Mercedes barracks and hospital where Lieutenant Richmond Hobson and the crew of the *Merrimac* were imprisoned.

Another military objective lay four miles north of El Pozo hill, the village of El Caney, the southern edge of which was protected by formidable wired entrenchments, six wooden blockhouses, a stone fort and stone church (where Cortez was said to have prayed en route to his conquest of Mexico in 1519). The garrison there, something over five hundred men commanded by General Joaquín Vara del Rey, would pose a threat to the flank of any army advancing on Santiago and it would have to be captured.

A prominent feature of the San Juan Heights seen by those eyeing the terrain from El Pozo was a low hill at the northernmost sector of the series of rises. The Cubans said there were a number of old, iron sugar cane–refining cauldrons on its summit and, in the absence of a name on the maps, it was dubbed Kettle Hill. San Juan Hill, the one name that would reverberate after the campaign, lay a short distance south behind Kettle. It was the highest of the hills at about 125 feet, and the most dangerous. There was a large brick blockhouse on its summit, wire entanglements and rifle entrenchments encircling it.

Santiago's defending garrison, estimated at about ten thousand men, were scattered in pockets around the city from Dos Caminos del Cobre, a mile to the north of the city proper, to Las Cruces, a point midway down the eastern shore of Santiago Harbor.

Among the many who peered toward Santiago from El Pozo during the hiatus between battles was William Randolph Hearst, proprietor of the *New York Journal*. He had come to Siboney via Jamaica on a large steam yacht, trailed by a large entourage of reporters, photographers and gofers, to try his hand at war correspondence. He rode up to El Pozo on a large white horse on May 27, dressed in a wrinkled linen suit and jaunty straw boater, smiling and shaking hands and greeting the military men, excited and animated to actually see the war he believed he'd created. He got the lay of the land from General Shafter himself—who apparently subdued his press animosity in the presence of one of the greatest opinion-makers of the day. Afterward, in a story Hearst wrote for his paper, he described the rotund commander as a "bold, lion-headed hero, massive as to body—a sort of human fortress in blue coat and flannel shirt."

Those advancing from Siboney to El Pozo traversed the Las Guásimas battleground and saw the detritus of the fight still blighting the roadway and brush: a sad congeries of abandoned knapsacks and blanket rolls, cartridge shells, boots, canteens, blood-soaked dressings and items of clothing. The passersby also necessarily saw the clearing and its graves marked with stones and pebbles in the shape of a crude cross.

One who stopped at the rude Rough Rider cemetery was Captain Allyn Capron, Sr., commander of the Fourth Artillery. The veteran regular army officer stood at length at his son's grave. Charles Johnson Post told a poignant story about the elder Capron, recalling that the artilleryman, after learning of his son's death, "would crawl into his dog tent and we could hear the clink of the bottle against his tin mess cup . . . you could hear the captain murmuring. . . . There was a sob in it." Post said, "From where we sat on the trench berm we could hear it. 'I'll get 'em, Allyn, I'll get 'em, goddam 'em.' "

After a few days ashore, Shafter fled to his tent and cot, prostrated by the heat. His gouty leg and huge bulk made it impossible for him to mount a horse without a makeshift ladder and even then he could suffer it only briefly. He was more comfortable sitting in his outsized buggy, his wrapped foot propped up, under a shade tree. But supine or sitting, in his buggy or new headquarters tent on the north of the Santiago road and behind El Pozo hill, he managed to put together the final plans for the advance, determined to take Santiago quickly. The hurricane season was upon his army, the rains along the coast and the phantom fevers that accompanied them, were already claiming officers and men and the situation could only get worse.

On the 25th, the Rough Riders moved up the road past the village of Sevilla and closer to El Pozo hill and made their camp in marshy ground, a place infested with mosquitos, tarantulas and scorpions, close to one of the little tributaries of the Aguadores River. Foreign observers and attachés, correspondents and regular army officers came to visit Wood and Roosevelt and their celebrated regiment, but the troopers awaiting the word to move forward had no such diversions. Food supplies were now adequate—soggy hardtack, greasy bacon wrapped in sacking, dried beans, tinned beef, watery coffee—but the sudden rains doused cook fires and made it difficult to make the primitive meals.

The two basic, elementary commodities that raw troops treasure more than food, shelter, clothing, or news—coffee and tobacco—were in short supply, as they had been since leaving Tampa. What coffee could be found was in the form of greenish, partially roasted beans that had to be mashed between stones with a rifle butt, then boiled to make a thin, amber-colored, nearly tasteless brew. The volunteers learned some tobacco tricks from the regular army men, such as getting double duty from a piece of borrowed chaw: It was chewed to tastelessness, then dried and smoked in a pipe. But the treasured pipe tobacco—Piper Heidsick, Green Turtle and Black Jack (licorice and molasses flavored)—could be found only among the regulars, who had the experience and foresight to load up with it in Tampa, and it was almost impossible to bargain for.

Richard Harding Davis, a tailor-made cigarette smoker, summed up the matter: "I have to confess that I never knew how well off I was until I got to smoking Durham tobacco and I've got only half a bag of that left. The enlisted men are smoking dried horse droppings, grass, roots and tea."

Worse than smoking manure or gagging down sodden hardtack was the interminable *waiting,* waiting for orders, waiting to move, waiting to attack. Stephen Crane's hero in *The Red Badge of Courage* spoke for every trooper in Cuba on the eve of battle when he said, "This waiting was an ordeal to him. He was in a fever of impatience. He considered that there was denoted a lack of purpose on the part of the generals."

That the attack on Santiago would be launched on July 1 became generally known in the steamy camps around El Pozo two days before the march. Davis wrote his father on June 29, "We expect to move up on Santiago the day after tomorrow, and it's about time, for the trail will not be passable much longer. It rains every day at three o'clock for an hour and such rain you never guessed. It is three inches high an hour. Then we all go out naked and dig trenches to get it out of the way."

On the 30th, Shafter, in his headquarters a mile east of El Pozo Hill, called a meeting of his divisional commanders to go over the final plans.

He had decided to detach one of his divisions, that commanded by General Henry Lawton, plus the independent brigade commanded by General Bates, and one battery of field artillery of four 3.2-inch guns under command of Captain Allyn Capron, Sr., to advance on El Caney, four miles north of El Pozo. Lawton would move into position that night, camp, and attack at dawn. There were believed to be five hundred Spanish troops defending El Caney, most concentrated at the stone fort—called El Viso—and Lawton said, optimistically as it turned out, that he should be able to capture the fort and the entire position in three hours or less.

While Lawton's five-thousand-man force was engaged, Shafter's plan called for an opening bombardment of the San Juan

Heights by Captain George Grimes's battery of 3.2-inchers, firing
from in front of El Pozo, 2,500 yards from the enemy trenches.
This cannonade would be followed by the launching of Shafter's
other two divisions west on the Santiago road with the dismounted cavalry leading the way, the Rough Riders in the van,
crossing the San Juan River and deploying on the right toward
Kettle Hill. Meantime, General Jacob Kent's First Division would
follow, deploying on the left of the San Juan Heights. The two divisions, about eight thousand men, would more-or-less simulta-
neously make a frontal assault on the rifle pits on the ridges. The
object was to capture them and the fortifications protecting the
city while Lawton's force, after capturing El Caney, would come
south in a flank march and assist those advancing on the far right,
the Kettle Hill side, of the San Juan Heights. The three divisions,
it was envisioned, would pour over the last defensive works and
into the city.

Davis later described these proposed movements as "resembling a pitchfork, with its prongs touching the hills of San Juan.
The long handle of the pitchfork was the trail over which we had
just come, the joining of the handle and the prongs was El Pozo.
El Caney lay half-way along the right prong, the left was the trail
down which, in the morning, the troops were to be hurled at San
Juan."

("Hurled" was an apt word. Shafter later admitted, "There
was no attempt at strategy and no attempt at turning their [the
enemy's] flanks. It was simply going straight for them.)

One added feature of the plan was to have a brigade of Michigan infantry volunteers march west along the coast from Siboney
to the town of Aguadores, make a feint to pin down the Spanish
force there and prevent it from moving north to reinforce the San
Juan defenders.

Shafter's greatest fear—the rains and attendant fevers—
proved well-founded when Generals Joe Wheeler and Sam Young
fell ill with malaria and had to be replaced on the eve of the ad-

vance to Santiago. General Samuel S. Sumner was selected to take
over Wheeler's dismounted cavalry division and Colonel Leonard
Wood took command of Young's brigade. (Wood's promotion to
brigadier general of volunteers became official on July 9.)

Roosevelt now took command of the Rough Riders. "It was
among the signal days of my life," he said.

The Rough Riders broke camp at noon on the 30th for the short
march to their assigned position in front of El Pozo. Each man
carried a filled canteen and three days' rations along with his Krag
and ammunition. Mules were brought forward to haul the pneumatic dynamite gun and the Colt rapid-firers, and the regiment
drew up in a column beside the ten-foot-wide Santiago road at the
rear of the First and Tenth Cavalry regulars and waited as the
other regiments passed.

Roosevelt rode at the head of his dismounted troopers, his
pince-nez glinting in the sunlight (spare pairs sewn into his campaign hat), wearing a dark blue cavalryman's blouse with yellow
U.S.V. shoulder straps, khaki trousers, shiny cordovan boots, a
blue-and-white polka-dotted bandanna around his neck and another suspended from his hat as a Dick Davis–like puggaree.

At three o'clock the regiments were notified of the advance
and by four were on the move along the congested trail, the
Rough Riders following the cavalry regulars, Kent's infantry following the Rough Riders, all bogging down on the road in a series of frustrating stoppages. It rained, as usual, on Davis's
timetable, turning the pitiful road into a muddy porridge, bogging down man, beast, ammunition cart and ambulance wagon.

In the softening sunlight, as the troops slogged ahead, Army
Signal Corps observers began ascending in their varnished silk
balloon, a monster airship that arrived in Siboney on the transport
Rio Grande. The balloon and its components had been carried to
the front in six wagons; it was equipped with a telephone system,

a cable and windlass, guide hawsers, and was inflated by a huge generator and 180 steel tubes of hydrogen.

By eight, the march was halted; at midnight, to the north, Lawton's division made camp and slept a short distance down the road from the El Caney fortifications.

Sentries and vedettes were posted, fires extinguished, the creak and rumble of wagons stilled. On both sides of the road, as far as the eye could see, lay a stupendous scatter of bedrolls, shelter halves, horse and mule remudas, gun parks and command tents. As the chilly night of June 30 drew on, the occasional snorts of the animals and a murmur of voices among sleepless men broke an otherwise eerie silence as over thirteen thousand men—plus the correspondent corps, Cuban rebel officers, foreign observers and dignitaries—waited, three miles from the portals of Santiago de Cuba.

XII

CROWDED HOUR

1

"Captain . . . a bullet is sure to hit you!"

Henry Lawton's division rose in a ground fog at sunrise on Friday, July 1, and after a "prison breakfast"—hardtack and water—the men were deployed in a semicircle around the southern approaches to El Caney. Allyn Capron's four field guns were positioned on a small rise 2,400 yards from the ring of Spanish entrenchments, blockhouses and El Viso fort and opened fire at seven. The boom of the light artillery, the sharp crackle of Mauser fire, and the deeper popping of Krags and Springfields were plainly heard at El Pozo where officers peered through their field glasses at the white plumes of cannon smoke rising in the north.

On a loaf-shaped hill in front of El Pozo, Captain George Grimes's four-gun battery waited. Stephen Crane, positioned on El Pozo, peered west and saw Grimes's target—"hills that resembled the sloping orchards of Orange County in summer. . . . Here and there, too, along the crests of these curving hillocks were ashen streaks, the rifle pits of the Spaniards." At eight,

Grimes's cannoneers yanked their lanyards, there was a series of metallic bangs, the cannon blowing giant white smoke rings and sending their 3.2-inch shells hurtling toward the Spanish lines some 2,500 yards distant—too far to be effective. Quickly the battery was enveloped in billowing clouds of smoke, pinpointing their position for the return fire from the enemy's gun emplacements, the first shell from which landed on a slope behind El Pozo, killing a number of Cuban insurgent soldiers and injuring several American troopers lying in wait below the hill. Four Rough Riders were wounded in the first return-fire shrapnel bursts from the Spanish guns and one trooper, Fred E. Champlin of Flagstaff, Arizona, age thirty, a rancher and a private in Buckey O'Neill's troop, died of his wounds. Wood's horse took a shrapnel fragment in its chest and went down and Roosevelt felt the sting of a chunk of metal that raised a walnut-sized welt on his wrist.

Grimes's men kept up their fire for forty-five minutes and during the cannonade, Shafter directed General Sumner to advance with his cavalry division to the edge of the woods, a short distance in front of El Pozo, and await further orders. Sumner led the Third, Sixth and Ninth Cavalry regulars, and the Rough Riders, down the narrow trail and left instructions for the First and Tenth Regiments to follow.

"It was a very lovely morning," Roosevelt said, "the sky of cloudless blue, while the level, shimmering rays from the just-risen sun brought into fine relief the splendid palms which here and there towered above. . . ."

By nine, Shafter, his adjutant, Colonel E. J. McClernand, and the other officers at the command post, realized that Lawton's division was facing stiff resistance and that the two- or three-hour estimate to take El Caney was off schedule. With the possibility that El Caney might be reinforced, Shafter determined to push on to battle and ordered General Kent's division to advance. By mid-morning the rutted road was clogged by a sweating, grumbling army of over eight thousand men trudging along in columns, four abreast, then in narrower places two, hemmed in by jungle and brush, the trail crisscrossed by fords of the Aguadores River and its myriad tributaries. A mile and a half ahead lay the enemy trenches.

After Sumner's and Kent's divisions were twenty minutes into their advance, the Spanish artillery fire slackened and Wood formed up his brigade, with the Rough Riders in the lead, and followed Sumner's First Brigade in columns of four down the slope of the woods toward the ford of the San Juan River. The Rough Riders' objective was to reach a point on the line in front of the San Juan Heights where the regiment would "connect" with Lawton's division, it ostensibly having overrun the enemy at El Caney and marched southwest to join the main fight.

The Spanish small-arms fire was desultory at first but increased in intensity as the advance toward the heights continued. "Our orders had been of the vaguest kind," Roosevelt said, "being simply to march to the right and connect with Lawton—with whom, of course, there was no chance of our connecting. No reconnaissance had been made, and the exact position and strength of the Spaniards was not known."

Adding to the confusion in the midmorning march was the well-intentioned work of Colonel George M. Derby of the Signal Corps balloon detachment. In the absence of an on-ground reconnaissance and in an effort to locate alternate trails for Kent's and Sumner's divisions, Derby went aloft in the observation balloon directly over the First and Tenth regulars, packed together at the San Juan River ford. The effect of the rise of the immense balloon was immediate: It drew a raking Spanish fire, small arms and artillery, on the troops below it. Richard Harding Davis watched the bag "blundering down the trail" fifty feet above the palm tree tops, and said it was "an invitation to the enemy to kill everything beneath it." Roosevelt was furious: "Of course it was a special target for the enemy's fire," he said. "I got my men across before it reached the ford. There it partly collapsed and remained, causing severe loss of life. . .," and Wood considered the balloon incident "one of the most ill-judged and idiotic acts I have witnessed."

Derby did notify his superiors that he had identified a trail to the left of the Aguadores which would relieve the congestion at the river crossing. Kent's division took advantage of this alternate route, serving as the left and center of the eventual line, with Sumner's division at center and right, at the San Juan Heights.

Roosevelt led the Rough Riders in a column toward the San Juan River—an ankle-deep, easily fordable stream—and before ten o'clock reached a sunken lane, fenced on each side, which led directly to two hills, the closest of which, on the right, was surmounted by some ranchlike buildings and sugar-refining pots. The Spanish fire from these hills, and from distant trenches, sniper positions in the brush and jungle in and around the hills, was intense and unrelenting, pinning the regiment down. "I got the men as well-sheltered as I could," Roosevelt said. "Many of them lay close under the bank of the lane, others slipped into the San Juan River and crouched under its hither bank, while the rest lay down behind the patches of bushy jungle in the tall grass. The heat was intense and the men were already showing signs of exhaustion."

In the heavy volley firing, the Rough Riders suffered several casualties, among them Lieutenant Horace Devereaux of K Troop, the Princeton football star, who was shot in the arm, and Ernest E. Haskell, a West Point cadet on summer leave and serving as an acting second lieutenant with Wood's staff, who took a Mauser bullet in the abdomen. Trumpeter Emilio Cassi of Troop A lost his bugle in the rush for cover and sprinted up and down the line in the hail of lead looking for it, and artist-correspondent Frederick Remington, sticking close to the Rough Riders, dropped to the ground and lost his sketchbook in the guinea grass.

Like correspondent Edward Marshall, shot through the spine at Las Guásimas, and many others who served in the Santiago battles, Roosevelt was fascinated by the Spanish Mauser fire and the peculiarities of the Mauser bullet. These .45-caliber slugs, driving in sheets from the trenches, trees, and grass, he said, made "a peculiar whirring or rustling sound; some of the bullets seemed to pop in the air, so that we thought they were explosive; and, indeed, many of those which were coated with brass did explode, in the sense that the brass coat was ripped off, making a thin plate of hard metal with a jagged edge, which inflicted a ghastly wound." The bullets ordinarily made a small clean hole which healed quickly, he said. "One or two of our men who were shot in the head had the skull blown open, but elsewhere the wounds from the minute steel-coated bullet, with its high velocity, were certainly nothing like as serious as those made by the old large-calibre, low-power rifle." He continued, with a clinician's indifference if not precision, to assert that "if a man was shot through the heart, spine, or brain he was, of course, killed instantly; but very few of the wounded died—even under the appalling conditions which prevailed, owing to the lack of attendance and supplies in the field hospitals with the army."

During the pinning-down below Kettle Hill, a Mauser bullet caused what Roosevelt called, "The most serious loss that I and the regiment could have suffered."

Captain William Owen "Buckey" O'Neill, mayor of Prescott, lawman, newspaperman, Populist politician, Grand Canyon explorer, called "the most many-sided man Arizona ever produced," had a theory. It was, Roosevelt said, "that an officer ought never to take cover—a theory which was, of course, wrong, though in a volunteer organization the officers should certainly expose themselves very fully, simply for the effect on the men. . . ." Examples of this crack-brained notion had been set at Las Guásimas by men with regular army experience who ought to have known better, such as Leonard Wood and Alexander Brodie (who was shot by Mauser fire for his foolhardy disregard for the enemy), and by Roosevelt himself, an eternal amateur whose normal clear-headedness was clouded by fanciful views of war in general and specifically of leading men in battle.

But if the "theory" was not of Buckey O'Neill's authorship, he became its best-remembered, and deadest, practitioner on the morning of July 1, 1898, while the Rough Riders awaited a signal to attack the Spanish outposts on Kettle Hill.

At about ten, O'Neill was strolling in front of his hunkered-down men, smoking his eternal cigarette, when somebody in Woodbury Kane's Troop K shouted at him through the din of the enemy fire, "Captain, *get down,* a bullet is sure to hit you!" O'Neill, so the story goes, laughed and said, "Sergeant, the Spanish bullet has not been made that will kill me." He continued his pacing and chatting with his troopers and then strolled over to say something to Captain Robert Howze, one of Sumner's aides. K Trooper Jesse D. Langdon, crouched in the grass nearby, happened to glance toward the two men when a bullet struck O'Neill—in the mouth and out the back of his head, it was later determined. The dashing captain stiffened, then crumpled to the ground. "Even before he fell," Roosevelt said, "his wild and gallant soul had gone into the darkness." Langdon's unadorned recollection: "He was dead before he hit the ground."

As O'Neill's corpse was dragged under a tree to await a burial detail, Roosevelt's orderly, "a brave young Harvard boy" from Salem, Massachusetts, named Sanders, dropped in the heat and later died. His replacement, a trooper whose name Roosevelt never discovered, was told, in his first and last order, to make his way back along the trail to "ask whatever general he came across if I could not advance, as my men were being much cut up." The new orderly stood up to salute, then pitched forward across Roosevelt's knees, "a bullet having gone through his throat, cutting the carotid."

Roosevelt's third orderly that day, Trooper Henry Bardshar, an

Arizona miner in Buckey O'Neill's troop, despite several tests, managed to survive his assignment.

2

"I waved my hat and we went up the hill."

At the bloody ford of the San Juan River, the Rough Riders crouched in the searing hundred-plus heat for hours while staff officers galloped up and down the trail amidst shrapnel bursts and raking Mauser enfilades, seeking orders while casualties mounted. "Men gasped on their backs," Richard Harding Davis wrote, "like fishes in the bottom of a boat, their heads burning inside and out, their limbs too heavy to move."

While waiting for orders, while casualties mounted, while Lawton's division was still occupied at El Caney, other units moved into attack positions below the San Juan Heights. The Rough Riders had the right of the line of attack, the First and Tenth Cavalry regulars slightly behind. In front of Roosevelt's troopers were arrayed the Ninth on the right, the Sixth in the center and the Third Cavalry on the left. To the far left of those advancing on Kettle Hill, Kent's five infantry regiments occupied a position directly in front of San Juan Hill.

Something had to give. Shafter's aide-de-camp, Lieutenant John D. Miley, was among those begged for orders, since he represented the Fifth Corps commander, but the best he could offer was the statement, "The heights must be taken at all hazards. A retreat now would be a disastrous defeat." It appears that General Sumner obtained from Miley, a mere lieutenant, the authority to advance on the San Juan Heights and got the word to those awaiting on the front line.

"I had sent messenger after messenger to try to find General Sumner or General Wood to get permission to advance," Roosevelt said, "and was just about making up my mind that in the absence of orders I had better 'march toward the guns,' when Lieu-tenant Colonel Dorst [Joseph H. Dorst, Fourth Cavalry] came riding up through the storm of bullets with the welcome com-mand 'to move forward and support the regulars in the assault on the hills in front.' "

It was past noon when Roosevelt sprang on his horse. Then, he said, "my 'crowded hour' began."

He first rode to the rear of his regiment—"the position in which the colonel should theoretically stay"—shouting orders and encouragement and forming his men in columns of troops, extending them in skirmish lines along the sunken roadway with Captain Micah Jenkins, the regular army officer from Young's Is-land, South Carolina, leading the first squadron, "his eyes," Roo-sevelt said, "literally dancing with joyous excitement."

At first, Roosevelt gave some thought to going into the fight on foot, as at Las Guásimas, but decided he would not be able to cover the ground and "superintend matters" except on horseback and so rode Little Texas back and forth among his troopers so "I could see the men better and they could see me better." As he rode and reined, barking orders to his captains and lieutenants, he came across one trooper crouched behind a bush, seemingly un-able to move. Roosevelt ordered the man to his feet, "jeering him and saying, 'Are you afraid to stand up when I am on horse-back?' " The man rose, then fell forward on his face, "a bullet having struck him and gone through him length-wise," in Roo-sevelt's unlikely speculation. The colonel opined that the bullet had been meant for him.

Unlike Las Guásimas, which Roosevelt said he "had not en-joyed at all because I had been so uncertain as to what I ought to do," he could actually see the Kettle Hill defenders "and I knew exactly how to proceed. . . . I waved my hat and we went up the hill in a rush."

The Rough Riders moved forward on the double with Roo-sevelt galloping along at the front—the position in which the

colonel should theoretically not be—and within minutes all pre-
tense of order dissolved in the moblike rush toward Kettle Hill,
the Ninth regulars in the front and the First on the left making the
charge intermingled with Roosevelt's troopers, followed by the
Third, Sixth and Tenth Regiments, the latter suffering the greatest percentage of casualties among its officers—eleven out of
twenty-two.

Richard Harding Davis, close to his hero, observed Roosevelt
"mounted high on horseback, and charging the rifle-pits at a gal-
lop and quite alone." He described Roosevelt wearing "on his
sombrero a blue polka-dot handkerchief, a la Havelock, which, as
he advanced, floated straight behind his head, like a guidon," and
said the colonel's intrepidity "made you feel that you would like
to cheer." Stephen Crane likened the Mauser fire to the "noise of
a million champagne corks" and called the advance "the best moment of anybody's life."

Near the foot of the hill, the crouching Rough Riders ran into
the left wing of the Ninth Cavalry regulars and some men from
the First lying down in the grass and firing up toward the Spanish entrenchments while their officers paced to and fro in front of
them. Roosevelt found a captain and notified the man that he
had been ordered to support the regulars in an attack on the hill
and that this could not be done by firing from the grass but only
in a mass rush to the summit. The officer explained that he could
not charge without orders. "I asked him where the Colonel was,"
Roosevelt said, "and as he was not in sight, said, 'Then I am the
ranking officer here and I give the order to charge. . . .' " When
the captain hesitated, Roosevelt said, "Then let my men through,
sir," and rode past them with his troopers in his wake. "Their attention," he claimed, "had been completely taken off the Spanish
bullets, partly by my dialogue with the regulars, and partly by the
language I had been using to themselves as I got the lines forward,
for I had been joking with some and swearing at others, as the exigencies of the case seemed to demand."

As the Rough Riders moved past, "It proved too much for the regulars," he said, "and they jumped up and came along, their officers and troops mingling with mine, all being delighted at the chance."

A similar bottleneck, this one involving infantry volunteers, had occurred earlier on the left of the line, in front of San Juan Hill. There, a battalion of the Seventy-first New York Volunteer Infantry, ordered in the vanguard of the assault, withered under the terrific enemy fire from the heights and after an artillery shell burst among them, killing twelve men, turned back, running into the advancing units behind them. General Kent, the divisional commander; Brigadier General Hamilton S. Hawkins, commanding the brigade in which the Seventy-first was one of three regiments; and other officers, managed to prevent the situation from becoming a mêlée but a number of volunteers had to be ordered out of the line and to lie down in the grass so that Hawkins's other regiments could pass.

The Rough Riders' move up Kettle Hill was accidentally coordinated with the regulars on Roosevelt's right and left. "The whole line," he said, "tired of waiting and eager to close with the enemy, was straining to go forward; and it seems that different parts slipped the leash at almost the same moment." The wire fence along the sunken roadway was hacked apart with bayonets, the posts knocked down, and the Rough Riders, mixed with troopers of the Ninth and Tenth Cavalry, began the run, shouting and cheering. Sumner's aide, Captain Robert Howze, who had been sent a message from Sumner to take and hold the hill "against all hazards," witnessed the Rough Riders charge "under a galling fire," and said Roosevelt "jumped through the fence and by his enthusiasm and courage succeeded in leading to the crest of the hill a line sufficiently strong to capture it."

Roosevelt, on horseback, outdistanced his men at first, except for his orderly, Henry Bardshar, "who had run ahead very fast in order to get better shots at the Spaniards," whose heads could be

seen peering above rifle pits and earthen parapets and the win-
dowsills of the ranch buildings around the summit. At another
fence about forty yards from the top, Roosevelt jumped off Little
Texas and turned the horse loose to wander back behind the lines.
He ran up the hill with Bardshar, the two stopping to crouch and
shoot amid a storm of bullets from the outbuildings and trenches
above.

In a zig-zagging crouched run, with frequent stops to aim and
fire their Krags, the Rough Riders made their way to the hilltop
and scattered over the summit and slopes to find cover in the
grass, outbuildings and around the iron sugar cane kettles. Bullets
and time-fuse artillery shells continued to fall among them even
as the former Kettle Hill defenders—probably under three hundred soldiers in all—fled to join their comrades on the San Juan
Heights five hundred yards to the west.

There were 2,522 men, regulars and volunteers, commanded
by Sumner, Wood and Roosevelt, in the charge up Kettle Hill
and much discussion later about who had been first to reach the
summit. The Ninth Cavalry regulars believed they were ahead of
everybody else and probably were; the honor of planting the first
guidons on the summit went to Troops E, F and G of New Mexico Territory, commanded by Captains Frederick Muller and Maximiliano Luna of Santa Fe, and William H. H. Llewellyn of Las
Cruces.

"As for the individual men," Roosevelt wrote later, "each of
whom honestly thought he was first on the summit, their name
was legion."

3

"It's the Gatlings, men . . ."

Securing Kettle Hill provided no respite for the Rough Rid-
ers or any of the other units on and around its summit. On the

slopes of the San Juan Heights men lay exhausted in the broiling heat under the scything volley fire from the Spanish trenches and blockhouses. Ammunition was running low and many of the wounded lay exposed awaiting stretcher bearers. There were no orders and each regimental commander was left to make his own way. Shafter, now suffering from heat exhaustion in addition to his other ailments, sat in his headquarters tent behind El Pozo Hill shouting orders to aides and officers, dispatching couriers, receiving them, trying to assess his battle with too little information. He had no reinforcements. Lawton was still occupied at El Caney, supported by General Bates's reserve brigade, over five thousand men trying to flush five hundred defenders from their wooden blockhouses and stone forts.

At about one in the afternoon, Joe Wheeler rose from his sickbed, determined to take the field and rejoin his cavalry division. He sent a message to Shafter asking if the commanding general contemplated attacking the entrenchments on the San Juan Heights. The answer came back: yes.

Indeed, a frontal attack seemed the only option. No help could be expected from Lawton, no time could be spent on serious tactical planning under the galling fire from the enemy trenches, and the casualty lists were lengthening.

Richard Harding Davis summed up the situation neatly and correctly: "There was only one thing to do—go forward and take the San Juan hills by assault." The decision, he said, "was desperate as the situation itself," to send men to charge earthworks "held by men with modern rifles, and using modern artillery, and to attack them in advance and not in the flanks." These, he opined in the definitive voice of the correspondent-as-tactician, "are both impossible military propositions." But, he added, nothing in the campaign had thus far been conducted according to military rules, "and a series of military blunders had brought seven thousand [actually 8,400] American soldiers into a chute of death from which there was no escape except by taking the enemy who held it by the throat and driving him out and beating him down."

Atop Kettle Hill, Roosevelt looked toward the San Juan trenches and blockhouses on his left and had "a splendid view" of Kent's infantrymen, led by Brigadier General Hawkins, climbing the hill. The frontal assault was taking place before his eyes and, he said, "Obviously the proper thing to do was to help them." He gathered the Rough Riders to begin a volley fire on the Spanish defenders while he sought out General Sumner for permission to advance on San Juan Hill in support of Kent's regiment.

At a critical juncture in the agonizingly slow move up the slopes of the San Juan Heights, at about 1:30 in the afternoon, a strange new sound rose above the fire-crackerlike popping of rifle fire and flat metallic bang of light artillery. This was a hollow, crisp *chunkchunkchunkchunk* drumming that was at first thought to be enemy machine gun fire. Roosevelt listened a moment and recognized the sound coming from the left, somewhere in front of San Juan Hill. "It's the Gatlings, men," he yelled.

Every man who fought in the San Juan battle remembered the Gatlings and how they turned the tide that afternoon of July 1.

Lieutenant John H. "Blackie" Parker (the nickname for his luxurious black beard), West Point '92, and his crew, on a sort of roving commission, had manhandled the four-gun battery to the front against the odds. The guns had to be floated on pontoons borrowed from the Engineer Corps to Daiquirí beach and the mule-drawn teams belabored along the rutted, littered Santiago road to the San Juan River ford and across. They arrived at the front with a weirdly impeccable timing, as Kent's regiments were making their advance on the heights under the incessant hail of fire from above them.

The "Gat" was a hammering death dealer, a scary gun with a scary sound. It consisted of eight .30-caliber barrels arranged around a rotating cylinder turned by a crank. The mechanism sat on a light artillery caisson, balanced on a swivel that could be easily rotated, elevated or depressed. As the crank was turned, each barrel fired, ejected the spent cartridge and automatically reloaded. The rate of fire depended on how fast the crank was turned, but the gun could fire up to fifteen rounds a second, nine hundred a minute, 3,600 a minute with the four guns firing at once, and a disciplined Gatling crew such as Parker's could clear a jungle with their guns, empty trenches, chop wooden block-houses to kindling, and kill and maim a large enemy force suddenly and quickly.

Parker's Gatlings raked San Juan Hill, about six hundred yards distant, for about eight minutes without letup and had an instantly devastating effect. The Spanish return fire slackened and the defenders began pouring out of their rifle pits and gun emplacements and fleeing behind the hills toward the next lines of defense at the Santiago outskirts. "There was never a more welcome sound than his Gatlings as they opened," Roosevelt said. "It was the only sound which I ever heard my men cheer in battle." He later added, "I think Parker deserved rather more credit than any one man in the entire campaign."*

Under Parker's death-dealing screen, Kent's blue-uniformed infantry approached the crest of San Juan Hill as the Rough Riders moved down Kettle Hill. Roosevelt impetuously ran ahead, jumped a wire fence, and found himself quickly separated from the main body of his regiment and had to return to gather them. "We didn't hear you," somebody shouted, "we didn't see you go, Colonel; lead on now, we'll sure follow you." Roosevelt found

---

*In a copy of a book sent to me by Rough Rider Jesse D. Langdon in February 1973, the inscription reads: "To my friend Dale Walker from Jesse D. Langdon, sole survivor of Rough Riders who followed 'Teddy' Roosevelt up Kettle & San Juan Hills to capture the Spanish trenches & Cuba on July 1, 1898, *under the protection of four Gatling guns manned by Lieut. Parker of the 26th U.S. Infantry.*"

Sumner and received permission to take his men and "make the charge." Sumner promised he would see to it that the other regiments followed.

"By this time everybody had their attention attracted," Roosevelt said, "and when I leaped over the fence again, with Major Jenkins beside me, the men of the various regiments which were already on the hill came with a rush, and we started across the wide valley which lay between us and the Spanish entrenchments."

They crossed the little valley in short sprints, stopping to kneel, fire and reload. At one point, ten yards ahead, two soldiers leapt from a trench and fired at Roosevelt and his orderly Henry Bardshar. "As they turned to run I closed in and fired twice, missing the first and killing the second," Roosevelt said. "My revolver was from the sunken battleship *Maine.*" Elsewhere he described drilling the Spaniard "neatly as a jackrabbit."

"They had no glittering bayonets, they were not massed in regular array," Richard Harding Davis, who made the charge with the Rough Riders, said. "There were a few men in advance, bunched together, and creeping up a steep, sunny hill, the tops of which roared and flashed with flame." He described men holding their guns pressed across their chests and walking "to greet death at every step, many of them, as they advanced, sinking suddenly or pitching forward and disappearing in the high grass." The others ran on, stubbornly, he said, "forming a thin blue line that kept creeping higher and higher up the hill. It was as inevitable as the rising tide. It was a miracle of self-sacrifice, a triumph of bull-dog courage, which one watched breathless with wonder."

The Rough Riders reached the first line of trenches and found them filled with dead bodies in the light blue and white uniforms of Spanish regulars. "There were very few wounded," Roosevelt said. "Most of the fallen had little holes in their heads from which their brains were oozing." He speculated that this was the result of the enemy soldiers standing in their trenches with only their heads showing above. Trooper Jesse Langdon also saw many of the bodies in the trenches and was appalled at the sight. "A lot of them were just kids," he said. And George Hammer of F Troop recalled a similarly awful sight, seeing the Gatling guns raking the trenches and causing the Spaniards' straw hats to jump in the air.

Roosevelt's "long-legged men"—Lieutenant John Greenway, an A Troop Arkansan who had been wounded at Las Guásimas; D Troop Second Lieutenant David M. Goodrich of Cambridge, Massachusetts; and William B. Proffitt of Prescott, Arizona, a private in Jim McClintock's troop—outdistanced the others as the Rough Riders pushed on and up the hill, the regiment becoming amalgamated in a jumble of regulars and volunteers, taking trench after trench, occupying deserted buildings and blockhouses, "driving the Spaniards through a line of palm-trees, and over the crest of a chain of hills," the colonel said.

With unfortunate timing, the Grimes light artillery battery on El Pozo hill, apparently detecting the advance of Kent's and Sumner's men up the San Juan slopes, opened fire. Some of the bursts landed dangerously close to the Americans when they were two-thirds of the way to the summit and frantic messages had to be signaled to El Pozo to cease fire. "We got no appreciable help from our guns on July first," Roosevelt said. "Our men were quick to realize the defects of our artillery, but they were entirely philosophic about it, not showing the least concern at its failure. On the contrary, whenever they heard our artillery open they would grin as they looked at one another and remark, 'There go the guns again; wonder how soon they'll be shut up,' and shut up they were sure to be."

Nor was the dynamite gun much help. It made a terrific coughing noise as it lobbed its explosive charge toward the enemy trenches but was wildly inaccurate. Charles Johnson Post, who saw it in action during the San Juan battle, said it was "a pocket-sized edition of the great dynamite guns of the U.S.S. *Vesuvius,*" and described the projectile, fired by compressed air, as having a screw propeller similar to that of a torpedo, to steady it.

The Colt rapid-firers, laboriously hauled on mule back to the front, did little better service than the dynamite gun. Ammunition for the Colts became a special problem since the guns could not handle Krag cartridges, although, ironically, captured Mauser ammunition fit and, being loaded with smokeless powder, were much sought after. Unfortunately the battle was over before the Colts— a good weapon, experts said—could prove their worth.

The Rough Riders reached the crest with elements of the Ninth and Tenth Cavalry regulars and Kent's Sixth and Sixteenth Infantry, the latter regiments having spearheaded the charge. Lieutenant Jules G. Ord of the Sixth Infantry, whose father had been a Civil War general, ran to the summit with his saber drawn and became the first man killed atop San Juan Hill.

Roosevelt reformed his regiment on the downslope of the hill, looking down on the city of Santiago de Cuba, and kept up the fire against the flank of the retreating Spanish force. During this critical period, Sumner's aide, Captain Robert Howze, came up with orders for Roosevelt—among the few he had received all day—to hold his position, in the favorite phrase of the day, "at all hazards," and not advance farther. The colonel had fragments of six cavalry regiments under his command for the rest of the day and night.

By 2:30 in the afternoon of July 1, the 8,400-man American force had possession of the San Juan Heights.

At four, the fight at El Caney—lasting ten hours instead of the proposed two—ended. Although Lawton's force had a ten-to-one superiority, the Spanish defenders hung on tenaciously behind their blockhouses and stone forts until, with no reinforcements in the offing, they ran out of ammunition. At last, the Twelfth Infantry of Adna Chaffee's brigade stormed and captured El Viso fort.

General Vara del Rey was dead; his 521-man defending force had been reduced at the end to 80 men. Two hundred and thirty-five Spaniards had been killed or wounded and 125 were taken prisoner. A few others escaped.

Lawton suffered casualties of 81 dead and 360 wounded. He would not be able to bring the balance of his force to the San Juan Heights until July 2.

XIII

LAST VOLLEYS

1

"I shall be very sorry to hurt you . . ."

The Americans teetered on the San Juan Heights that mid-afternoon of July 1, 1898, gaining a toehold so precarious that virtually any offensive move by the Spanish defenders could have pushed them back down the slopes. The enemy had not been routed but had retreated, overwhelmed by the numbers of Kent and Sumner's force, over eight thousand men against one thousand seven hundred in the initial assault, toward their heavily manned second line of trenches and defensive works on the eastern perimeter of Santiago. San Juan Hill and the other heights occupied by the Americans continued to be swept by rifle and artillery fire, so intense at times, Roosevelt said, that the men, on the "hither slope" of San Juan, "were lying flat on their faces, very rarely responding to the bullets, shells and shrapnel which swept over the hill-top."

Holding on "by their teeth and fingernails," as Richard Harding Davis put it, the Rough Riders, in lulls in the enemy fire, dug in, occupying abandoned enemy trenches and building new ones and traverses between existing trenches with captured spades and bayonets—"siege work" Roosevelt called it. Pickets were posted to watch for any sign of a counterattack, and sharpshooters were positioned to answer the popping Mausers causing havoc even on litter bearers carrying the wounded and Clara Barton's Red Cross workers wearing their bright red-and-white brassards.

Moving the wounded off the heights and down trail became a particularly perilous business. Mule-drawn ammunition and ration wagons were used as ambulances and, loaded with battle casualties, often came under volleys of enemy fire as they made their way over the chuck-holed road to dressing stations behind the San Juan River and the field hospital near Shafter's headquarters. The wounded from the El Caney fight were also arriving at the primitive tent hospital and Shafter was shocked at the number of men he saw coming in their bloodied uniforms and dressings.

On the "hither slope," Roosevelt tried to keep his men together, keep them low, keep them alive. He knew the battle had not ended, was anxious in the waning sun about spending the night on the heights with no food or blankets, about moving his wounded and trying to keep up a semblance of defensive fire on the enemy emplacements and sniper nests below his fragile position.

In this critical time he perceived a problem among the "colored infantrymen" of the fragmented Ninth and Tenth Regiments which had mixed with his volunteers in the charge up the San Juan slopes and were now under his immediate command. "None of the white regulars or Rough Riders showed the slightest sign of weakening," he later wrote of the incident, "but under the strain the colored infantrymen (who had none of their officers) began to get a little uneasy and to drift to the rear," to assist with the wounded and to find their regiments and officers. "This I could not allow," he said, "as it was depleting my line." What he said he did to stop it was a characteristic instance of Rooseveltian vainglory.

He "jumped up," he said, "and walking a few yards to the rear, drew my revolver, halted the retreating soldiers, and called out to them that I appreciated the gallantry with which they had fought and would be sorry to hurt them, but that I would shoot the first man who, on any pretence whatever, went to the rear." Now, Roosevelt said, his own men "had all sat up and were watching my movements with the utmost interest" as he ended his threat by saying, in a windy monologue that smacked of a nickolodeon movie subtitle, "Now, I shall be very sorry to hurt you, and you don't know whether or not I will keep my word, but my men can tell you I always do." Whereupon, he said, "my cowpunchers, hunters and miners solemnly nodded their heads and commented in chorus, exactly as if in a comic opera, 'He always does; he always does.' "

The resemblance to a comic opera—actually a cheap minstrel show—hamhandedly composed by Roosevelt himself—he insured by his denouement to the episode: "This was the end of the trouble, for the 'smoked Yankees'—as the Spaniards called the colored soldiers—flashed their white teeth at one another, as they broke into broad grins, and I had no more trouble with them, they seemed to accept me as one of their own officers."

Roosevelt may have misapprehended what these regular army men, many of them "Buffalo Soldier" veterans of Indian campaigns, were grinning about. It may have been the sight and sound of this unmistakably amateur warrior peering through his prince-nez and berating them in his tinny Harvard accent for trying to rejoin their regiments of professional soldiers led by professional officers. Furthermore, their "drifting to the rear" had been for the purpose of finding entrenching tools.

The one man present in the San Juan battle who knew the Tenth Regiment better than anyone else, had a far different view of their conduct than Roosevelt's. Lieutenant John J. Pershing had commanded a troop of the Tenth at Fort Assiniboine, Montana Territory, in 1896, leading his Buffalo soldiers in the dan-

gerous work of rounding up renegade Cree Indians and escorting
them back across the Canadian border. His leadership was remarkable enough to come to the attention of Nelson A. Miles, the
topmost general of the army, who summoned then Lieutenant
Pershing to Washington to serve as his aide-de-camp. During his
assignment with Miles, Pershing was sent to New York to attend
a military tournament at Madison Square Garden, during which
he was introduced to the city's police commissioner, Theodore
Roosevelt. The two found much common ground—especially in
their interest in Indian dialects—and formed a lifelong friendship
that was apparently undisturbed by their differing opinions on
the conduct of the men of the Tenth at San Juan.

Pershing, at the time of the Santiago campaign, was a West
Point instructor and had difficulty getting into the action. He
considered resigning his commission and asking his friend Roosevelt for an appointment with the Rough Riders. But his superiors at the academy gave him permission to personally plead his
case to Secretary Alger. He did so and, perhaps with the help of
Miles, was granted a billet as quartermaster in his old Tenth Regiment where, for his stern but steady command of "colored
troops" and his loyalty to them, he was affectionately called "Black
Jack."

With the Second Squadron of the Tenth in the advance on the
San Juan Heights, Pershing and his men ran the slopes close on
to the Rough Riders and he vividly remembered the "gallant advance" of his soldiers from Kettle Hill through the grass and
brush, across a stream and under the barbed-wire entanglements,
holding steady "regardless of the casualties."

"Our troopers halted and laid down but momentarily to get a
breath and in the face of continued volleys soon formed for attack
on the block houses and entrenchments," Pershing wrote, describing how his men crept through the tall grass and brush, in the
small valley between Kettle and San Juan Hills, "crawling when casualties came too often, courageously facing a sleet of bullets," and

how they clung to the rises "ready to spring the few remaining yards into the teeth of the enemy."

The charge, he said, "continued dauntless in its steady, dogged, persistent advance until like a mighty resistless challenge it dashed triumphant over the crest of the hill and fired a parting volley at the vanishing foe. . . ."

He said of the hoisting of the Stars and Stripes above San Juan, "This was a fine time for rejoicing. It was glorious," and while he won a Silver Star for valorous conduct under severe enemy fire in leading his men in the attack, he gave the credit to his troopers. "They had again fought their way into the hearts of the American people," he said.

Roosevelt credited the officers of the Ninth and Tenth Regiments, all of whom were white, saying, "Under their leadership the colored troops did as well as any soldiers could possibly do."

He was loved by his Rough Riders but he had few admirers in the regular army, who considered him a showboating amateur and politician climbing the Washington ladder over the bodies of better men. And the regulars were dubious of any officer who seemed to have a personal retinue of newspapermen. One of the few correspondents in Cuba besides Stephen Crane not caught up in "the effulgence of Teethadore," was Poultney Bigelow of *Harper's*. He referred to Roosevelt as "our cowboy Napoleon."

As the afternoon wore on it became clear that the Spanish forces, now in their second line of defensive works, were not going to mount a serious counterattack—at least on the first day of battle. In the entire engagement, Roosevelt said, he saw only one desultory offensive movement by the Spaniards and that occurring in the afternoon after the Americans had taken the San Juan Heights. "In this case," he said, "they actually did begin to make a forward movement, their cavalry coming up as well as the marines and reserve infantry, while their skirmishers, who were always bold, redoubled their activity." The offense, if it could be called that, was stopped cold by the heavy fire from the American troops on the heights, which drove the Spanish force back to its trenches. Parker's Gatling battery, brought up the hill and now positioned on the right of the Rough Riders, did its customary deadly .30-caliber work raking the enemy lines, making it suicidal for massed troops to attempt to retake San Juan.

At dusk on July 1 the enemy fire waned and, except for sporadic sniper shooting, died out by nightfall.

2

"And death often smote them."

General Joe Wheeler, still shaky with the malaria that kept him out of the action on the heights, came to the front in the late afternoon and as senior divisional commander surveyed the American positions and sent a message back to Shafter: "The lines are now very thin as so many men have gone to the rear with the wounded, and so many are exhausted. . . . We ought to hold tomorrow, but I fear it will be a severe day."

It was to be a severe night as well. While Shafter was sending a tentatively optimistic cable to Secretary Alger about the initial successes on the heights, the shaken victors there were hungry, exhausted, cold and nervous. On the slopes the wounded lay in agony, many of them hidden in the high grass and difficult to find and move.

"We have carried their outer works, and are now in possession of them," Shafter's cable to the War Department said. "There is now about three-quarters of a mile of open country between my lines and the city."

In his command post behind El Pozo, Shafter was personally experiencing the awful truth of the duke of Wellington's remark after Waterloo that "The next dreadful thing to a battle lost is a battle won." The general was burdened with casualties and with the realization that the Spanish defenses around Santiago were stronger than anticipated and that he had no heavy artillery to punch through them. Now, too, hurricane weather lurked, malaria was rampant—he had contracted it himself—and a yellow fever epidemic seemed a certainty. He was sending what reinforcements he had to the heights but knew he could not capture the city as he had hoped, in a seamless rush from the San Juan River, over the heights and into the eastern Santiago perimeter.

Now, too, he was haunted by the possibility that if the Spanish forces at Manzanillo were to move east to reinforce the Santiago garrison, the Americans could be driven off the San Juan Heights and the supply depot at Siboney placed in peril.

In fact, although Shafter would not learn the extent of it for several days, the Spanish defenders at Santiago were in even direr straits and unable—or perhaps unwilling—to mount a counterattack or make an offensive move of any kind. The commander of the Santiago forces, General Arsenio Linares, severely wounded in the San Juan fight, had his own burdens of sick and wounded and, as well, critical shortages of food and ammunition. Lawton's force on the north had captured the town of Cuabitas, the main fresh water supply source for the Santiago garrison and Linares, as well as his successor, General José Toral, also had to contend with a morale problem. This was created by the masses of civilian refugees leaving the city and trudging east toward the American lines. In the days to come, correspondent Stephen Crane watched the exodus of "this great, gaunt assemblage, the true horror of war," and said, "The sick, the lame, the halt and the blind were there. Women and men, tottering upon the verge of death, plodded doggedly onward."

In truth, the Spanish defense of Santiago, seen in the aftermath of the San Juan Heights fighting, was inexplicably botched. At the beginning of the American advance on the heights, Linares had, according to figures Roosevelt gathered from the British consul in Santiago, six thousand troops in the city—four thousand of them regular army soldiers, the others volunteers, marines and sailors. Linares had dispatched over five hundred of this force to defend El Caney and under one thousand to man El Morro and other for-tifications along Santiago Harbor. Yet, of four thousand or more troops available to defend the San Juan Heights, only about one thousand two hundred were positioned there on July 1, scarcely more than five hundred of which, with poor artillery support, were stationed at San Juan Hill, the key to the entire defensive works.

Just as Shafter sent reinforcements to the heights in the after-noon and evening of July 1, General Toral pulled men from gar-risons northwest of the city (a vicinity by then controlled by Calixto García's insurgent forces) and other outlying districts, brought his reserve forces up, and managed to put over five thou-sand additional men in the second-line trenches east of the city by the day after the battle.

But by then the San Juan Heights, potentially impregnable if defended by great numbers and great guns, had been lost to the Americans. Close to thirty-five percent of Linares's original fight-ing force of one thousand two hundred on the heights—includ-ing sixteen officers—were dead, and, after the toughest resistance of the July 1 action, he had lost El Caney, outnumbered there ten-to-one by Lawton's force.

The defense of Santiago de Cuba was marked by a sort of melancholy inertia and a pervasive despair among the Spanish armed forces, land and sea. The first mordant note of this had been sounded as early as April 29, seven days after the United States declared war, and it had come from one of Spain's most dis-tinguished military officers, Admiral Pascual Cervera. On that date, as he received orders to lead his seven-ship squadron from the Cape Verde Islands to the Caribbean, he had plaintively cabled Madrid, "I shall do all I can to hasten our departure, disclaiming all responsibility for the consequences."

Generals Linares and Toral seemed to share Cervera's pessimism and Shafter and his army benefitted enormously by it and the defensive posture taken by the Spaniards throughout the campaign. The Fifth Corps faced potential calamity from the moment the first boats approached the beach at Daiquirí, but the village and its Mount Losiltires blockhouse had been abandoned and the American force, as helpless and vulnerable as a turtle on its back, was able to continue its scramble ashore unmolested. Nor was the march to Siboney contested, nor the subsequent landings there. At Las Guásimas only a small rearguard of Spanish troops fleeing toward Santiago had engaged the Americans and, after a brief skirmish, broke off what might have been an utter rout of Young and Wheeler's raw, disorganized troopers. And at San Juan, last bastion of the defenses of Santiago, the heights were undermanned with too few artillery pieces and those employed too small; reinforcements and reserves were called forward too late to be effective; there was shortsightedness in ammunition supplies, food and water reserves; and, once chased from the heights, serious counterattacking plans never seem to have been entertained. And finally, the strategic outpost of El Caney—certainly tenable, if not impregnable, with proper man- and gun-power—was defended with too small a force.

Leonard Wood had it right when at Daiquirí he said the Americans were very fortunate to be going to war "with a broken-down power, for we would surely have had a deuced hard time with any other."

The irony of the situation, at the end of the second day of fighting on the heights, was that Shafter seemed prepared to snatch defeat from the jaws of victory: He polled his officers on the idea of a strategic retreat.

The rumor of a retreat spread by some mysterious trench telegraph among the men holding the heights. "One smelt disaster in the air," Richard Harding Davis said. "The alarmists were out in strong force and were in the majority."

Roosevelt heard the rumor on the night of July 1 while his troopers, under desultory sniper fire, were digging rifle pits with bayonets and captured spades and improving their precarious foothold on San Juan Hill. Two officers of the Third Cavalry made their way to the Rough Riders' trenches to tell him about the rumor and to protest it, if it turned out to be true. Roosevelt agreed with them and said, "it would be far worse than a blunder to abandon our position." He said later, "there was not a man on the crest who did not eagerly and devoutly hope that our opponents would make the attempt [at a counterattack], for it would surely have been followed, not merely by a repulse, but by our immediately taking the city."

Joe Wheeler heard the rumors too, and when he came to the front late in the day to resume command of the cavalry division, undertook to "discountenance" any idea of withdrawal. "He had been through too much heavy fighting in the Civil War to regard the present fight as very serious," Roosevelt said, "and he told us not to be under any apprehension, for he had sent word that there was no need whatever of retiring. . . ."

But Wheeler was called to a meeting with Shafter the next day and learned more about the rumor he had discountenanced.

At nightfall the Rough Riders had been fourteen hours without food, other than nibbling on mealy hardtack and washing it down with swigs of tepid canteen water. The captured Spanish buildings on Kettle and San Juan Hills yielded a pot of beef stew, another of rice and boiled peas; some loaves of rice bread were found, some salted flying fish, tinned preserves and a demijohn of rum. The food was divided among the men but, Roosevelt said, "did not give very much to each." He did not mention who got the rum but said the repast "freshened us all." Another discovery was made by Trooper Warren Crockett, a former revenue agent from Georgia, who found a supply of coffee beans abandoned by the Spaniards and spent the night pulverizing and brewing them for his exhausted comrades.

At about midnight, the Rough Riders finished their trench work. The firing had ceased and the American positions on the heights and those of the Spanish in their defensive lines fell quiet. Some of the Rough Riders had found blankets in the captured buildings but most simply curled up in their rifle pits and slept in the cool and dewy night in their filthy and sweat-soaked uniforms. Roosevelt, his orderly Henry Bardshar, and D Troop Lieutenant David Goodrich of Cambridge, Massachusetts (promoted that day for gallantry in action), slept huddled together.

The day had been costly. Roosevelt estimated the number of Americans in the San Juan Heights battle at about 6,600 men, of which 1,071 were killed or wounded. (The most dependable modern historian of the war, David F. Trask, gives the total casualties on July 1, counting those at El Caney, as 1,385, of which 205 were killed, 1,180 wounded. Of this number, Kent's infantry on the heights lost 89 killed and 489 wounded and Sumner's cavalry division lost 35 killed and 328 wounded; Lawton's division at El Caney suffered 81 dead and 363 wounded. In all, casualties amounted to about ten percent of the American force.)

Spanish numbers were disputable. Roosevelt estimated Linares and Toral's force on the heights at about 4,500 and the killed and wounded there and at El Caney totaling 1,200. (Trask gives 1,700 as the number of Spanish troops engaged on July 1, including those at El Caney, and casualties at 593, of which 215 were killed.)

Of the 490 Rough Riders engaged in the battle (52 others were either ill and in the hospital behind the lines or on guard duty at Siboney), 89 fell as casualties, 13 of which were killed or subsequently died of wounds on July 1 and 3 others were killed the next day. In all, Roosevelt's demiregiment suffered a fifteen percent casualty rate, highest in the cavalry division.

It was a heavy loss and a heavy responsibility. "I freely sent men for whom I cared most, to where death might meet them," he wrote, "and death often smote them—as it did the two best officers in my regiment, Allyn Capron and Bucky O'Neill." But the losses were assuaged, according to his ultimate tenet that in a time of war, "The life, even of the most useful man, of the best citizen, is not to be hoarded if there be need to spend it.

"I felt, and feel, this about others," he said, "and of course also about myself."

He had pride in his casualties and in the rapidity with which the Rough Riders took the field of battle: "In less than sixty days the regiment had been raised, organized, armed, equipped, drilled, mounted, dismounted, kept for a fortnight on transports, and put through two victorious aggressive fights in very difficult country," he said.

3

"I am seriously considering withdrawing . . ."

The firing resumed early on July 2, while the ground fog was still rising in what would be a blisteringly hot day. The mist concealed the enemy for a brief time as the sun climbed and the Spanish rifle and light artillery fire, while not comparable to the intensity of the day before, was incessant and nerve-wracking. In their trenches on the summit and city-side of the San Juan Heights, the Americans awoke hungry and under fire.

On the slopes of San Juan Hill, Roosevelt gave his Rough Riders some relief from their trench duty by establishing a six-hour watch, then waiting for a lull in the firing to send replacements for the cramped, hungry men in the noxious ditches—some of which had been occupied on July 1 by Spanish defenders. Getting food to those on the firing line proved to be a dangerous problem, too. When some cases of hardtack were brought up the hill, the Oklahoma bronc-buster "Little Billy" McGinty grabbed one and sprinted toward the trenches under a pelting enemy fire and tum-

bled into the ditch unwounded but with the box holed by Spanish bullets. Another Oklahoma trooper, Dick Shanafelt, ran the
gauntlet later, carrying pails of coffee to his trench mates.

The Spanish artillery fire remained desultory that morning but
one shell exploded close enough to Roosevelt to give him a dirt
bath. D Troop Second Lieutenant Robert Ferguson, a New
Yorker, was nearby when it happened and watched the colonel
stand and nonchalantly brush himself off. "I really believe now
they can't kill him," Ferguson decided.

The American's light artillery pieces had been removed from
the hill after the first day's fighting, replaced on the Rough Riders' side of the line by the dynamite gun and Sergeant William
Tiffany's Colt rapid-firers. Both these weapons were trouble
prone. The dynamite gun, operated by Rough Rider Sergeant
Hallett P. Borrowe of Jersey City, New Jersey, being pneumatically
charged, left no telltale white smoke cloud when fired and made
a splendid noise when its dynamite charge exploded, but it was
notoriously inaccurate and jammed easily. Tiffany's tripod-
mounted Colts were heavy and cumbersome and had to be drawn
by mules—in short supply on and around the heights—and,
worse yet, could not handle Krag cartridges. Captured Mauser
ammunition worked but was never in sufficient quantity to keep
the guns busy.

Roosevelt put the dynamite gun and Colts under Lieutenant
John Parker's command and said Parker developed the same fa-
therly interest in them as he did his beloved Gatlings.

The first day's fighting filled General Shafter with foreboding.
The casualties drifting back to dressing stations, the field hospital
and the hospital ships anchored off Siboney horrified him; reports
of the reinforcements joining General Toral's force along the
perimeter of Santiago were especially worrisome. (Roosevelt believed that on July 2 the Spanish troops defending the city actu-

ally outnumbered the Americans, who, he said, had eleven thousand men in the San Juan Heights trenches after Lawton's El Caney infantrymen joined up.)

On the morning of July 2, Shafter sent an urgent, somewhat anguished message to Admiral Sampson, whose squadron roamed in blockade formation outside Santiago Channel. "Terrible fight yesterday," the general wrote. "I urge that you make effort immediately to force the entrance to avoid future losses among my men, which are already very heavy. You can now operate with less loss of life than I can."

The exchange of wired dispatches between the two commanders, a frustrating business for each man, created a rift between the two services and a controversy not to be settled until long after the war ended.

Sampson's attitude had not changed since the beginning of the campaign when Spanish Admiral Pascual Cervera's seven-ship "fleet" was discovered snugly at anchor in Santiago Harbor: the entrance to the harbor could not be "forced" until the channel was cleared of mines and this touchy and lengthy operation could only take place after the army captured the Morro, the other forts and the shore batteries lining the entrance. The desperate little mission of June 3 past, when Lieutenant Hobson and his crew took the old collier *Merrimac* into the channel, proved the point: The *Merrimac* had been sunk by Spanish artillery before it could block the narrow channel neck.

Shafter could not absorb Sampson's rationale. "I am at a loss to see why the Navy cannot work under a destructive fire as well as the army," he messaged the admiral.

Sampson patiently explained the perils of such an operation as Shafter proposed. If any of the American ships were sunk in the harbor by mines or shore battery fire, the entire venture might end in defeat and the army would be in worse shape than at present. "It was my hope," Sampson said, "that an attack on your part of these short batteries, from the rear, would leave us at liberty to drag the channel for torpedoes [mines]."

They ended their exchange by agreeing to meet the next day at Siboney, where Shafter would by then have reestablished his headquarters, to discuss the situation.

Meantime, while newspaper dispatches from the front were already being printed describing the San Juan fight and especially the casualties that resulted from it, the War Department bombarded the general with appeals for a detailed report on the July 1 battle.

"We have the town well invested on the north and east, but with a very thin line," Shafter cabled Secretary Alger. "Upon approaching it we find it of such a character and the defenses so strong it will be impossible to carry it by storm. . . ." He then inserted an idea that chilled Alger and all but one of Shafter's own generals: "I am seriously considering withdrawing about five miles and taking up a new position on the high ground between the San Juan River and Siboney. . . . I have been unable to be out during the heat of the day for four days, but am retaining the command."

At seven on the evening of July 2, Shafter called his generals together for a council at his El Pozo headquarters. He was literally prostrate with heat exhaustion, fever and gout, and had to be carried to the meeting reclining on a door taken from a nearby farmhouse, which was laboriously lugged to the tent by six strong soldiers. He told the assembled commanders that a "great many" of his aides and staff officers were of the opinion that "we cannot hold the position and that it is absolutely necessary for us to retreat in order to save ourselves from being enfiladed by the Spanish lines and cut off from our supplies." He told of his fear that enemy reinforcements might be coming from Manzanillo on the west, possibly others from Holguín in the north and the Guantánamo area on the east, and said in such an eventuality, "an attack by the Spanish with a few fresh troops would result in our utter defeat."

Of the generals present at the council—Joe Wheeler, Jacob Kent, Henry Lawton and John C. Bates—only Kent agreed with the idea of withdrawing from the San Juan Heights. The others strongly opposed the idea, and as a result, Shafter agreed with the majority to hold on, at least for the present.

In Washington, Alger did not yet know this; his last message from his army commander had to do with "seriously considering withdrawing," and this Alger regarded as very disturbing. His response was to leave the decision to Shafter but to hint strongly that "the effect upon the country would be much better" if the general could hold the San Juan Heights and not fall back.

As to reinforcements, Shafter was assured he could have whatever he needed and that they would be underway as soon as the transports to carry them were secured.

Shafter's disturbing proposal came close to causing his replacement as commanding general in Cuba. President McKinley, Adjutant General of the Army Henry C. Corbin, Secretary Alger and others who had favored Shafter's appointment at the outset were now worried that his ill health might be standing in the way of his steadfastness. As a result of this concern, General Nelson Miles was ordered to Cuba to assess the situation and, if necessary, to take over the army command there.

On the San Juan Heights, as the second day of the battle wore on, the firing on both sides again died away although the Rough Riders were harassed throughout the day by sniper fire which, Roosevelt said, "caused us a great deal of annoyance and some loss." The snipers, most of them perched in trees, fired at anything that moved but Roosevelt believed they aimed particularly at such defenseless targets as Red Cross and medical personnel and the wounded being carried in litters off the hillsides. A select number of Rough Rider sharpshooters and experienced woodsmen were assigned the duty to hunt down as many of these snipers as they could find and to show them no quarter. They killed eleven without suffering a casualty. In this risky work, Roosevelt singled out two of his Arizonans, William B. Proffitt, a ranchman out of Prescott, and Richard E. Goodwin of Phoenix, a miner, both from Captain Jim McClintock's Troop B, as being especially proficient and tireless.

That night, both sides built cook fires and watched each other. The Americans thought there might be a night attack and were ready for it, but no offensive move was made from the enemy lines below the heights.

In his command "bomb-proof" as the night wore on, Roosevelt wrote his friend Henry Cabot Lodge: "Tell the President for Heaven's sake to send us every regiment and above all every battery possible. We have won so far at a heavy cost; but the Spaniards fight very hard and charging these entrenchments against modern rifles is terrible. We are within measurable distance of a terrible military disaster; we *must* have help—thousands of men, batteries, and food and ammunition." Despite military taboos against such practices, he could not avoid inserting criticism of Shafter ("Our general is poor; he is too unwieldy to get to the front") and an honor for himself: "I commanded my regiment, I think I might say, with honor. We lost a quarter of our men. For three days I have been at the extreme front of the firing line; how I have escaped I know not; I have not blanket or coat; I have not taken off my shoes even; I sleep in the drenching rain, and drink putrid water. . . ."

XIV

VICTORY
___

1

"Clear for action!"

There would be sporadic rifle and artillery fire for another week, but except for the talking and the paperwork, the war ended on July 3, a day in which so much happened it was difficult to sort out the details and credit the coincidences.

Early that morning, at Shafter's headquarters at Siboney, while awaiting the arrival of Admiral Sampson to discuss the inter-service strategy and cooperation necessary to capture Santiago, the general had a discussion with his adjutant and chief aide, Colonel Edward J. McClernand. This officer, who had been at Shafter's side from the beginning of the formation of the Fifth Corps in Tampa, knew and respected his commander. McClernand believed that Shafter's proposal for a withdrawal from the San Juan Heights was never a serious option and that if the general, ill and debili-tated, could find some rest, the whole idea of falling back would be abandoned and Shafter would pursue his original goal: to hold on until the starving and demoralized Spanish defenders realized they had no choice but to capitulate.

On the morning of July 3, McClernand walked to the command tent and found Shafter lying awake on his cot. "General," the adjutant said, "let us make a demand on them to surrender." McClernand said Shafter "looked at me for perhaps a full minute and I thought he was going to offer a rebuke . . . but finally he said, 'Well, try it.' "

By 8:30, McClernand had the message written, approved and signed by Shafter. It was addressed to the General José Toral, Commanding General of the Spanish Forces, Santiago de Cuba, and was taken into the city and delivered to Toral under a white truce flag. The terse message read: "I shall be obliged, unless you surrender, to shell Santiago de Cuba. Please inform the citizens of all foreign countries, and all women and children, that they should leave the city before 10 o'clock tomorrow morning."

The Spanish fire on San Juan Hill resumed at first light that morning and in the Rough Riders' camp, Roosevelt again selected his best sharpshooters to slip into the brush and jungle between the opposing lines and search out and kill any snipers found. Another of Roosevelt's favorites in this work was the Alsatian, Fred Herrig of Kalispel, Montana, a corporal in Troop K, who Roosevelt knew from hunting expeditions in the Badlands along the Little Missouri River. Herrig was a guide, scout, expert marksman and hunter and considered the search for Spanish snipers a "holiday" from the suffocating heat and filth of the trenches.

Roosevelt also visited the wounded in Dr. Rob Church's little tent hospital under the shoulder of a slope at the rear of San Juan Hill. Church himself was sick with fever and had little in the way of medicines or supplies to treat the wounded and fever-ridden men under his care. Roosevelt said the condition of the wounded in the big field hospitals in the rear—the biggest in abandoned buildings at Siboney—"was so horrible, from the lack of attendants as well as of medicines, that we kept all the men we possibly could at the front."

Before the sniper-hunting expedition could be launched, the troops on the San Juan Heights were notified to cease fire, that a demand of surrender had been sent into Santiago under a flag of truce. The order was passed through the ranks at about noon.

About an hour later, the men in the trenches along the heights heard the faint, deep booming of heavy guns, heavier than any field artillery, coming from several miles away, south of Santiago.

Admiral William T. Sampson's squadron lay in its customary semicircle six miles off the Santiago Channel entrance that Sunday morning, with the Morro Castle at the center of the arc, the ships spread out four or five miles on either side. Nearest the shore on the far west of the entrance lay the armored cruiser *Brooklyn,* commanded by the second-ranking officer after Sampson, Commodore Winfield Scott Schley; then next to the *Brooklyn,* the battleships *Texas* and *Iowa* (the latter commanded by a celebrated Civil War veteran and Roosevelt friend, Captain Robley Dunglison "Fighting Bob" Evans), then the battleship *Oregon* and Sampson's flagship, the armored cruiser *New York;* on the east side of the arc lay the battleship *Indiana* and the converted yachts *Vixen* and *Gloucester* (the latter J. P. Morgan's *Corsair,* refitted and renamed and on loan by the financier to the navy).

At about nine, Sampson's *New York* broke from the arc and with signal flags indicating "disregard movements of commander-in-chief," steamed east along the coast toward Siboney, seven or eight miles distant, where the admiral was to rendezvous with Shafter.

At 9:30, just as the *New York* disappeared in the distance, General Quarters alarm bells clattered, bosun pipes shrilled, "Clear for action!" orders were shouted through megaphones and crews scurried to battle stations on the ships of the American Squadron. An amazing thing was happening: Under full steam, down Santiago Channel toward the open sea, came the Spanish Fleet, Admiral Cervera's flagship *Infanta María Teresa* in the lead, resplendent in a new coat of black paint, battle flags fluttering at the masthead, black smoke billowing from its funnels. Behind the flagship at ten-minute intervals steamed the armored cruisers *Vizcaya, Cristóbal Colón, Almirante Oquendo* and the torpedo boats *Furor* and *Plutón.*

Emerging into the sea, Cervera led his Cape Verde fleet west along the coast under close pursuit and heavy fire from the American warships. On the *Brooklyn,* its signal pennants ordering "Follow the flag," Commodore Schley, in command of the American Squadron in Sampson's absence, stood on a wooden platform next to the conning tower giving quiet orders to his executive officer as he watched the procession of blockade-running Spanish ships. In the first hour of the fight, the flagship and the cruiser *Oquendo,* wooden decks afire, were run aground six miles west of Morro Castle; at around eleven, the *Vizcaya,* crippled and ablaze, ran onto the sandbanks off Aserraderos and the torpedo boats had been sunk or disabled. At two P.M., the last Spanish cruiser, the *Cristóbal Colón,* was caught seventy-five miles west of Santiago by the *Oregon,* which fired its murderous thirteen-inch guns until the Spanish ship ran down its colors and surrendered after careening hard aground.

The sea fight lasted four hours and every Spanish ship had been sunk, disabled or beached in flames. Admiral Cervera, who had lived his nightmare, lost 6 ships, 323 men killed, 151 wounded and 1,813 taken prisoner—including himself, shaken but uninjured and treated with elaborate courtesy on board the *Gloucester.* The Americans suffered light ship damage, one sailor killed and two wounded.

When the battle began, the *New York* was eight miles east of the channel, close to the Siboney beach, the ladder down for the admiral to descend to his launch. After somebody on deck yelled, "Smoke in harbor! The fleet is coming out!" Sampson ordered the ship to steam up and get underway but he arrived in the battle zone too late to take part in the action. From the *Brooklyn,*

Schley signaled, "We have gained a great victory." Sampson's response was a cold, "Report your casualties."

The two naval officers never had a kind word for each other after that. Sampson, whose subsequent report to the Navy Department did not even mention Schley, had suffered the greatest disappointment of his life. Through a perversely fateful timing, he had missed the battle that could have shaped his career and made it enduring in naval annals. Schley, whose own career was marred by the public controversy that ensued from the Santiago fight, at least had the courtesy to say that the victory "seems big enough for all of us."

In Washington on Monday morning, the Fourth of July took a more than usual celebratory turn when a cable from General Shafter to the War Department arrived at one o'clock which not only confirmed the destruction of the Spanish Fleet but advised that he had demanded the surrender of Santiago de Cuba. In the meantime, he wrote, "I shall hold my present position."

Later that day the newspapers were saturated with news of the naval victory and at noon on July 5, Sampson's cable arrived at Alger's office. Sampson wrote as if he had history books on his mind and did not want to clutter them with such trivia as not being present in the action or the fact that his second-in-command had conducted the battle: "The fleet under my command," he wrote, "offers the nation as a Fourth of July present the whole of Cervera's fleet. It attempted to escape at 9:30 this morning. At 2 the last ship, the Cristóbal Colón, had run ashore seventy-five miles west of Santiago and hauled down her colors."

2

"A kind of nondescript arrangement"

General José Toral, in the early evening of July 3, rejected Shafter's surrender demand. "It is my duty to say to you that this city will not surrender," his message said, "and that I will inform the foreign consuls and inhabitants of the contents of your message."

But the annihilation of Cervera's fleet was celebrated by the men in the trenches and gave everyone, from Washington to the San Juan Heights, renewed confidence that the war was nearing its end. Shafter told Joe Wheeler, "Now that the fleet is destroyed I believe the garrison will surrender, and all we have to do is hang on where we are and very soon starve them out."

Toral permitted the foreign consuls and their families to leave the city and these dignitaries, after entering the American lines, asked Shafter to postpone the bombardment of Santiago until July 5 to allow time for other noncombatants to make their way out. Shafter agreed.

During the truce, "a kind of nondescript arrangement," Roosevelt called it, Toral's defenders were reinforced by some 3,600 men arriving from Manzanillo, 150 miles east of Santiago. This development, a long-standing worry of Shafter's, did not dampen his conviction, stated to Alger, that he could "hold my present line and starve them out." The general had reinforcements of his own promised (he asked for another 15,000 men). His artillery at El Pozo was being improved. Morale was high. Casualties were being cared for at last. Supplies and matériel were being moved up to the heights overlooking the city. And now, Shafter felt, Sampson's (actually Schley's) triumphant sea fight would enable the navy to make a sortie on the west side of Santiago to finish the job he had started on the east. He messaged Sampson: "Now, if you will force your way into that harbor the town will surrender without any further sacrifice of life. My present position has cost me 1000 men and I do not wish to lose any more." But Sampson again demurred, saying such a proposal showed "a complete misapprehension of the circumstances which had to be met." (Historian Walter Millis provided a scorning summation of this general-admiral impasse: "General Shafter, evidently, was still under the impression that fighting ships were supposed to fight. The Admiral could not possibly entertain so gross a violation of theory.")

Shafter, after his communications with Sampson, his appeals to the War Department, and after leaking his communications to the press to embarrass the navy, concentrated on General Toral and a peace by capitulation.

During the cease-fire the Americans brought up stores and medical supplies from Siboney and reinforcements for the medical staff at the front. Clara Barton and three Red Cross physicians made their way to the heights, helped with the wounded and prepared hot meals for them. The medical help gave the Rough Riders' regimental surgeon Rob Church a respite to recover from the fever that had progressively weakened him since his heroic exertions at Las Guásimas ten days ago.

Roosevelt at last had a chance to wash and shave and change his socks and visit the Rough Rider wounded—over eighty men in the field hospitals behind the lines. When time permitted, he moved his command tent an appropriate distance from the trenches and "lived a little apart," he said, "for it is a mistake for an officer ever to grow too familiar with his men, no matter how good they are; and it is of course the greatest possible mistake to seek popularity either by showing weakness or by mollycoddling the men."

But he mollycoddled more than he admitted. Rations were improved in the lull in the fighting and Roosevelt, learning the military art of cumshaw, improvised ways to provide such luxuries as canned tomatoes, condensed milk, beans, rice, flour, oatmeal and tobacco, sometimes paying for them out of his own, or borrowed, money. "My regiment did not fare very well," he said, "but I think it fared better than any other."

He supervised policing their camp, and the gathering together of a four-day supply of rations for each man in the event the fighting resumed. He helped reinforce the trenches, dig latrines, build "bomb-proofs" (makeshift shelters, often as simple as a brush cover over a trench), sand-bagged bastions, traverses for connecting trenches, and improved positions for the Gatling and Colt guns.

On July 6, upon authorization by the military governor of Cuba, Captain General Ramón Blanco y Erenas, and agreement by General Shafter, an exchange of prisoners was made. Lieutenant Richmond P. Hobson and his seven crewman from the *Merrimac* were taken from the Santiago *cuartel* (a barracks, in this case one serving as a jail) and in the afternoon marched—blindfolded— through the streets of the city toward a prearranged rendezvous point in the American lines. Toral's escort party delivered the prisoners under a white flag to two American officers—one of them Colonel John Jacob Astor. The *Merrimac* men, freed after thirty-three days in prison, marched triumphantly along a cordon of cheering soldiers singing "When Johnny Comes Marching Home." Richard Harding Davis witnessed the scene:

> The trail up which they came was a broad one between high banks, with great trees meeting in an arch overhead. For hours before they came, officers and men who were not on duty in the rifle-pits had been waiting on these banks, broiling in the sun. . . . Hobson's coming was one of the most dramatic pictures of the war.

The slim, handsome Hobson, who had weathered his captivity well and had valuable information to share, was taken to Shafter's command tent for a conference. (Stephen Crane witnessed this meeting and could not resist adding a cruel line to his report: "The general sat in his chair, his belly sticking ridiculously out before him as if he had adopted some form of artificial inflation.") In the meeting, Hobson, who had studied Santiago's defenses from his cell in the Morro Castle and later from the *cuartel* deeper in the city, advised the general against assaulting Santiago from the fortified eastern perimeter and said he thought the best plan would be an attack from the south after the city was "reduced" by naval bombardment.

Although he received it graciously, this was not a new idea to Shafter. Later, Hobson recalled that "My words seemed to make but little impression on the general, and I concluded that it would be best to urge the matter through the admiral."

The eleven days that followed the release of the *Merrimac* crew were filled with a growing apprehension that the Santiago defenses were strong enough for Toral and his forces to hold out indefinitely while more reinforcements, ammunition, food and water arrived in the city—that the war might go on until the Americans were decimated by malaria and yellow fever and forced to leave the island.

Toral intimated as much in an exchange of messages on July 8, when he offered to evacuate the city provided he could march his defenders unmolested to the town of Holguín, northwest of Santiago. He told Shafter he held a good defensive position, had water stored in cisterns, ammunition and food, and that the only effect a bombardment of the city would have would be to kill and wound innocent civilians.

Shafter's dithering over this proposal, which he too quickly endorsed and sent to the War Department, earned him a stern and disapproving cable from Adjutant General Corbin in Washington: "The Secretary of War orders that when you are strong enough to destroy the enemy and take Santiago that you do it." Shafter was cowed by this unequivocal order. He notified his superiors that "Instructions of the War Department will be carried out to the letter," and notified Toral that the bombardment of the city would begin on the afternoon of July 10, unless the Spanish general surrendered unconditionally.

Some reinforcements—volunteer infantry from Illinois and

the District of Columbia, and added artillery support—began arriving soon after this ultimatum and on schedule, on the afternoon of the tenth, Sampson's battleships *Indiana, Brooklyn* and *New York* opened fire on the city from outside Santiago Channel. The eight-inch guns worked for an hour that day and over three hours on the morning of the 11th but the effect was negligible: some houses were destroyed but most of the shells landed harmlessly in the bay.

The Rough Riders, in their San Juan entrenchments, were under fire again on the 10th, but Roosevelt thought it "evident that the Spaniards did not have much heart in it." The answering fire, he said, came mostly from his sharpshooters, although the Colts and Gatlings put one Spanish artillery emplacement out of commission. Even the dynamite gun occasionally managed to fling a charge close enough to an enemy trench or blockhouse to cause the Spaniards to "show themselves and give our men a chance to do some execution."

The firing stopped by nightfall and Roosevelt's troopers, untouched by the day's bullets and shells, found shelter in the folds, trenches, bomb-proofs, brush and jungle on the heights, and made their meals.

3

"Having soundly thrashed the enemy"

The fighting fizzled out on July 11. General of the Army Nelson A. Miles reached Shafter's headquarters at Siboney that day and trench talk had it that Miles, Shafter and Toral were negotiating and that Spain was poised to sue for peace.

The army's general-in-chief had reached the Cuban coast full of energy and ideas—sharply in contrast with Shafter, who was ill, worn out and despairing. Miles had worked out a plan to land a force on the west side of Santiago Channel which, coordinated with a bombardment from Sampson's ships, would enfilade and overrun the Spanish shore batteries and capture Santiago from its bayside. He had shared this strategy with the admiral and Sampson thought so highly of the plan that he assigned Lieutenant Richmond Hobson to coordinate it. Hobson, from his *Merrimac* experience of trying to run the channel, and from his observations of the shore defenses while a prisoner in Morro Castle, had become everybody's authority on the seaward side of the city.

The daring scheme was never implemented. Shafter was opposed to it and seems to have convinced Miles that progress was being made in negotiations with General Toral and that this approach needed to be exhausted before any resumption of battle and a possibly unnecessary loss of life. Moreover, Shafter had a new card to play, an amazing idea from the War Department: Secretary Alger had authorized Shafter to tell Toral that if he would surrender unconditionally, the Spanish forces in Cuba would be shipped back to Spain at the expense of the government of the United States.

Miles, Shafter and their aides parleyed with Toral and his aides between the lines on July 13 and, with Miles doing the talking for the American side, set forth the terms. The talk produced an extension of the truce and some optimism that the Spaniards wanted out: Toral spoke of the need for a "solution" and used the word "honor." Words had to be agreed upon and from his hospital bed in Santiago, Toral's predecessor, General Arsenio Linares, employed some portentous ones in a message to Madrid. He wrote that the situation in Cuba "is fatal; surrender inevitable; we are only prolonging the agony. . . ."

While words were being debated in preparation for a new parley, Roosevelt received orders to move his troopers, with one of Parker's Gatling guns, out of their rifle pits and bomb-proofs north to help guard the El Caney road. That night of the eleventh a sudden storm swept over the El Caney camp, pelting the sodden bivouac with rain, blowing down shelter halves and extinguishing cook fires. Roosevelt's tent was knocked flat at an inopportune time, after its sole occupant had stripped to the buff for the first time in a fortnight. "I felt fully punished for my love of luxury when I jumped out into the driving downpour of tropic rain," he said, "and groped blindly in the darkness for my clothes as they lay in the liquid mud." He made his way to the cook tent where Bert Holderman, an Indian Territory private in Troop L, wrapped him in blankets. The colonel spent the night curled up on a table Holderman had scrounged from an abandoned Spanish building.

Like every other officer in the field, Roosevelt worried about the idleness of his men, the hammering rains which were visiting them more and more frequently now, and the rising number of fever cases in the ranks and among the officers. Scuttlebutt had it that General Miles might lead an expedition to Puerto Rico and Roosevelt hoped his regiment might take part it—it would energize his men, occupy them physically and mentally. In the meantime, he could only fret at the inactivity, the absence of orders, the burgeoning sick list, the incessant rain, the incompetence of their high leadership. "It is criminal to keep Shafter in command," he wrote to Cabot Lodge. "He is utterly inefficient, and now he is panic struck . . . tacking and veering."

He kept up a semblance of activity by following a War Department suggestion that the regiments move their camps every few days, believing this would help reduce the fever rolls. Unfortunately, it didn't.

Now, too, there was a yellow fever scare. As early as July 9 there were reports of cases of the dreaded febrile disease in the ramshackle hospital buildings in Siboney, among the Cuban rebels and the refugees pouring out of Santiago. The *Chicago Tribune* reported 200 cases of "yellow jack" (the nickname deriving from the yellow quarantine flag that warned of its presence) in "army hospitals in Cuba," and Roosevelt said yellow fever rumors created "a perfect panic among some of our own doctors, and especially in the minds of one or two generals and of the home authorities."

There was ample reason to fear it. The yellow fever mortality rate was a minimum of one-in-five and as high as fifty percent in some areas of Cuba in the hurricane season. The disease had horrendous complications—fever, jaundice, internal bleeding, liver and kidney failure, a vomiting of blood—*el vomito negro* was the Spanish term for it. It was well known in the port cities of the southern and eastern United States, coming in the spring and summer months, dying out with the frost, and there had been numerous periodic yellow fever epidemics, one of which, in 1878, had killed more than twenty thousand people in the Mississippi Valley between Memphis and the Gulf of Mexico. Clara Barton had witnessed it and nursed its victims in Florida in 1887.

Theories on the origins of the fever ranged from unsanitary conditions to swamp miasmas, and although theories that mosquitos carried the disease had been proposed as early as 1848, and a particular mosquito, the *Aëdes aegypti* had been identified in 1881 as the carrier, there was no cure, and little effective treatment available in 1898 for those stricken.

Fortunately for the Americans, the disease was never as prevalent as imagined and was confused with other fevers—malaria and typhoid in particular. Roosevelt said that "whenever we sent a man to the rear he was decreed to have yellow fever, whereas, if we kept him at the front, it always turned out that he had malarial fever, and after a few days he was back at work again."

While a high number of men in his regiment suffered from malaria and dysentery, Roosevelt himself managed to remain healthy throughout the campaign. Stephen Crane took note of this and also the colonel's efforts on behalf of his men, and paid him high tribute in the *New York World:* "This fellow worked for his troopers like a cider press," Crane said. "He tried to feed them. He helped build latrines. He cursed the quartermasters. . . .

Let him be a politician if he likes. He was a gentleman down there."

The "let him be a politician" comment may have been Crane's nod to the newspaper notices, beginning after the San Juan battle, of a movement afoot back home to have Roosevelt nominated for the governorship of New York.

Shafter may have been "tacking and veering" but despite having the nettlesome General Miles peering anxiously over his shoulder, and the secretary of war buffeting him with urgent messages, he was making progress with the commander of the Spanish forces. Toral's proposal that he be permitted to evacuate Santiago and move his army to Holguín was turned down flatly in Washington by no less a personage than the commander-in-chief himself. President McKinley, keenly sensitive to the attitude of voters, saw such a move as a sign of weakness and inimical to ending the war. Unconditional surrender would be the only terms acceptable, with the United States agreeing to ship the enemy garrisons home to Spain.

On July 14, Toral notified Shafter that he was awaiting word from Madrid to negotiate "capitulation on the basis of repatriation" and both sides appointed "commissioners"—Joe Wheeler, Henry Lawton, Lieutenant John D. Miley, Shafter's inspector-general, on the American side—to discuss the terms.

After this penultimate parley, the Spanish commissioners returned to Santiago to report to Generals Toral and Linares the details of the arrangements and to await the final sanction from Madrid to proceed with the surrender. Shafter meantime said he was "thunderstruck" that Toral was giving up much more than the 11,500-man army in Santiago and environs: He would also be surrendering 7,000 men stationed around Guantánamo, 3,500 at San Luís, north of Santiago, and another 1,500 scattered in small units around the province. Here was a gift of 12,000 men Shafter said "were absolutely beyond my reach."

Leonard Wood, now a brigadier general of the volunteer cavalry under Joe Wheeler, was satisfied that the war was ending in
negotiation rather than in a larger expenditure of lives, but he
had little patience with either his cavalry commander or Shafter.
In a letter to his wife on July 15 he wrote that Wheeler was running "a news correspondence stand," and that, "while a dear old
man is no more use here than a child." He said, "Having soundly
thrashed the enemy we are now in a struggle with nature," and
railed about the "appalling mismanagement" of the campaign:
"Shafter was not out of his ship until *three days* after my first fight
[Las Guásimas] and did not see the battlefield of Santiago until
four days after the fight." He called the artillery support of the
troops attacking the San Juan Heights "a howling farce," and said
the entire war was "absolutely sickening."

It ended in the late afternoon of July 16 with the commissioners
on each side signing the articles of capitulation. (The word "surrender," by mutual agreement, was not employed.) The formal
ceremony took place the next morning in Santiago's great plaza
with Toral saluting as Spanish flags were hauled down from the
city's military and governmental buildings. Arms were stacked in
the arsenal (sixteen thousand rifles, one hundred cannon, eighteen
Maxim machine guns, three million rounds of ammunition), after
which Shafter and his top officers rode through the city observ-
ing its defenses.

One gentlemanly touch in the ceremonies was the presenta-
tion by Shafter to Toral of the sword and spurs of General Joaquín
Vara del Rey, the commander at El Caney who had been killed in
Lawton's assault.

At eleven, the Americans were invited to a lunch at the city's
palacio with Spanish municipal officials, the archbishop of Santiago, consuls and high-ranking military officers. Thousands of people gathered in the plaza as the cathedral clock chimed twelve and
the American flag was hoisted above the city. A twenty-one-gun

salute was fired by Captain Capron's artillerymen, followed by the band of the Sixth Cavalry striking up "Hail, Columbia."

In twenty-three days, a little over a week of fighting and two of negotiating, the Americans had won Santiago—and thereby, all of Cuba—and ended four hundred years of Spanish hegemony on the island.

In a poignantly sad and disgraceful development in the final act of the Cuban campaign, Calixto García was conspicuously absent from the Santiago ceremonies. Shafter had determined that if the general and his rebels were allowed into the city, they would commit "reprisals" against the Spaniards. Thus the valiant old rebel, who had been fighting for Cuban freedom when Shafter was chasing Comanches and Kickapoos in east Texas, gathered his tattered soldiers and retired sullenly into the jungle. "We are a poor, ragged army," he said before departing, aiming his words at the Americans, "as ragged and poor as was the army of your fore-fathers in their noble war of independence, but like the heroes of Saratoga and Yorktown, we respect our cause too deeply to dis-grace it with barbarism and cowardice."

Of this wretched development, Margaret Leech, McKinley's biographer, has observed that the breach at Santiago might have been avoided "if Shafter had granted to García a tithe of the diplo-matic consideration he had lavished upon Toral."*

---

*At the behest of Leonard Wood, García visited the United States during the win-ter of 1898 and even had an interview with President McKinley. García died in Washington on December 11, 1898, at the age of seventy-one.

XV

HOME
━━━━

1
"The death rate will be appalling."

The fever and worsening weather problems faced by Shafter's army in Cuba after the surrender occupied the War Department, the army and the news correspondents for three weeks; the plight of those left behind in Tampa, including Major George Dunn's Rough Riders, were ignored.

Dunn had succeeded Major Henry Hersey in command of New Mexico troops C, H, I and M, the 475 officers and men—a hundred less than shipped out to Cuba on June 14—who remained in Tampa. It was a thankless, rankling, frustrating business for the Denver native and no less so for the troopers under his command. Roosevelt acknowledged that those left behind "felt the most bitter heartburn," and said, "To the great bulk of them I think it will be a life-long sorrow," but he had no real idea of the emptiness of his statement that "those that stayed were entitled to precisely as much honor as those that went."

"It was no honor to stay behind," said Frank Brito, who served in Captain George Curry's H Troop of New Mexicans. "Tampa was a hell-hole. We were there, waiting, thinking we would get over to Cuba, or maybe Puerto Rico, and nothing happened. A lot of us got sick and a lot got in trouble in Tampa. No wonder. We were there over two months with nothing to do but get sick and get mad."

The Tampa camp, a fever hole comparable to Santiago and its outstations, originally lay three miles west of the city, near the bay where pools of stagnant water gave birth to clouds of mosquitos. As well, since there were twelve hundred horses and mules picketed near the camp, the men attending them were feasts for swarms of voracious botflies. The Rough Riders were eventually moved to higher ground but morale had already seriously deteriorated and no number of marksmanship contests, roping and riding matches and similar artificial diversions could override it. Major Dunn and his officers were liberal in granting passes to town but repeated fights and small riots in the cheap cafes, saloons and cribs in the red-light districts brought about a curtailing of this favor. Malaria and dysentery took a high toll among the idle men and some, tired of make-work drills and pretending to fight the enemy while slapping mosquitos among the palmetto groves and sand dunes, deserted.

There were three exciting moments in the Rough Riders' forsaken Tampa camp, those who were there remembered: the three times Major Dunn was ordered to place the men on alert—after the Las Guásimas fight, after the San Juan Hill battle, and during General Miles's Puerto Rican expedition. But nothing came of any of them. The next most anxious time, Trooper Frank Brito recalled, was the day the Rough Riders' mascot, the mountain lion Florence, escaped from her cage and panicked the horses before being recaptured.

In early August, Dunn's forlorn gang of they-also-servers received orders to depart for the island—Long Island, New York—via the Florida Central and Peninsular Railroad.

* * *

On the other island, during the postsurrender period when his troopers were at least as sick and restless as those left in Tampa, Roosevelt wrote, "We did everything possible to keep up the spirits of the men, but it was exceedingly difficult because there was nothing for them to do. They were weak and languid, and in the wet heat they had lost energy, so that it was not possible for them to indulge in sports or pastimes." In a letter to Cabot Lodge he said there were fifteen hundred cases of malarial fever in the army in Cuba and, using a curious simile, said the men were "ripe for dying like rotten sheep."

He hoped that his men might play a role in the Puerto Rican campaign and thus be able to quit the fever camps around Santiago but the Rough Riders were not needed—nor, as it turned out, was the army General Miles led to the island.*

Roosevelt himself, enjoying the fortune that follows some of the bold, remained fever-free and healthy and during the interminable days of waiting—for orders to Puerto Rico, or home—tried to find some respite from the languor of the steaming camps between Siboney and Santiago. The capital, which he called "the quaint, dirty old Spanish city," with its narrow streets, ramshackle shops and single decent café, he found a bore although he enjoyed his visits to the Governor's Palace where his old walking companion, Brigadier General Leonard Wood, now presided as military governor. That assignment had given Roosevelt command of Wood's cavalry brigade and the responsibilities, but not the rank, of a brigadier general.

Late in July, Fitzhugh Lee, the former consul in Havana and now a major general of volunteers, invited Wood, Roosevelt,

---

*On July 25, eight days after Toral's surrender of Santiago, Miles and 3,300 men landed at Guánica on the southwest coast of the island. Eighteeen days later, with his force then numbering 15,000 men and with the general directing an overland march of four columns toward the capital at San Juan, Puerto Rico fell to the Americans when the peace settlement was announced.

Henry Lawton, and several other officers, on an excursion to ex-
amine the Morro Castle, guarding the channel entrance to Santiago Bay. The party wandered among the castellated battlements
and dungeons ("where we found hideous rusty implements of
torture," Roosevelt said) of the ancient fortress, and inspected
the old cannon on its ramparts which had been little affected by
Sampson's bombardments.

"Afterward I had a swim," Roosevelt said, "not trusting much
to the shark stories."

Lieutenant John C. "Jack" Greenway of Buckey O'Neill's
troop, a Yale athlete who had been slightly wounded at Las Guásimas, accompanied the colonel on this swim and gave a fuller account of it. He said Roosevelt wanted to see the hulk of
Lieutenant Richmond Hobson's *Merrimac,* which lay in the harbor not too far from one of the Spanish shore batteries. As soon
as Roosevelt and Greenway slipped into the water to swim out to
the wreck, Fitzhugh Lee began waving his arms and "doing a war
dance" on a parapet of the Morro, shouting at the pair in the
water. Greenway told Roosevelt that Lee had spotted sharks pa-
trolling near the sunken collier. Roosevelt's reaction, according to
Greenway:

> "Sharks," says the colonel, blowing out a mouthful of water,
> "they" stroke "won't" stroke "bite." Stroke "I've been" stroke
> "studying them" stroke "and I never" stroke "heard of one"
> stroke "bothering a swimmer." Stroke. "It's all" stroke "pop-
> pycock."

As Roosevelt finished his stroke-and-talk shark discourse,
Greenway said, "a big fellow, probably not more than ten or
twelve feet long, but looking as big as a battleship to me, showed
up alongside us. Then came another, till we had quite a group.
The colonel didn't pay the least attention. . . ."

The two finally reached the hulk and Roosevelt examined it closely. Greenway pretended a deep interest while warily cocking an eye on the circling sharks, his mind occupied with getting back to shore.

They did, miraculously without incident and to Fitzhugh Lee's immense relief. Greenway had witnessed the almost supernatural luck Roosevelt carried with him throughout the campaign. He couldn't get sick and neither Spaniards nor sharks could kill him.

On July 31, Roosevelt and all senior line and medical officers of the Fifth Corps were summoned by Shafter to a conference at Wood's quarters in the Governor's Palace in Santiago. Those gathered were unanimous in their conviction that the army was in grave danger of further decimation by fever and disease and that the War Department's directive on moving the camps to higher ground was not the answer. Shafter wanted a record of the meeting made, the document to contain the consensus that except for a minimal holding force the army must be shipped home.

Since none of the regular army officers wished to put their careers on the line by drafting such a paper, Roosevelt, who appears to have been invited for the purpose, volunteered to write it, adopting corrections and suggestions by the generals in attendance.

The proceedings and cover letter were dated August 3, the former signed by all the officers, the cover letter written and signed exclusively by Roosevelt.

Both documents were leaked to the press and created a fiery newspaper–War Department debate on the state of the army in Cuba, fueled particularly by the blunt and impertinent language of Roosevelt's letter. In a document made available to the world in the midst of delicate negotiations with Spain to end the war, he had written, "The army is disabled by malarial fever to such an extent that its efficiency is destroyed. . . . To keep us here, in the opinion of every officer commanding a division or a brigade, will simply involve the destruction of thousands." He added, with the serene omniscience and candor possessed exclusively by the politician serving as temporary soldier, "There is no possible reason for not shipping the entire command North at once," and "Persons responsible for preventing such a move will be responsible for the unnecessary loss of many thousands of lives."

Roosevelt's screed infuriated Alger (who briefly contemplated calling for its author to be court-martialled) and President McKinley, among others, and was believed by many old army officers to be tantamount to treason. The president cabled Shafter that the letter was "most unfortunate from every point of view. . . . No soldier reading that report if ordered to Santiago but will feel that he is marching to certain death." Hearst's *New York Journal* also pounced on the matter, as did other newspapers coast-to-coast, lambasting Roosevelt for his egotism and his besmirching of the army in Cuba, its victories and sacrifices and the memory of its dead. Some papers supported Roosevelt, calling his letter "courageous" and crediting him with "saving the Fifth Corps" by his daringly forthright revelations.

In fact, Roosevelt's blunt conclusions were shared by Shafter and his senior officers and two days before the letter fell into the hands of the Associated Press, plans were being made to ship the army home. On August 1, Alger had authorized the movement of "some of Wheeler's dismounted cavalry" to Montauk Point, Long Island, with the proviso that all men ill with fever were to be declared free of communicable disease before debarking from Cuba. Preliminary arrangements were also made to move the troops from Tampa to Montauk Point and, on August 3, the date of Roosevelt's letter, Shafter had appealed to Alger for the immediate transport of the army back to the United States. "If it is not

done," he said, "I believe the death rate will be appalling." On the
same day Alger issued orders that all troops not required for duty
in Cuba be transported home "rapidly."

2

"I've had a bully time and a bully fight."

On the morning of August 7, the merchant steamers carrying
the Fifth Army Corps ran down Santiago Channel past the deserted shore batteries, the hulk of Hobson's *Merrimac,* the walls
of Morro Castle, and into the open sea. The string of battered
transports plowed the blue-green waters past the beached derelicts
of Cervera's fleet and moved east along the coast past Siboney and
Daiquirí where, just forty-seven days ago, the army had first set
foot on the beaches of the Ever-faithful Isle. Late that evening the
flotilla butted through the Windward Passage, headed west toward the edge of the Great Bahama Bank where Columbus's
Ragged Island lay, and home.

The Rough Riders and a squadron of the Third Cavalry regulars shared the transport *Miami.* General Joe Wheeler was on
board and put the management and policing of the ship under
Roosevelt's charge, an assignment that proved difficult on the
first three days at sea. The *Miami* had scarcely slipped past the
Morro when Roosevelt was notified by the transport's captain
that the ship's stokers and engineers were getting drunk on liquor
smuggled on board by the soldiers. A search of the ship turned up
about seventy flasks and bottles, which were confiscated, many
thrown overboard. The drunkenness, Roosevelt said, ended
abruptly even though the ship's belowdecks crew remained
"sullen and half mutinous" and had to be watched.

Not much had changed in the War Department's muddled
methods of moving troops on the high seas and the voyage home

was reminiscent of the voyage out from Tampa Bay on the *Yucatan*. Wheeler, being the only general aboard, had quarters to himself, but the other officers, Roosevelt said, "slept in a kind of improvised shed, not unlike a chicken coop with bunks, on the aftermost part of the upper deck." The troops would have welcomed the coops; instead, they had their customary sweltering, stinking, belowdecks "sardines in a can" billets. Moreover, in other echoes of the *Yucatan* experience, the water aboard was tainted, there was no ice, disinfectants, or vegetables, and when cases of tinned beef were presented as a dietary option, that not fed to the outward-bound sharks was now fed to the homeward-bound ones.

Since there was no provision for tending the sick, they were isolated on the main deck and cared for by regimental surgeon Robert Church and Chaplain George Brown. Five Rough Riders, all malaria victims, had been left behind in Santiago until cleared of quarantine, but several fever-stricken troopers had relapses and other suffered from other tropic diseases. One, Rough Rider private George Walsh of Troop A, a forty-three-year-old San Franciscan, died of dysentery. On the first night ashore at Daiquirí, Walsh had gotten drunk on rum he had bartered from Cuban rebels and the next day marched to Siboney in the sun. "He never recovered," Roosevelt said coldly, "and was useless from that time on." Somewhere off the north coast of Cuba, the trooper's body, sewn into a hammock weighted with iron shot, was buried at sea while Third Cavalry band members played a dirge.

But bright and sunny weather eased the eight-day passage to Long Island and the time was passed mostly in talking, not only of the war in Cuba, but of wars longer past—General Wheeler told many excellent tales of his "great war" between the states—plus tales of yacht races and voyages around Cape Horn, of sporting and hunting, Indians and outlaws.

On the afternoon of the 14th, the *Miami* steamed through the still waters of the sound and along the low, sandy bluffs of Long

Island, dropping anchor off Montauk Point, at the extreme north-eastern tip of the island. A gunboat came out to greet them, bringing news: Commodore Dewey and Major General Wesley Merritt, in command of the Eighth Army Corps, had forced the surrender of Manila and ended the war on the Pacific front and President McKinley had signed a peace protocol with Spain.

At eleven the next morning a tug nudged the *Miami* against the Montauk pier. Joe Wheeler, his white beard neatly trimmed, his blue uniform spotless, waved his campaign hat at the crowd and walked down the ramp, a huge sheathed machete hanging from his belt in lieu of a cavalry saber. Roosevelt debarked in his rumpled khakis and pinned-up campaign hat, his *Maine* pistol in a holster at his side. He was met at dockside by General Sam Young, felled by malaria in Cuba and now commander of the camp. Roosevelt's wife Edith was there with fourteen-year-old Alice, and sons Ted and Kermit. Also awaiting him was what he called a "manly letter" from the secretary of war. Alger apologized for mistakenly thinking that Roosevelt had leaked his "destruction of thousands" letter to the press. He praised the colonel as "a most gallant officer" who "in the battle before Santiago showed superb soldierly qualities," and invited Roosevelt to visit him in Washington. "No one will welcome you more heartily than I," he said.

Roosevelt told reporters of "feeling disgracefully well." "I've had a bully time and a bully fight," he said. "I feel as big and strong as a bull moose."

The troopers coming down the gangplank did not. Most looked haggard and weak as they smiled and waved their hats at the crowd of well-wishers gathered at dockside. Dr. Church and his helpers had managed to keep most of the demi-regiment healthy on the voyage home, but thirty Rough Riders were on the sick list, most weak and ill from dysentery and other malarial fever symptoms. Some had to be carried from the *Miami* on stretchers, others limped ashore supported by their comrades. Among the men who had served closest to him in the campaign, Roosevelt said, only Color Sergeant Albert Wright remained in good health. Henry Bardshar, the colonel's faithful orderly, "was a wreck, literally at death's door," his body servant Marshall and trooper Bob Wrenn, the tennis star from Chicago, were also weak and ill and would spend the month remaining before mustering-out on the sick list.

The camp at Montauk, named in honor of Colonel Charles A. Wykoff, killed on July 1 in front of the Thirteenth Infantry at San Juan Hill, turned out to be the perfect place for rest and recuperation. Occasional rain squalls and winds smacked the camp, blowing down tents, but most often the August days were breezy, sunny and clear. The food was good and abundant—milk, eggs, oranges—"and any amount of tobacco," was available, Roosevelt said. The sick and wounded were cared for by the Red Cross, volunteers from New York hospitals and philanthropic and patriotic societies, and after passing quarantine inspections, many of the eastern seaboard residents were given leave and made their way home.

Several Rough Riders died at Montauk or in other hospitals. J. Knox Green of G Troop, a native of Rancho, Texas, died at Camp Wykoff "because of sickness which originated in the line of duty" on August 15; Stanley Hollister, the champion track and field star from California, succumbed to typhoid fever at Fortress Monroe, Virginia, on August 17 and on the same day, E Trooper Alfred Judson of New York City died at Montauk. On August 19, Frederick W. Gosling of Troop H, born in Bedfordshire, England, died at Wykoff; Private Alexander Wallace of Troop A died of typhoid in a Brooklyn hospital on August 31; Private Edwin E. Casey of Las Cruces, New Mexico Territory, an H trooper, died of unnamed causes at Wykoff; and Private Frank H. Clearwater of Troop C died in Corpus Christi, Texas, on September 2 of "typhoid malaria."

Roosevelt, and indeed all the Rough Riders, were particularly saddened by the news that the popular New Yorker, Lieutenant William "Willie" Tiffany, had died in Boston on August 26. The wealthy socialite, who had wrestled the Colt rapid-firers to the front and scrounged Mauser ammunition for them, had been left behind in Santiago, suffering from yellowjack, when the *Miami* steamed home with his regiment. Roosevelt thought highly of Tiffany and must have reflected on the sad irony that this valuable officer had accompanied him on the trip out to Morro Castle on July 26 and now, a month to the day later, lay dead in a Boston hospital.

Another sad affair was the reunion at Camp Wykoff of the Rough Riders who served in the Santiago campaign and the four troops that had stayed behind at Tampa under Major George Dunn's command. Roosevelt hinted that the Tampa troopers were "bitter" over their fate and tried valiantly to salve it over. "Of course those who stayed had done their duty precisely as did those who went," he said, and while "no distinction of any kind was allowed in the regiment between those whose good fortune it had been to go and those whose harder fate it had been to remain," he admitted that "the latter could not be entirely comforted." Perhaps especially since he persisted in making the distinction himself.

He made a trip home to Oyster Bay at the end of August for a reunion with his family at Sagamore Hill but he had little privacy there as throngs of well-wishers and newspapermen insisted on seeing him and shaking his hand. He was repeatedly asked to talk about his future plans, about politics and the increasing momentum to have him declared as a Republican candidate for the New York governorship. He refused all these entreaties. "I will not say a word about myself," he declared, "but I will talk about the regiment forever." He would soon have to abandon the first promise, but he kept the last one.

General Shafter arrived at Montauk on September 1. On that day the War Department notified Joe Wheeler, who had now replaced

Sumner as commander at Camp Wykoff, that eleven regiments, including the Rough Riders, would be mustered out at a date to be named soon.

On Saturday, September 3, President McKinley visited the camp, accompanied by Vice President Garret A. Hobart, Secretary of War Alger and other cabinet members and Washington dignitaries. After a twenty-one-gun salute, the president visited Shafter, who was still shaky from the aftermath of malaria, and the camp hospital where Wheeler's daughter Annie, a nurse who had served in Cuba with Clara Barton, became McKinley's guide. During his tour of the camp facilities, the president spotted Roosevelt and stepped out of his carriage for a chat. Roosevelt struggled to get his gauntlet off to shake hands, finally attacking and pulling it free with his famous teeth.

McKinley inspected the troops at noon and made a vigorous and heart-warming speech that brought a rousing cheer. "You have come home after two months of severe campaigning," he said, "which has embraced assault, siege, and battle, so brilliant in achievement, so far-reaching in results as to command the unstinted praise of all your countrymen." Of the dead he said, "Their memories will be perpetuated in the hearts and histories of a generous people."

3

"This peculiarly American regiment"

The mustering out began on September 13 and on that day Roosevelt was working on papers in his tent when Major Alexander Brodie came to pay a visit and to ask the colonel to step outside. He found the regiment formed up in a hollow square waiting for him. On a table in the center of the square sat a bulky object covered by a blanket. Brodie led the colonel to the table where Private William S. Murphy, a Caddo, Indian Territory, volunteer in

Troop M had the honor of presenting to Roosevelt "a very slight token of admiration, love and esteem." The blanket was whisked off to reveal a splendidly detailed bronze sculpture of a cowboy on a bucking horse, a work by Frederick Remington, the correspondent-artist in the Cuban campaign and Roosevelt's friend.

He was deeply touched at the gift and gave an eloquent extemporaneous speech in which he said, "I am proud of this regiment beyond measure," and paid tribute to the "backbone" of it, "the men of the West and Southwest," and the appropriateness of the Remington sculpture to symbolize these volunteers. He spoke of the vivid memories the regiment had brought home from the campaign, not of personal exploit or suffering, but of those who died—such as Allyn Capron, Buckey O'Neill and Hamilton Fish—and he mentioned the "men of color" who fought beside the Rough Riders and the "tie which we trust will never be broken." The speech, interrupted several times by the cheers of his troopers, he ended by saying:

> Nothing could possibly happen that would touch and please me as this has. . . . I would have been most deeply touched if the officers had given me this testimonial, but coming from you, my men, I appreciate it tenfold. It comes from you who shared the hardships of the campaign with me, who gave me a piece of your hardtack when I had none, and who gave me your blankets when I had none to lie upon. To have such a gift come from this peculiarly American regiment touches me more than I can say. This is something I shall hand down to my children, and I shall value it more than the weapons I carried through the campaign.

After the impromptu ceremony he shook each man's hand, spoke a few words to each trooper and at the end, chatted at length with Nicholas Fish and his wife, Hamilton's parents, who stood in line with the others.

* * *

On September 15, 1898, four months after it was organized in San Antonio, Color Sergeant Albert Wright lowered the regimental colors for the last time, ending what Roosevelt called the "life of a regiment of as gallant fighters as ever wore the United States uniform."

The Rough Riders received their seventy-seven dollars mustering-out pay and scattered to the four winds home.

On October 3, the Fifth U.S. Army Corps was officially disbanded at Camp Wykoff.

By the end of 1898, the official casualty figures of the war were totaled: 5,462 total deaths among officers and men in all camps and theaters of war; of this number the battle casualties amounted to 1,983, of which number 379 had been killed in action or died of wounds.

Of the Rough Riders, thirty-seven percent of those who got to Cuba were either killed, wounded or stricken with disease.

In the Treaty of Paris, signed on December 10, 1898, Spain relinquished sovereignty over Cuba and ceded to the United States Puerto Rico, Guam in the Mariana Islands, and, for a twenty-million-dollar payment, the Philippines. During the next year, the United States divided the Samoan Islands with Germany and took possession of Wake Island atoll between Hawaii and Guam.

On December 30, Major General Samuel S. Sumner, in Camp Mackenzie, Georgia, and Major General of Volunteers Leonard Wood, commanding the Department of Santiago de Cuba, each wrote to the U.S. Adjutant General, Henry C. Corbin, in Washington. Sumner's letter recommended "Hon. Theodore Roosevelt, late Colonel First United States Volunteer Cavalry, for a Medal of Honor, as a reward for conspicuous gallantry at the battle of San Juan, Cuba, on July 1, 1898." He said that "Colonel Roosevelt by his example and fearlessness inspired his men, and

both at Kettle Hill and the ridge known as San Juan he led his
command in person. I was an eye-witness of Colonel Roosevelt's
action." Wood's letter was similar, recommending Roosevelt for
a Medal of Honor and basing his recommendation "upon the fact
that Colonel Roosevelt, accompanied only by four or five men, led
a very desperate and extremely gallant charge on San Juan Hill,
thereby setting a splendid example to the troops. . . ."

Letters by others followed, each from eyewitnesses to Roosevelt's gallantry at San Juan, each asking the adjutant general to
sponsor awarding of the Medal of Honor to Colonel Roosevelt.

Corbin apparently sent the letters to War Secretary Alger but
he took no action of them.

Edith Carow Roosevelt said that failure to win the medal was
one of the bitterest disappointments of her husband's life.*

---

*Forty-seven years later, Roosevelt's son, Brigadier General Theodore Roosevelt,
Jr., earned the Medal of Honor for his valorous conduct at Utah Beach, Nor-
mandy, on D-day. Theodore Junior died of heart failure on July 11, 1944, age
fifty-six. The medal was awarded posthumously.

EPILOGUE

"I will talk about the regiment forever," Roosevelt said at Sagamore Hill in August 1898, and he was true to his word. In June 1899, while governor of New York, he traveled by train out to Las Vegas, New Mexico Territory, for the first reunion of the Rough Riders, held on the first anniversary of the Las Guásimas battle. The celebrated newspaper editor William Allen White of the Emporia, Kansas, *Gazette,* accompanied Roosevelt and wrote about the adulation the colonel received en route from Albany to the tiny New Mexico town. Six hundred of his regiment were present to see and hear him and he spent thirty-six hours among them, talking virtually nonstop.

In the two decades that followed, he kept up a keen interest in the welfare of the men of his Rough Riders, their problems, scandals, accomplishments, peregrinations and deaths. He tended to forgive the most egregious sins of his troopers, as exemplified by the case of Ben Daniels, the former Dodge City sheriff and member of Troop D. Daniels was imprisoned for murder some years after the war but when finally freed, Roosevelt asked former Rough Rider major Alexander Brodie, now governor of Arizona Territory, if he could find work for the old lawman. Brodie complied and, so the story goes, appointed Daniels a prison warden.

In 1906, during his presidency, Roosevelt received from Secretary of War William Howard Taft the nomination of a Yale man for a government post in the Southwest. In a droll memorandum to Taft, the president wrote, "I guess Yale '78 has the call, as there seems to be no Rough Rider available and every individual in the Southern District of the Indian Territory (including every Rough Rider) appears to be either under indictment, convicted, or in a position that renders it imperatively necessary that he should be indicted."

Privately, he wrote of his post-'98 "boys," those from the ranks at least, as "great big, goodhearted, homicidal children," and "children of the dragon's blood."

He also assiduously defended the regiment against its occasional critics. When *New York Herald* correspondent Stephen Bonsal, in his 1899 book, *The Fight for Santiago,* revived the idea that the Rough Riders had been ambushed at Las Guásimas, Roosevelt delightedly stepped into the fray. "Mr. Bonsal was not present at the fight," he said with gleeful finality, "and, indeed, so far as I know, he never at any time was with the cavalry in action. He puts in his book a map of the supposed skirmish ground; but it bears to the actual scene of the fight only the well-known likeness borne by Monmouth to Macedon." His devastating rebuttal went on for several printed pages, including supporting material from Leonard Wood and Richard Harding Davis.

In his own book, *The Rough Riders,* published in 1900, Roosevelt wore out his mental thesaurus in describing his troopers' "courage," "great hardihood," and "soldierly conduct," their "self-reliant," "self-sufficient," "eagerness," "devotion," "bravery," "boldness," "enterprising natures," "resolution," "intelligence," "gallantry" and "fortitude." And, there was enough of the personal pronoun in the book to elicit from Finley Peter Dunne's Chicago newspaper column this commentary from the Irish sa- loon-keeper "Mr. Dooley" to his barfly friend Hennessy:

> This here book . . . fell fr'm th' lips iv Tiddy Rosenfelt. . . . They has been some discussion as to who was th' first man to r-reach th' summit iv San Joon Hill. . . . "I will say f'r th' binifit iv pos- terity that I was th' only man I see. An' I had a tillyscope." I have thried, Hin- nissy, [Mr. Dooley continued] to give you a fair idee iv th' contents iv this re- markable book. . . . If I was him I'd call th' book "Alone in Cubia."

Roosevelt, who could take a joke, wrote to Dunne, "I regret to state that my family and intimate friends are delighted with your review of my book."

His political star, which seemed always in the ascendant, had a comet's impetus and brilliance after the war. He was elected governor of New York in 1899, vice president in 1900 and, upon William McKinley's assassination in September 1901, rose to the presidency at age forty-three, to the dismay of convervative Re- publicans. Senator Mark Hanna of Ohio, McKinley's closest ad- visor and confidante, told a Chicago newspaper editor during the president's funeral, "I told him it was a mistake to nominate that wild man. . . . I asked him if he realized what would happen if he should die. Now look, that damned cowboy is President of the United States."

Hanna, who died in 1904, lived long enough to see what that damned cowboy—the man so fond of the West African proverb, "Speak softly and carry a big stick; you will go far"—could do.

After his presidency (1901–1909) and his Nobel Peace Prize

in 1906 for arbitrating the end of the Russo-Japanese War, he headed an African safari (which produced fourteen thousand specimens, rhinos to rodents, for the Smithsonian Institution), took a European tour, made an unsuccessful "Bull Moose Party" presidential bid in 1912, and a harrowing expedition to trace the River of Doubt in Brazil in 1914. (During this awful adventure, Roosevelt suffered from an abcessed leg, malaria and dysentery, fell into a delirium, muttered over and over, "In Xanadu did Kubla Khan a stately pleasure-dome decree" from Coleridge's poem, and contemplated suicide rather than be a burden to his partners.)

"The old lion," as his son Archie called him, rose up a final time when the United States entered the war in Europe in April 1917. He inveigled Secretary of War Newton Baker on his idea of raising not a mere regiment, as in 1898, but a *division* of Rough Rider–inspired volunteers to fight in France. He had in fact been making plans for such an organization since the war erupted in August 1914, even to compiling lists of men—including some who had fought in the Rough Riders—who he would ask to serve. He said if the War Department would supply the arms and supplies, he would do the rest: raise the money, give the division six weeks' training at Fort Sill, Oklahoma, and prepare them for more intensive training in France before leading them over the top. But Newton Baker was not Russell Alger and politely rebuffed these entreaties. Roosevelt then went over the secretary's head and directly to the White House to present his case personally to President Woodrow Wilson. "If Wilson gives me the division," Roosevelt wrote to Cabot Lodge, "I shall serve him with single-minded loyalty." This was no small promise, given his attitude toward Wilson, a man he considered even more spineless than McKinley, and as well a "sophist," a "pacifist," "a trained elocutionist," a "logothete" and "neither a gentleman or a real man." Wilson, Roosevelt sneeringly said, "waged peace" when war was the clear and proper course.

Their session together on April 9, 1917, was polite, but tense and uncomfortable for both. Ultimately, Wilson said the army's general staff was opposed to volunteer troops. (General John J. Pershing, who was to lead the American Expeditionary Force in France, opposed formation of any volunteer units in his command.) While Roosevelt continued to elaborate on his idea for the division and Wilson neither approved nor denied its formation, the old Rough Rider knew the answer. He wrote his long-time friend, novelist Owen Wister, "The Administration is playing the dirtiest and smallest politics. I don't think they have the slightest notion of letting me go."

He was right.

Denied his own last chance for it, Roosevelt continued to view military glory as a noble ambition even when his son Quentin, age twenty, was killed in aerial combat behind German lines in July 1918. "I would not for all the world have had him fail fearlessly to do his duty and tread his allotted path, high of heart, although it led to the gates of death," Roosevelt wrote to French premier Georges V. Clemenceau.

The old lion died of a pulmonary embolism in the early morning hours of January 6, 1919, at Sagamore Hill, at age sixty.

Postscript: In 1914, at a time when Winston S. Churchill was serving as First Sea Lord in the British cabinet, Roosevelt wrote a friend, "I never liked Winston Churchill," but asked the friend to extend his congratulations to the sea lord for his quick mobilization of the British Fleet after the German invasion of Belgium. Alice Roosevelt Longworth said the two men had first met in Albany in 1899 when her father was governor of New York. There is no record of it, but they must have talked about their Cuban experiences—Churchill's in 1895, Roosevelt's in 1898. The source of Roosevelt's dislike for Churchill is a mystery for they were like-minded in many ways and each a man of the century.

After his military governorship of Cuba ended in 1902, Leonard Wood, promoted brigadier general in the regular army, in 1904 received the appointment (by President Roosevelt) as governor of Moro Province in the Philippines, then in 1906, now as a major general, to the command of the army's Philippine Division. He returned to Washington in 1910 and with the outbreak of the war in Europe became a steadfast proponent of "preparedness," standing firmly in Roosevelt's camp and in opposition to Wilson's determination to keep America out of the war.

Wood declared himself a candidate for the presidency in 1920 and sought the Republican nomination, but at the convention at the Chicago Coliseum in June that year, a stalemate was broken on the tenth ballot and Warren G. Harding of Ohio won the nomination.

Harding appointed Wood governor-general of the Philippines in 1921. The first and least-known colonel of the Rough Riders died there on August 7, 1927, after surgery for a brain tumor.

William Rufus Shafter, "quite likely the most cruelly maligned general officer of courage, competence and patriotism in our history" (as historian Stewart Holbrook called him), returned to San Francisco after the war and resumed command of the army's Department of California, a post he had given up when called to Washington to lead the Fifth Corps in Cuba. He retired from the army in 1901 after forty years' continuous service, beginning as an enlistee in the Seventh Michigan Infantry in the Civil War, and made his home with his only child, a daughter, on a small farm near Bakersfield, California. He died there on November 13, 1906.

He had returned home from Cuba with little personal glory, wrote his "The Capture of Santiago de Cuba" for *Century* magazine (February 1899) matter-of-factly, and took the criticism in the yellow press, much of it outrageous, stoically.

Holbrook wrote that Shafter was good-humored, even jolly, in private and among friends and trusted colleagues, but gruff and grim to others, soldiers and civilians, especially politicians and newspapermen. Novelist Stewart Edward White, who knew him intimately and served as his literary executor, said Shafter was one of the few really noble men he had ever known, "Deeply patriotic in the best sense, thoughtful, generous, and direct in all dealings both private and public." White added, "Never, although doubtlessly hurt by them, did Shafter mention the name of any reporter or newspaper who had a part in defaming him."

Shafter's commander-in-chief, William McKinley, had the last word, almost an epitaph, for the beleaguered old soldier: "Instead of waiting for what he wanted," the president said at a peace rally in Omaha after the war, "he took what he could get, and brought back what he went for."

"Fighting Joe" Wheeler served briefly as a brigadier general of volunteers in the Philippines in 1899–1900, then returned home and retired. He traveled in Mexico and Europe, became a friend of British field marshal Lord Roberts (the "Bobs" of Kipling's poem) and a familiar Bobs-like figure—tiny, white-bearded, standing straight and sharp as a bayonet, clearly a soldier, whether in uniform or mufti—in military exercises in France, Germany and England. He died in Brooklyn, New York, on January 25, 1906.

Of the two correspondents most identified with the Rough Riders, Stephen Crane had the briefest life but made the most durable contribution as a man of letters. He died after suffering tubercular hemorrhages, in Badenweiler, Germany, on June 5, 1900, at age twenty-nine.

Richard Harding Davis's glittering career as war correspondent continued another sixteen years. He worked in the Boer War in South Africa, in the Russo-Japanese War, in Mexico during its revolution, and covered the opening guns of World War One, writing some of the most memorable dispatches in the history of journalism from Brussels and Louvain in 1914. He spent a year on the Western Front but after being prohibited from covering the war from the trenches, returned home to his wife and family. He died on April 11, 1916, a week before his fifty-third birthday, in Mount Kisko, New York. "He was as good an American as ever lived and his heart flamed against cruelty and injustice," Roosevelt wrote of him.

Soon after the war, Captain Buckey O'Neill's widow, Josephine Schindler O'Neill of Prescott, Arizona, contacted Rough Rider chaplain Henry A. Brown, then in the regular army in Santiago, and asked him to locate her husband's grave for the purpose of eventual disinterment and reburial in the United States. Brown, who had helped bury O'Neill on the morning of July 1, 1898, found and remarked the grave. In the spring of 1899, Chaplain Brown, Buckey's brothers Eugene and John, and former Rough Rider captain L. B. Alexander of Jim McClintock's Troop B, visited the San Juan battlefield and the grave in the woods below Kettle Hill. The body was exhumed and found to be "in a good state of preservation"; positive identification was made from the black celluloid matchcase found in Buckey's tunic pocket which contained a folded slip of paper on which he had written his name, rank and Prescott address.

William Owen "Buckey" O'Neill was reburied on May 1, 1899—the first anniversary of Dewey's victory at Manila Bay—at Arlington National Cemetery, with nearly two hundred friends and admirers in attendance.

In 1911, Congress appropriated funds to remove the hulk of the *Maine* from Havana Harbor. The remains of sixty-four bodies were found in the hull of the ship and transported to Arlington for burial in a grave marked by the *Maine*'s topmast.

The wreckage was towed out to sea in February 1912; her sea cocks were opened and the tragic ship, its name an enduring battle cry, sank to the bottom of the Atlantic.

In 1976, Rear Admiral Hyman G. Rickover, the father of the nuclear submarine, and other navy specialists, studied the 1898 Court of Inquiry reports and the additional 1911 data on the *Maine*. These authorities reported finding no evidence that an external explosion caused the destruction of the ship. Rickover's conclusion was that the evidence "is consistent with an internal explosion alone," and concluded that the cause of the explosion was probably the heat from a coal bunker fire adjacent to an ammunition magazine.

The first annual Rough Riders' reunion in Las Vegas, New Mexico, in June 1899, drew 600 former troopers. The 1948 fiftieth anniversary reunion convened in Prescott, Arizona, Buckey O'Neill's town. That year there were 107 Rough Riders still living.

In 1973, the seventy-fifth anniversary year of the Cuban campaign, there were three authentic Rough Rider veterans living. Two of them died in that diamond anniversary year, the last survived two years beyond it.

Oldest of the survivors was Dr. George Hamner of Bay Pines, Florida, who was age ninety-nine and nine months when he passed away in a veteran's hospital on February 6, 1973. He was born on May 23, 1873, at Faber's Mill, Virginia, and had enlisted in the regiment in Santa Fe, assigned to Captain Maximiliano Luna's Troop F of the New Mexico contingent. He saw action at both Las Guásimas and in the Kettle Hill–San Juan battle. He earned a doctor's degree in medicine at the University of Virginia after the war, served in the Medical Corps of the American Expeditionary Force in World War One, and continued to practice until the last day of 1961.

Frank C. Brito of Las Cruces, New Mexico, died on April 22, 1973, in a nursing home in El Paso, Texas, at age ninety-six. Brito returned to active service in 1916 with an infantry company of the National Guard after Francisco "Pancho" Villa and a band of his rebel soldiers raided the New Mexico border town of Columbus. He also served as a fireman, jailer and deputy sheriff of Doña Ana County, New Mexico.

"I figure twenty-two Brito men have fought for this country," he said toward the end of his life. "My brother Joe was killed in the Philippine Insurrection. Two of my boys went though World War Two. Four of my grandsons are now in Vietnam."

Jesse D. Langdon liked to say that he was the first Rough Rider sworn in (in San Antonio, by "the Colonel himself," within a day or two after Roosevelt's arrival at Camp Wood on May 15, 1898) and the last to be mustered out. He had taken a furlough from Camp Wykoff on Montauk Point when the regiment disbanded there on September 15, 1898, and received his discharge at Fort Yates, Dakota Territory, on December 7.

To the end of his life he never had a negative thought or said a negative thing about "the Colonel," nor would he entertain such things from others. When asked to recommend a book on the regiment, he had no other suggestion than Theodore Roosevelt's *The Rough Riders* and even had a form letter made up with that book alone listed, to send to those who wrote to him.

The things he remembered most vividly about his service with Troop K at Las Guásimas and San Juan were the death of Buckey O'Neill at Kettle Hill (which he witnessed), the work of "Blackie" Parker's Gatling guns on the Spanish trenches, the Spanish dead— "A lot of them were just boys—just kids"—he saw in the rifle pits defending Santiago, and how the colonel was always in front of his men—"We had to run to keep up with him," Langdon said, "and running up Kettle Hill wasn't easy."

After the war he traveled with a troupe of Rough Riders in Buffalo Bill Cody's Wild West Show, worked as a veterinarian, an unlicensed physician in a Washington state community seventy miles from the nearest doctor, surveyor, plumber, builder, mechanical engineer, inventor (claiming eighty-nine patents) and economic theorist. The latter calling reached fruition in a book, begun in 1905 and published in 1972, titled *Taxless Government via Effort Money.*

Langdon, still tall and erect in his nineties, his hair long and snowy, his profile hawkish, his hands huge and strong, outlived all the others and between Frank Brito's death in April 1973, and his own, on June 28, 1975, at the Veteran's Hospital at Castle Point, New York, was "the last Rough Rider."

SOURCES

Twenty-five years ago, while researching a biography of Buckey O'Neill of Arizona, I made contact and interviewed, in person and by mail, the three surviving Rough Riders—the men to whom this book is dedicated. My notes and correspondence from these interviews are a unique, in the strictest sense of the word, source. Other primary material derives from the William R. Shafter Papers (Stanford University Library); James McClintock Papers (Phoenix Public Library); and the William O. O'Neill Collection (Sharlot Hall Museum, Prescott, Arizona).

In preparing to write *The Boys of '98*, I sought to find and make the greatest use of the memoirs, published or unpublished, of the men who actually served in the First U.S. Volunteer Cavalry Regiment in the spring and summer of 1898. I discovered, however, that there are few of these, a peculiar thing considering the highly "personal" nature of the Rough Riders and the great public fascination with the regiment and its colorful, charismatic leader. But Roosevelt's *The Rough Riders* (1902), the principal first-person source (despite its exasperating sketchiness), is one of only two such book-length memoirs from officers of the regiment and the other, Tom Hall's *The Fun and Fighting of the Rough Riders* (1899), is not reliable. Hall, a lieutenant and regimental adjutant, had a poor reputation in the regiment that extended from San Antonio to San Juan. (See chapter 11.)

From the Rough Rider ranks I have made use of *Gun Notches* (1931) by Tom Rynning, a sergeant in Arizona's Troop B; David Hughes's unpublished memoir of his service, also in Troop B (Arizona Pioneers Historical Society, Tucson); the James B. Mc-Clintock papers and the William O. O'Neill papers.

One first-person book containing a terrific sidelines view of Roosevelt and his Rough Riders is Charles Johnston Post's undoubted classic, *The Little War of Private Post*. He was a private in the Seventy-first New York Volunteer Regiment, a unit that was thrown together with the Rough Riders from Tampa days throughout the Santiago campaign. Post, a newspaper artist, told his story with great humor and insight. No book by any participant at Santiago gives a better picture and sense of what it was like to slog along the mud-rutted wagon roads between Daiquirí and the San Juan Heights, choking down hardtack and sowbelly in a pummeling rain, and dodging mosquitos, land crabs—and mainly, bullets—in a war everybody forgot far too soon.

Fortunately, there were other eyewitness sources for the Rough Riders' work in Cuba, principally those of the newspaper correspondents who followed the regiment so assiduously. Richard Harding Davis attached himself to Roosevelt early and stayed with him until the end of the fighting. Davis was so identified with the regiment, Roosevelt praised him so unstintingly in dispatches, in his book on the regiment, in his *Autobiography,* and in personal letters, there is reason to doubt Davis's credibility as an objective reporter—especially considering his abrupt about-face on the matter of the Rough Riders' "ambush" at Las Guási-mas. But he was a shrewd, tested observer, a marvelous writer and a born reporter, and his writings on the Cuban adventure, before, during, and after the war, are quite priceless.

Stephen Crane, too, especially since he was often in Roosevelt's camp without being in Roosevelt's "camp," was the eternal outsider, a thoroughly fearless reporter oblivious to the repercussions of what he wrote. Reading Crane is an education by itself. Not only are his dispatches vivid and first-person personal (in the spirit of war correspondence in the 1890s), but very economical—as his controversial dispatch on the Las Guásimas skirmish (see chapter 11)—in contrast to his loquacious colleagues, such as Davis. Reading Crane's reportage from Cuba in '98 is an eerie experience, an admirable example of life imitating art: He seemed to write of war experiences *before* actually living them. His classic novel of the Civil War, *The Red Badge of Courage,* published four years before the Spanish-American War, presages events, scenes, people—some of them weirdly identical—he witnessed and experienced in Cuba.

Other correspondents whose work has been invaluable include Edward Marshall, Murat Halstead, George Kennan, Burr McIntosh, Stephen Bonsal, Caspar Whitney, Frederick Remington, Poultney Bigelow, James Creelman, George Bronson Rea, and Winston S. Churchill. I'm also indebted to two books that should occupy premium space in any collection on the war correspondence of the era: *The Correspondents' War* by Charles H. Brown, and *The Yellow Kids* by Joyce Milton.

On the Spanish-American War in its entirety, there is no better work than David Trask's splendidly organized and lucidly written book, but I also admire G. J. A. O'Toole's clever approach to the subject and his novelist's eye for color; Walter Millis's spirited and plain-spoken *The Martial Spirit;* and Russell A. Alger's early, and indispensable, work by the man who headed the War Department in the White House throughout the 1898 campaigns in Cuba and the Philippines.

Among works expressly on the Santiago campaign, Herbert H.

Sargent's exhaustive 1907 work remains a classic; John Cameron Dierks's *A Leap to Arms* is a more readable, and briefer, account; and on the Rough Riders, the modern books by V. C. Jones, Charles Herner and H. Paul Jeffers, have been immensely helpful.

The three primary Roosevelt sources I have employed are his *The Rough Riders,* his *Autobiography,* and *The Letters of Theodore Roosevelt.* In addition to these, there are the biographies. Surely no president, not even Lincoln, has been the subject of such a wealth of brilliant books, even the most balanced seeming to attest to Edith Wharton's likening his blazing energy to that of radium and Henry Adams comparing the velocity of his career to a hurtling freight train. I am partial to Henry Pringle and Edmund Morris, but William Harbaugh's *Power and Responsibility* is to Roosevelt what Margaret Leech's *In the Days of McKinley* is to McKinley—a masterpiece of probing the inner workings, especially the political and philosophical ones, of a complex man. Nathan Miller's 1992 biography is also excellent, as are the books by Stefan Lorant and H. Paul Jeffers. Special appreciation needs to be given to Mark Sullivan's six-volume *Our Times,* especially the 1937 *The Turn of the Century* volume. There exists no better or valuable history of the Roosevelt-Wilson era than these masterpieces, each a joy to read.

And finally, among published works, I had the good fortune to find a copy of a very scarce and primary work, published by the War Records Office of the War Department in 1902, *The Official and Pictorial Record of the War with Spain and the Philippines.* This massive book—12 × 17 inches in size, 650 pages in length— is a meticulous record of the entire war, with a special emphasis on all the military units, regular and volunteer, that fought in it. The book stands up well, nearly a hundred years after it was printed in a limited edition, presumably for governmental distribution, soon after the assassination of President McKinley.

BIBLIOGRAPHY

Alger, Russell A. *The Spanish-American War*. New York: Harper & Brothers, 1901.

Azoy, Col. A. C. M. *Charge! The Story of the Battle of San Juan Hill*. New York: David McKay, 1961.

———. *Signal 250!: The Sea Fight Off Santiago*. New York: David McKay Co., 1964.

Beer, Thomas. *Stephen Crane*. New York: Alfred A. Knopf, 1923.

Berryman, John. *Stephen Crane: A Critical Biography*. New York: Farrar Straus Giroux, 1950.

Brown, Charles H. *The Correspondents' War: Journalists in the Spanish-American War*. New York: Charles Scribner's Sons, 1967.

Carlson, Paul H. *"Pecos Bill": A Military Biography of William R. Shafter*. College Station: Texas A&M University Press, 1989.

Churchill, Winston S. *A Roving Commission: My Early Life.* New York: Charles Scribner's Sons, 1930.

Crane, Stephen. *The Portable Stephen Crane* (ed. by Joseph Katz). New York: Viking, 1969.

Curry, George. *George Curry, 1861–1947: An Autobiography.* Albuquerque: University of New Mexico Press, 1958.

Davis, Charles Belmont, ed. *Adventures and Letters of Richard Harding Davis.* New York: Charles Scribner's Sons, 1918.

Davis, Richard Harding. *The Notes of a War Correspondent.* New York: Charles Scribner's Sons, 1911.

———. *The Cuban and Porto Rican Campaigns.* New York: Frederick Stokes, 1899.

Dierks, John Cameron. *A Leap to Arms: The Cuban Campaign of 1898.* Philadelphia: J. B. Lippincott, 1970.

Dyer, John P. *From Shiloh to San Juan: The Life of "Fighting Joe" Wheeler.* Baton Rouge: Louisiana State University Press, 1961 (revised edition).

Freidel, Frank. *The Splendid Little War.* Boston: Little, Brown, 1958.

Gould, Lewis L. *The Spanish-American War and President McKinley.* Lawrence: University Press of Kansas, 1982.

Hagedorn, Hermann. *Leonard Wood: A Biography.* New York: Harper & Brothers, 1931 (2 volumes).

———. *The Rough Riders: A Romance of Theodore Roosevelt and the Spanish War.* New York: Harper & Brothers, 1927.

Hall, Tom. *The Fun and Fighting of the Rough Riders.* New York: Frederick Stokes, 1899.

Halstead, Murat. *The Story of Cuba: Her Struggles for Liberty.* Chicago: Franklin Square Bible House, 1898.

Harbaugh, William H. *Power and Responsibility: The Life and Times of Theodore Roosevelt.* New York: Farrar, Straus and Cudahy, 1961.

Herner, Charles. *The Arizona Rough Riders.* Tucson: University of Arizona Press, 1970.

Holbrook, Stewart H. *Lost Men of American History.* New York: The Macmillan Co., 1947.

Jeffers, H. Paul. *Colonel Roosevelt.* New York: John Wiley & Sons, 1996.

Jones, Virgil C. *Roosevelt's Rough Riders.* New York: Doubleday, 1971.

Kennan, George. *Campaigning in Cuba.* New York: The Century Co., 1899.

Lane, Jack C. *Armed Progressive: General Leonard Wood.* San Rafael, Calif.: Presidio Press, 1978.

Leech, Margaret. *In the Days of McKinley.* New York: Harper & Brothers, 1959.

Lodge, Henry C. *Selections from the Correspondence of Theodore Roosevelt and Henry Cabot Lodge, 1884–1918.* New York: Charles Scribner's Sons, 1925.

Lorant, Stefan. *The Life and Times of Theodore Roosevelt.* Garden City, N.Y.: Doubleday, 1959.

Manchester, William. *The Last Lion: Winston Spencer Churchill, Visions of Glory, 1874–1932.* Boston: Little, Brown, 1983.

Marshall, Edward. *The Story of the Rough Riders.* New York: G. W. Dillingham, 1899.

McClure, Alexander K. and Charles Morris. *The Authentic Life of William McKinley*. n.p.: 1901.

McIntosh, Burr. *The Little I Saw of Cuba*. New York: F. Tennyson Neely, 1899.

Miley, Lieutenant L. D. *In Cuba with Shafter*. New York: Charles Scribner's Sons, 1899.

Miller, Nathan. *Theodore Roosevelt: A Life*. New York: William Morrow, 1992.

Millis, Walter. *The Martial Spirit*. New York: Houghton Mifflin, 1931.

Milton, Joyce. *The Yellow Kids: Foreign Correspondents in the Heyday of Yellow Journalism*. New York: Harper & Row, 1989.

Morgan, Ted. *Churchill: Young Man in a Hurry, 1874–1915*. New York: Simon & Schuster, 1982.

Morris, Edmund. *The Rise of Theodore Roosevelt*. New York: Coward, McCann & Geoghegan, 1979.

Morris, Sylvia Jukes. *Edith Kermit Roosevelt: Portrait of a First Lady*. New York: Coward, McCann & Geoghegan, 1980.

O'Connor, Richard. *Black Jack Pershing*. New York: Doubleday, 1961.

The Official and Pictorial Record of the War with Spain and Philippines. Washington, D.C.: War Records Office, 1902.

Otis, James. *The Boys of '98*. Boston: Dana Estes & Co., 1898.

O'Toole, G. J. A. *The Spanish War: An American Epic, 1898*. New York: W. W. Norton, 1984.

Post, Charles Johnson. *The Little War of Private Post*. Boston: Little, Brown, 1960.

Pratt, Julius. *Expansionists of 1898*. Baltimore: Johns Hopkins Press, 1936.

Pringle, Henry F. *Theodore Roosevelt: A Biography*. New York: Harcourt, Brace & World, 1931.

Roosevelt, Theodore. *An Autobiography*. New York: Macmillan, 1913.

———. *The Letters of Theodore Roosevelt,* edited by Elting E. Morison. Cambridge, Mass.: Harvard University Press, 1951–54 (8 volumes).

———. *The Rough Riders*. New York: Charles Scribner's Sons, 1902.

Rynning, Thomas H. *Gun Notches: The Life Story of a Cowboy-Soldier*. New York: J. B. Lippincott, 1931.

Sargent, Herbert H. *The Campaign of Santiago de Cuba*. Chicago: A. C. McClurg, 1907 (3 volumes).

Spiller, Roger J., ed. *Dictionary of American Military Biography*. Westport, Conn.: Greenwood Press, 1984 (3 volumes).

Sullivan, Mark. *Our Times: The Turn of the Century*. New York: Charles Scribner's Sons, 1937.

Swanberg, W. A. *Citizen Hearst*. New York: Charles Scribner's Sons, 1961.

———. *Pulitzer*. New York: Charles Scribner's Sons, 1967.

Thrapp, Dan L. *Encyclopedia of Frontier Biography*. Glendale, Calif.: Arthur H. Clarke Co., 1988 (4 volumes).

Trask, David F. *The War with Spain in 1898.* New York: The Free Press, 1981.

Walker, Dale L. *Death Was the Black Horse: The Story of Rough Rider Buckey O'Neill.* Austin, Texas: Madrona Press, 1975. (Reprinted as *Rough Rider: Buckey O'Neill of Arizona.* Lincoln: University of Nebraska Press, 1997.)

Weems, John Edward. *The Fate of the Maine.* New York: Henry Holt, 1958.

White, Trumbull. *Our War with Spain for Cuba's Freedom.* Chicago: Imperial Publishing Co., 1898.

Young, James Rankin. *History of Our War with Spain.* n.p., 1898.

INDEX